MINUTES

OF THE

EIGTH ANNUAL CONFERENCE

YOUNG PEOPLE'S SOCIETY OF CHRISTIAN ENDEAVOR

HELD IN

FIRST REGT. ARMORY HALL,

PHILADELPHIA, PA.,

JULY 9 - 11 1889.

WITH ADDRESSES AND PAPERS READ AT THE CONFERENCE.

First Fruits Press
Wilmore, Kentucky
c2015

First Fruits Press
The Academic Open Press of Asbury Theological Seminary
204 N. Lexington Ave., Wilmore, KY 40390
859-858-2236
first.fruits@asburyseminary.edu
asbury.to/firstfruits

MINUTES

OF THE

Eighth Annual Conference

OF THE

YOUNG PEOPLE'S SOCIETY

OF

CHRISTIAN ENDEAVOR,

HELD IN

FIRST REGT. ARMORY HALL, PHILADELPHIA, PA.,

Tuesday, Wednesday and Thursday, July 9, 10 and 11, 1889.

WITH ADDRESSES AND PAPERS READ AT THE CONFERENCE.

PUBLISHED BY
THE UNITED SOCIETY OF CHRISTIAN ENDEAVOR,
No. 50 BROMFIELD STREET, BOSTON.

Winship, Daniels & Co.,
PRINTERS,
150 Pearl St., Boston.

PREFATORY NOTE.

Great pains have been taken to make this report of the Eighth Annual Convention of the Societies of Christian Endeavor as accurate and complete as possible, and, in an unusual degree, it is believed that it will be found of interest and value. In one or two instances, where the speakers had no manuscript and where, through a misunderstanding, the address was not fully taken by the stenographers, the speeches are not given in full, but in almost every case the addresses are printed without any abbreviation, and as revised by the authors themselves.

It may disappoint some that the names and statistics of the societies are not included in this year's report, but our societies are now so numerous that it was found to be practically impossible to print these tables, without increasing the price of the report so largely as to put it beyond the reach of many who desire it, besides entailing a large and unnecessary expense upon the United Society.

Hearty thanks are due to the authors of the papers herein printed, for the use of their manuscripts and for their kindness in revising them, and also to Mr. William Shaw, the treasurer of the United Society, for his zeal and labor in preparing for and hastening the publication of this report. It is now sent forth in the hope that it may enlarge and perpetuate the blessed influences of a convention of which one of the least important things to say is that "it was beyond a doubt the largest delegated religious convention ever held in America." F. E. C.

MINUTES OF THE EIGHTH ANNUAL CHRISTIAN ENDEAVOR CONVENTION.

TUESDAY, JULY 9.

AFTERNOON SESSION.

The eighth annual Christian Endeavor Convention assembled in the First Regiment Armory Hall, corner Broad and Callowhill streets, Philadelphia, Pa., Tuesday, July 9.

The convention was opened at 4 P. M. by Rev. S. W. Adriance of Massachusetts. Three thousand delegates were present at the opening session and joined in singing that grand old hymn, "All Hail the Power of Jesus' Name." Mr. W. J. Van Patten, president of the convention, was prevented by sickness from being present, and Rev. F. E. Clark, D. D., was unanimously chosen to fill his place.

The opening prayer was then offered by Rev. Mr. Nichols of Nova Scotia.

Rev. Bartlett Foskett, of Minneapolis, was elected scribe of the convention, with H. A. Field, of Massachusetts, as assistant.

Rev. Theodore Shaffer, of New Jersey, was elected time-keeper.

By vote of the convention, the appointment of committees was left with the president.

After the hymn, "Christ for the World we Sing," President Clark introduced Rev. J. T. Beckley, D. D., president of the Pennsylvania Union, who welcomed the convention in an admirable address, outlining the Christian Endeavor idea and the principles for which it stands. He was followed by Bishop W. R. Nicholson, D. D., in behalf of the city churches, whose earnest words made a deep impression upon the convention.

An eloquent response to these addresses of welcome was delivered by Rev. S. V. Leech, D. D., of Albany, N. Y.

At the conclusion of his address, the following Committee on Credentials was appointed by the chair: —

F. W. Weber of Pennsylvania, Augustus V. Heely of New York, C. J. Frye of New York, W. S. Burns of Missouri, Thos. C. Baldwin of New Hampshire.

The benediction was then pronounced by Rev. Chas. F. Deems, D. D., of New York City.

Evening Session.

The evening session opened at 7.30 o'clock with a devotional and praise service, led by Rev. Ralph W. Brokaw of Massachusetts, who read the 13th chapter of I. Corinthians, and offered up a fervent prayer for the Holy Spirit's presence during the convention.

Rev. Jas. L. Hill of Massachusetts read a letter from General Secretary Ward, expressing his sincere regret at his inability to attend the convention.

This was followed by the report of Secretary Ward, which was read by the same brother. Sincere regret was expressed on every side that our beloved secretary could not be with us, and many fervent prayers were offered for his speedy recovery to health and strength.

Two verses of "Onward, Christian Soldier," were sung, and then President Clark introduced Rev. George H. Wells, D. D., of Montreal, who delivered the convention sermon from Ephesians, vi : 11, "Put on the whole armour of God."

The sermon seemed to lift every one up into a higher, purer atmosphere, and its inspiring thought was reflected in all the succeeding sessions.

The president announced the following committees: —

On Business. — Rev. H. B. Grose, Pennsylvania; Rev. R. N. McKaig, D. D., Minnesota; E. G. Dean, New York; E. E. Towner, Vermont; Miss E. D. Gates, Massachusetts.

On Nominations. — Rev. S. W. Adriance, Massachusetts; W. H. Pennell, Maine; Louis S. Gould, Nebraska; Miss Bettie Wishard, Indiana; John S. Smith, Nova Scotia.

On Resolutions. — Rev. J. L. Hill, Massachusetts; Rev. Mr. Dingwell, Connecticut; A. H. Frederick, Missouri; Miss Lucy P. Carey, Maine.

The session closed with two verses of "At the Cross." Benediction by Rev. Edward Noyes of Minnesota.

WEDNESDAY, JULY 10.

6.30 A. M. Prayer Meeting.

As a fitting prelude to the work of the day, and an index of the spirit of the convention, three thousand delegates gathered in the great auditorium at 6.30 A. M. for prayer. No one present will soon forget the solemn and impressive service. It was good to be there.

> "Heaven came down our souls to greet,
> And glory crowned the mercy-seat."

The service was conducted by Rev. O. H. Tracy of Maine.

Morning Session.

Promptly at 9 A. M. the gavel fell and President Clark opened the session by announcing the hymn, "Lord, we come before Thee now."

Rev. Dr. Bixby of Rhode Island read the Scripture and made the opening prayer. After singing "Nearer my God to Thee," Rev. C. A. Dickinson of Massachusetts, Rev. F. E. Marston, D. D., of Ohio, Rev. R. W. Brokaw of Massachusetts, Rev. S. W. Adriance of Massachusetts, and Rev. James L. Hill of Massachusetts, answered questions for the assembly.

Rev. C. A. Dickinson of Massachusetts was called to the chair.

Treasurer Wm. Shaw then read his annual report and that of the auditor. The report showed the expenditures of the year to have been $17,186.39, leaving a balance on hand of $498.53.

A half-hour praise service was then conducted by Rev. Nehemiah Boynton of Massachusetts, in which a large number participated.

At the conclusion of this service, the convention was invited to make its free-will offering for the work of the ensuing year. A large number of personal and society pledges were made. The offering amounted to $5,107.90. Dr. Wayland Hoyt of Philadelphia offered a fervent prayer of thanksgiving at the close.

The remaining portion of the morning session was devoted to the discussion of the following topic, viz.:—

"For What does the Christian Endeavor Movement stand?"

Rev. J. W. Chapman, D.D., of Albany, N. Y., opened the discussion with an address on "Loyalty to Duty." He was followed by Rev. Chas. F. Deems, D. D., of New York, upon "Loyalty to the Church." Rev. L. T. Chamberlain, D. D., of Brooklyn, followed upon "Loyalty to Christ."

These addresses following so quickly in the line of the convention sermon produced a powerful impression upon the assembly. They were cumulative both in interest and power. At the conclusion of these addresses, five thousand voices joined in singing "All Hail the Power of Jesus' Name." Benediction by Rev. J. R. Miller, D. D.

Afternoon Session.

Convention opened at 2 P. M. Prayer by Rev. Mr. Woodbridge of New York. Then followed reports from the States and Provinces.

MAINE, Rev. E. M. Cousins. — "Not ashamed of her child. Making steady progress."

UTAH, C. J. Parsons. — "Doubled in membership the past year. Utah a great field for Endeavor."

MARYLAND, Rev. Alex. Proudfit, D. D. — "Movement growing rapidly. Received new impulse from Chicago Convention."

CALIFORNIA, Rev. A. J. Cruzan. — "Reports progress. Much work to be done."

COLORADO, E. B. Clark. — "125 societies; gain of 50 since last convention. Denver wants next convention."

NOVA SCOTIA, Rev. Mr. Fisher. — "60 societies that are stirring up the churches at a great rate."

VERMONT, E. E. Towner. — "135 societies and 6 local unions."

ILLINOIS, C. B. Holdredge. — "Added 12,000 members; 700 changed from associate to active membership."

NEW HAMPSHIRE, Thos. C. Baldwin. — "130 societies, 4,000 members."

INDIANA, J. N. McCoy. — "160 societies, 7,000 members. Doubled the past year."

WASHINGTON, P. W. Willis, Walla Walla. — "Movement growing; 130 members in Walla Walla."

At this point the proceedings were interrupted by the reading of the following telegram from President Harrison: "President Harrison sends greeting to the convention. Public business prevents his attendance."

ONTARIO, Rev. G. H. Hobbleditch, — "100 societies, 7,000 members. Contemplating a union."

CONNECTICUT, Eli Manchester, Jr. — "335 societies, 23,000 members, 23 local unions."

NEW YORK, H. D. Jackson. — "1,500 societies, 80,000 members, 23 conventions, 6,000 conversions."

MICHIGAN, Robt. Murray. — "300 societies; 16 in Detroit and 1,000 members."

NEW JERSEY, F. D. Everitt. — "276 societies, 15,000 members; increased 53 per cent."

NEBRASKA, Rev. E. S. Ralston. — "Added 1,500 members in two years."

MISSOURI, A. H. Frederick. — "177 societies, 7,894 members; increased 60 per cent; wants next convention."

MINNESOTA, E. B. McClenahan. — "Wants the convention also; 200 societies, 4 local unions; increased 100 per cent."

PENNSYLVANIA, E. B. Weitzel. — "500 societies, 35,000 members."

IOWA, J. A. Mershon. — "260 societies, 9,000 members."

DELAWARE, H. J. Guthrie. — "21 societies, 976 members."

WISCONSIN, H. W. Nickerson. — "162 societies, 6,152 members."

OHIO, J. C. Beachman. — "465 societies; increased 265 last year."

MASSACHUSETTS, H. A. Field, State Secretary. — "743 societies, 50,000 members."

KANSAS, O. S. Davis.—"240 societies, growing rapidly."

FLORIDA, Mrs. M. L. Selden.—"25 societies, all doing missionary work."

RHODE ISLAND, H. E. Thurston.—"5 local unions, 70 societies, 3,500 members."

KENTUCKY, A. A. Hill.—"42 societies, 1,000 members."

A letter of regret from Gov. Beaver, who was unable to be present on account of the press of public duties and the Johnstown disaster, was read at this juncture.

The convention then rose and sang with wonderful enthusiasm the Endeavor Battle Hymn, "Onward, Christian Soldier."

Benediction by Rev. R. N. McKaig, D. D., of Minnesota.

The convention then adjourned to neighboring churches, for the discussion of practical Endeavor methods.

Meetings were held as follows:

AT 3.45 P. M.

In Arch Street M. E. Church (Audience Room); Conference on "The Work of the Lookout Committee." Led by Mrs. M. L. Selden, Gainsville, Florida.

In Arch Street M. E. Church (Lecture Room); Conference on "The Work of the Social Committee." Led by Miss Olive Blunt, Kansas City, Missouri.

In Thirteenth Street M. E. Church (Audience Room); Conference on "The Work of the Missionary Committee." Led by Mr. S. L. Mershon, Evanston, Illinois.

In Thirteenth Street M. E. Church (Lecture Room); Conference on "The Work of the Temperance Committee." Led by Rev. E. S. Ralston, Lincoln, Nebraska.

In Chambers Presbyterian Church (Audience Room); Conference on "The Work of the Prayer-meeting Committee."

In Chambers Presbyterian Church (Lecture Room); Conference on "The Work of the Sunday School Committee." Led by Mr. C. H. Parsons, Salt Lake City.

AT 4.30 P. M.

In Arch Street M. E. Church (Audience Room); Conference on "Prayer-meeting Methods." Led by V. Richard Foss, Portland, Maine.

In Arch Street M. E. Church (Lecture Room); Conference on "Local and State Unions." Led by Rev. A. H. Hall, Meriden, Connecticut.

In Thirteenth Street M. E. Church (Lecture Room); Conference on "Junior Societies." Led by Miss Mary F. Dana, Manchester, New Hampshire.

In Chambers Presbyterian Church; Conference on "How can we help our Associate Members?" Led by Rev. D. N. Lowell, Rutland, Vermont.

These meetings were largely attended and of an informal character. Note-books were freely used and great interest was manifested in the discussions.

Many of the churches were densely crowded and large numbers stood during the entire sessions.

EVENING SESSION.

Convention opened at 7.30 with every seat in the great building occupied and many standing.

Rev. H. B. Grose of Pennsylvania presided. Rev. C. P. Mills of Massachusetts read the Scriptures and offered a fervent prayer. After singing, Mr. Mills presented to Pres. Clark the oldest copy of the first Christian Endeavor Constitution. At the conclusion of the presentation, the audience rose and sang, "Blest be the tie that binds."

President Clark was then introduced for his annual address. Rounds of applause greeted him as he stepped to the front of the rostrum. His address was partly reminiscent, full of inspiring thought and wise counsel, and closed by announcing as the motto for the coming year, "We are laborers together with God."

Chairman Grose then introduced Major-Gen. O. O. Howard, the Christian Soldier, whose earnest words were listened to with close attention, and awakened a responsive chord in every heart. Benediction by Rev. Dr. Conrad of Philadelphia.

THURSDAY, JULY 11.

PRAYER MEETING, 6.30 A. M.

For the better accommodation of the delegates, meetings were held in Arch Street M. E., Chambers Presbyterian and Beth Eden Baptist Churches, led respectively by J. E. Mershon of Iowa, E. B. McClenahan of Minnesota and C. B. Holdredge of Illinois.

These meetings were very largely attended and characterized by a spirit of sincere devotion.

MORNING SESSION, 9.00 A. M.

Promptly at nine o'clock Pres. Clark called the convention to order.

Rev. H. N. Kinney of Connecticut conducted the devotional service, reading from Luke xix, and made the opening prayer.

Pres. Clark, Rev. J. L. Scudder of New Jersey and Rev. H. N. Kinney of Connecticut answered the questions of the delegates.

Rev. Wayland Hoyt, D. D. of Philadelphia, was then introduced.

Dr. Hoyt addressed the convention on "The New Prayer-meeting," viz: The Christian Endeavor Prayer-meeting. The address was in Dr. Hoyt's best vein, and he was frequently interrupted by applause. At the conclusion of his address, the convention instructed the president to send the following telegram to Washington:—

"The United Societies of Christian Endeavor, in Eighth Annual Convention assembled, from 6,000 to 8,000 strong, gratefully express their thanks to President Harrison for his interest and sympathy. We crave for our Christian President God's utmost blessing."

Following this came an interesting paper from Rev. C. H. Farrar, D. D., of New York, on "Handshaking."

A paper on the "Value of Time" by Miss Ella Reinking of Iowa was then read by Rev. J. T. Kerr of New Jersey.

Miss Emily Wheeler of Harpoot, Turkey, addressed the convention upon "St. Paul's advice to the Sisters."

"The Society Interdenominational not Undenominational" was

next discussed by Rev. W. H. York of Syracuse and Rev. J. B. Helwig, D. D., of Ohio.

Rev. B. B. Loomis, Ph. D., of West Troy, N. Y. was then called to the chair to conduct "The Pastors' Hour." The hour was late and but thirty minutes were given to this topic. Among those who participated were Rev. J. H. Hanlon of New Jersey, Rev. J. L. Scudder of New Jersey, Rev. W. H. Tracy of New York, Rev. W. J. Peck of Long Island, Rev. J. P. Green of Baltimore and Rev. Dr. Lisk, who testified to the helpfulness and hopefulness of the Christian Endeavor movement.

Rev. H. B. Grose, Chairman of the Business Committee, then presented his report, which was unanimously adopted.

While the Scribe was making the customary announcements, the Hon. John Wanamaker entered the hall and the convention rose to do him honor.

Mr. Wanamaker was publicly vested with the badge of the society, after which he made a short address, testifying to his deep interest in the Endeavor movement.

A large number of telegrams from various religious organizations and missionary societies was then read, congratulating the convention and bidding it "Godspeed."

After a song the convention adjourned with prayer by Rev. Dr. Beaver.

AFTERNOON SESSION.

Arrangements had been made for an open-air mass-meeting at Fairmount Park, but the heavy rain of the morning and the threatening clouds and passing showers prevented the attendance of many of the delegates.

It was finally decided to hold the exercises in the banquet hall in Belmont Mansion, and at 3 P. M., Rev. J. T. Beckley, D. D., called the assembly to order.

After prayer by Rev. Mr. Carey of Japan, the presiding officer introduced Rev. J. W. Hamilton, D. D., of Massachusetts, who delivered an eloquent discourse on Temperance. Dr. Hamilton's address was full of stirring appeal and created a profound impression upon his audience.

At the conclusion of Dr. Hamilton's address, the sun shone forth so warmly and brightly, that it was decided to hold the rest of the meeting at the open-air stand.

Rev. S. W. Adriance led the audience in the "National Anthem," accompanied by the band of Belmont Mansion.

Mr. R. P. Wilder of New York was then introduced, and delivered an address upon the "Missionary Uprising." The theme and speaker were happily wedded, as all who know Mr. Wilder's work among the colleges of this country can heartily testify. All hearts were stirred by his earnest and impassioned utterance.

EVENING SESSION, 7.30 P. M.

Pres. Clark called the convention to order. The building was densely crowded, the doors were shut and large numbers refused admission.

Rev. J. L. Litch of Pennsylvania read the Scriptures and made the opening prayer. Sixty-five hundred voices joined in singing "Must Jesus bear the cross alone," and "We're marching to Zion."

Rev. S. W. Adriance then presented the following report for the nominating committee:—

President.—Rev. Francis E. Clark, D. D., Boston, Mass. Vice-Presidents.—Mr. W. J. Van Patten, Burlington, Vt.; Rev. J. E. Twitchell, D. D., New Haven, Conn.; Rev. Wayland Hoyt, D. D., Philadelphia, Pa.; Rev. C. F. Deems, D. D., New York, N. Y.; Rev. S. J. Niccolls, D. D., St. Louis, Mo.; Bishop Samuel Fallows, D. D., Chicago, Ill.; Rev. Robert Christie, St. Paul, Minn.; Rev J. K. McLean, Oakland, Cal.; Rev. Willard Scott, Omaha, Neb. Scribe.—Rev. Bartlett Foskett, Minneapolis, Minn. State Superintendents.—Alabama, Miss Lura E. Aldridge, Talladega; California, R. V. Watt, San Francisco; Colorado, Rev. G. W. Woodruff, Colorado Springs; Connecticut, Mr. Eli Manchester, Jr., New Haven; Delaware, Mr. E. M. Richmond, Wilmington; District of Columbia, Rev. Theron S. Hamlin, D. D., Washington; Florida, Mr. F. E. Nettleton, Lake Helen; Georgia, Rev. Wm. Shaw, Atlanta; Illinois, Mr. C. B. Holdredge, Bloomington; Indiana, Mr. W. J. Lewis, Evansville; Iowa, Rev. C. A. Towle, Cedar Rapids; Kansas, Rev. S. F. Wilson, Tonganoxie; Kentucky, Rev. S. S. Waltz, Louisville; Maine, Rev. J. M. Frost, Portland; Maryland, Rev. Alex. Proudfit, D. D., Baltimore; Massachusetts, Rev. C. P. Mills, Newburyport; Michigan, Rev. B. F. Sargent, Grand Rapids; Minnesota, Rev. Bartlett Foskett, Minneapolis; Missouri, Mr. Geo. B. Graff, St. Louis; Montana, G. C. Tilly, Helena; Nebraska, Rev. Edward S. Ralston, Lincoln; New Hampshire, Mr. Wm. P. Fiske, Concord; New Jersey, Rev. J. T. Kerr, Elizabeth; New York, Rev. H. W. Sherwood. Syracuse; Mr. Wm. G. Bassett, Rochester; C. J. Frye, New York; Nova Scotia, Mr. J. S. Smith, Halifax; Ohio, Rev. A. B. Christy, Hudson; Oregon, Rev. W. H. Landon, D. D., Portland; Pennsylvania, Rev. H. B. Grose, Pittsburgh; Quebec, Rev. Geo. S. Wells, D. D., Montreal; Rhode Island, Mr. H. Edward Thurston, Providence; South Carolina, Mr. J. L. Wilson, Society Hill; Tennessee, Mr. E. A. Palmer, Grand View; Texas, Mr. S. D. Scudder, San Antonio; Utah, Rev. J. Brainard Thrall, Salt Lake City; Vermont, Rev. D. R. Lowell, Rutland; Virginia, Rev. Mr. Hill; Washington, Rev. R. J. Mooney, Ellensburgh; Wisconsin, Rev. A. A. Burr; Wyoming, Mr. Marcus M. Mason, Cheyenne; Ontario, Rev. Samuel Lyle. Treasurer.—Wm. Shaw, 50 Bromfield Street, Boston, Mass.

The report was unanimously adopted.

Rev. Wayland Hoyt, D. D., read the decision of the United Society upon the place of holding the next convention, which was as follows:—

The Next Convention.

Christian Endeavor is one of the signal signs of the times. In several respects is this true.

First, in the surprisingly swift multiplication of the members allying themselves with it. This grand army, ranked and ready and aggressive for Christian work, recruits itself almost as rapidly as the moments fly. What a jump it is! How grateful we should be to God for it! A little more than a hundred members in 1881; more than half a million members in 1889!

Second, in the vast sweep of territory that Christian Endeavor has taken and is taking for its empire. Beginning in the most northern State of our union, it has pushed eastward and westward and southward until it has planted itself more or less numerously in every State and Territory of our great United States. Nor has even such a Utica been large enough to confine its powers. It has gone farther northward, into all the American dependencies of the British Empire. It has planted its flag in the Sandwich Islands. It has met the warmest welcome in Christian England. It has gathered beneath its banners societies in the most distant mission stations among the heathen.

Third, our great and glorious annual conventions. It is not too much to say that our conventions have grown to be the largest delegated gatherings of Christians in Christendom. Their enthusiasm is wonderful and contagious. Their reverence and orderliness are remarkable. Their prayerfulness and glad spirit of consecration seem to us to be a kind of renewed Pentecost. Of course, the holding of such conventions is to any community a great and impelling religious boon. No wonder it is most urgently desired north, south, east, west. The board of trustees desires to express its most grateful feeling for the beautiful and gracious enthusiasm of the members of Christian Endeavor, of which so many and such admirably argued invitations to this place and that are such evident symptoms.

Fourth, it can, therefore, be very easily seen that the decision as to the particular place of holding the convention as each year comes round, and so many and pressing invitations for it are presented, becomes a most complex matter. And the board of trustees desires to say that the only standard of decision has been and will be—as we know all members of the Christian Endeavor desire to be—where the convention will, everything considered, be most advantageous for the establishment and growth of Christian Endeavor for the year of that convention. And the board of trustees desires to say still further that while, of course, it would be unwise to make distinct and formal pledge or promise, in its judgment probably the best order of holding the conventions, for the future will be one year in a centre covering the great south and south-west, another year in a centre covering the great west and northwest, and another year in a centre covering the great east and northeast. Therefore, the board of trustees, after the most careful deliberation, and moved entirely by the motive above stated, which, we trust, will always be the only motive of decision, determined that, on the whole, and everything considered, the next International Convention of Christian Endeavor be held in St. Louis.

Rev. Jas. L. Hill of Massachusetts, then presented the report of the Committee on Resolutions.

RESOLUTIONS

Adopted by the Eighth Annual Convention.

These resolutions, reported by Rev. James L. Hill, chairman of the committee on resolutions, are both an expression of thanks for many kindnesses received, and a statement of the principles of the Society. They indicate, to a degree, the position that the Society will hold during the ensuing year:—

Whereas, All bills presented to the United Society for the vast expense incurred in the conduct of this convention are receipted bills; and

Whereas, There are two ways of doing a thing, and the friends who have here arranged for this great convention have found the most satisfactory and gratifying method; therefore, be it

Resolved, That we express our deep sense of obligation to the fifty societies of the Philadelphia Union for this welcome; to the "Committee of Nine" for the signal ability, unity of purpose and careful attention to details that has characterized their service, and for the scope, minuteness and completeness of all arrangements relating to this memorable meeting; to Prof. Wm. G. Fischer for his animated and inspiring leadership, which has secured such conspicuous results in our service of song; to the two hundred members of the Christian Endeavor choir; to Miss Walker, the organist, and Miss Knight, the pianist; to the board of officers of the Armory of the First Regiment of the Pennsylvania National Guards, for the use of this great and perfectly equipped building, and for their beneficent expression, "All that we have is for the time yours"; to Captain Muldoon, superintendent of this building, for personal supervision and attention; to his efficient corps of helpers for their patience with our throngs; to our trustee, an unnamed, but honorable and generous member of President Harrison's cabinet, for the gratuitous decoration of this beautiful building; to the churches that have opened their doors to our early meetings; to the Y. M. C. A. for proffered hospitality; to the Philadelphia papers, both morning and evening, for unprecedented courtesies; to the temporary postmaster for his unrequited labors; to the ushers who have been uniformly considerate and polite; to the courteous attendants upon our various bureaus of information, and to the scribes of the convention for their unwearying work.

Resolved, That we pledge to President Clark a renewal of our confidence, affection and support; that we emulate his devotion to the spiritual well-being of the young, and that, in reciprocation of his proposed sentiment, we enter into covenant, as much as in us lies, to be "laborers together with God."

Resolved, That the thanks of this convention having become so richly due, be heartily given to our faithful, vigilant, hard-working coadjutor, Mr. William Shaw, treasurer of the United Society, agent of its publishing department and representative of the trustees in business matters, for the mastery he has shown in the discharge of his multifarious duties.

Whereas, The usefulness of societies is sometimes impaired by the juiceless topics, often too hard, chosen for our prayer-meetings; therefore,

Resolved, That we recommend, without constraint, the adoption, whenever expedient, of the uniform topics selected by the United Society, and published always in THE GOLDEN RULE.

Whereas, Appeals from various organizations, Christian in character, and in themselves worthy of general sympathy and support, have been made to the United Society of Christian Endeavor for indorsement and aid; and

Whereas, the Young People's Society of Christian Endeavor is an organization in the church, and having as its specific object the development of spiritual life among the young people of the churches; therefore, be it

Resolved, That it is essential to the highest interests and permanency of the Young People's Society of Christian Endeavor that it hold strictly to its own lines of effort, as are laid down in its constitution, and be not in any wise diverted therefrom; that all special appeals for contributions to any outside cause be referred to the church officers as responsible for the general benevolence of the church; that the United Society be advised to deal uniformly with all applicants, declaring its adherence to its own great objects, and its conviction of duty to take upon itself no other burdens.

Resolved, That it is inexpedient to allow this society to be made auxiliary to any other, or to be used to further any other object than its own.

Whereas, intemperance recruits its ranks constantly from among the youth of our land, therefore, be it

Resolved, That the Societies of Christian Endeavor commit themselves definitely and unreservedly to the cause of personal abstinence from intoxicants, and to the work of undoing the power of the drunkeries that line the streets in many of our cities and towns.

Whereas, the observance of United Society Day has greatly promoted unity among us and a most desirable *esprit du corps;* therefore, be it

Resolved, That the universal observance of United Society Day be recommended for our societies in the years that are to come.

Whereas, each society of Christian Endeavor comes of some specific church, being of it is indebted to it, and always to be identified with it, and is to be recognized as having no separate existence whatever; therefore, be it

Resolved, That we pledge our loyalty to the pastor of that particular church with which we are severally connected, and that we regard it as no part of our work to break down denominational ideas, but that we go into that church with which we are allied, and there abide, doing its work in that place in the best way that may be disclosed to our united wisdom.

Whereas, the Society of Christian Endeavor is in its very spirit an aggressive missionary organization; therefore it is

Resolved, That we commit ourselves to co-operation with the missionary organizations of our respective churches, and that we work through them in expressing our spirit, and in applying our methods.

The Committee on Credentials presented the following report: —

"There are present in the convention 6,500 delegates representing thirty-one states and territories, Germany, Turkey, Canada, Ontario, Quebec and Nova Scotia."

A beautiful floral emblem bearing the motto of the Society for the coming year, "We are laborers together with God," was brought upon the platform by the Connecticut delegation and presented to Pres. Clark at this point by Rev. H. N. Kinney.

General Secretary Geo. M. Ward having resigned his position on account of sickness, the following resolution was presented by Rev. H. B. Grose: —

RESOLUTION OF TRUSTEES.

Whereas, On account of continued ill-health, our general secretary, George M. Ward, has felt it an imperative necessity to resign the office in which he has served for three years, therefore,

Resolved, That the trustees, regretfully recognizing the necessity, accept the resignation of the general secretary.

Resolved, That in taking this action, they would unanimously emphasize, with all possible intensity and sincerity, their appreciation of the devoted and self-sacrificing, exhaustive and efficient service rendered the cause of Christ and Christian Endeavor by the general secretary in the broad field assigned him. The trustees realize the multiplicity and urgency of the calls made upon him in every section and direction, the physical strain of travel by day and night and constant speaking, and would that it had been in their power to ease the burden and relieve the strain, thus preventing that physical prostration which was long ago foreseen and feared. They could not, however, change nature, nor repress the ardor of one whose heart ever urged him on, regardless of all but the needs of the work. The trustees appreciate the motive as well as the character, spirit and success, of the too arduous labor performed, and would place on record their hearty and unqualified approval of the consecration of the general secretary to his high duties. They express further their gratification at the cordial and fraternal feeling which has existed in mutual service, and which they trust no severance of official relations will interrupt. They believe that the call of Mr. Ward to the work was of God; they would express gratitude to God for raising up one who has stood before the young people as a representative of cultured, consecrated, Christian young manhood; who, in piety and prudence, in spirit and presence, has worthily illustrated the cause for which he has wisely and faithfully worked, and the type of Christianity which it is the supreme aim of Christian Endeavor to produce.

Resolved, That the trustees sympathize deeply with the retiring secretary in his present ill-health, and pray for his speedy and complete restoration; that they will cherish the memory of his worth and work, and hope that he may be spared to a future of conspicuous usefulness and honor.

Resolved, That an engrossed copy of these resolutions be presented to our brother, beloved in the Lord, and that they be printed in THE GOLDEN RULE.

After announcements, Rev. A. T. Pierson, D.D., of Philadelphia, was introduced. Dr. Pierson's address was upon "The World for Christ"

He was followed by Dr. O. P. Gifford of Boston on "Christ for the World."

The enthusiasm of the convention had reached its highest pitch, but the speakers were in full accord and hearty sympathy with the spirit of the hour.

The great needs of the world and the Christ "who supplies our every need" were pictured to the audience in a way never to be forgotten.

"Let us vote that by the help of God the Father, God the Son and God the Holy Ghost, we will see that every man on this earth learns the truth that Jesus Christ died for *sinners*," said Dr. Pierson.

"Christ is the exegesis of God and the world needs him. He is the Divine Dynamo that is to light up earth's darkness. We must step out of the forest of selfishness and yield ourselves to God, if we would hold up this Christ to a darkened world," said Dr. Gifford.

Rev. Jas. L. Hill of Massachusetts presented resolutions of sympathy for Wm. J. Van Patten, ex-president of the convention. Adopted.

A telegram was ordered, sent to him and to General Secretary Ward, embodying the same.

The business of the convention was now over; consecration hour had come. Rev. S. W. Adriance opened the service with an appeal for personal consecration. Prayers and testimony followed. While the audience sang "My faith looks up to Thee," the great assemblage rose, singly at first, then by dozens, by scores, by hundreds, till scarce any one of all the thousands remained seated, thus testifying anew their devotion to Christ.

Rev. Choate Burnham offered the consecration prayer, which was followed by a verse of "Cross and Crown."

"God be with you till we meet again" was sweetly sung by Miss Alice R. Moore, of Medford, Mass., the congregation joining in the chorus.

Pres. Clark then stepped forward and spoke tenderly to the departing delegates.

The convention rose to its feet.

"MIZPAH."

"The Lord watch between me and thee when we are absent one from another," devoutly came the prayer from the lips of the assembled throng, and the Eighth National Christian Endeavor Convention was over.

BARTLETT FOSKETT,
Scribe.

H. A. FIELD,
Assistant.

FINANCIAL STATEMENT

FREE-WILL OFFERING OF SOCIETIES.

CANADA —Montreal, Erskine Presbyterian,	$10 00	
Hamilton Christian Endeavor Union,	25 00	
Guelph Christian Endeavor Union,	1 00	
Toronto, Beverly Street Baptist,	2 50	
Toronto, Zion Congregational,	5 00	
		$43 50
COLORADO.—Denver, Central Christian,	$10 00	
Denver Christian Endeavor Union,	25 00	
Denver, 1st Congregational,	25 00	
		60 00
CONNECTICUT.—Ansonia Baptist,	$5 00	
Branford, 1st Congregational,	5 00	
Bridgeport, 1st Presbyterian,	10 00	
Bridgeport, 1st Congregational,	10 00	
Bridgeport, Park Street Congregational,	10 00	
Bristol Methodist,	5 00	
Bristol Congregational,	25 00	
Bristol Baptist,	2 00	
Cheshire Congregational,	4 00	
Collinsville Congregational,	10 00	
Danielsonville, Westfield Congregational,	15 00	
East Granby Congregational,	5 00	
Enfield Congregational,	10 00	
Forestville M. E.	1 00	
Glastonbury, 1st Congregational,	5 00	
Guilford, 3d Congregational,	2 00	
Hartford, Windsor Avenue Congregational	5 00	
Hartford, South Park M. E.	5 00	
Hawington,	2 00	
Higganum Congregational,	20 00	
Jewett City Congregational,	3 00	
Kensington Congregational,	5 00	
Kent Congregational,	5 00	
Manchester, North Congregational,	25 00	
Meriden, 1st Baptist,	5 00	
Meriden, 1st Congregational,	10 00	

YOUNG PEOPLE'S SOCIETY

Meriden, Centre Congregational,	$5 00
Middlefield Congregational,	2 00
Middle Haddam, 2d Congregational,	5 00
Milford, 1st Church,	10 00
Montville Congregational,	5 00
New Haven, 2d Congregational,	20 00
New Haven United,	20 00
New Haven, Davenport,	10 00
New Haven, Dwight Place Congregational,	10 00
New Milford Congregational,	5 00
Norwalk, 1st Baptist,	5 00
Norwich, 2d Congregational,	15 00
Northfield Congregational,	1 00
Plainville Congregational,	10 00
Plymouth Congregational,	12 00
Rockville, Union Congregational,	10 00
Simsbury Congregational,	10 00
Stamford, 1st Congregational,	10 00
Stamford Baptist,	10 00
Stamford Presbyterian,	10 00
Stamford Congregational,	5 00
Suffield, 2d Baptist,	10 00
Taftville Congregational,	1 00
Talcottville Congregational,	10 00
Terryville Congregational,	10 00
Thomaston, 1st Congregational,	25 00
Thomaston M. E.	5 00
Wallingford, 1st Congregational,	5 00
Waterbury, 2d Congregational,	5 00
Wethersfield Congregational,	2 00
Winsted, 1st Congregational,	2 00
Winsted M. E.	1 30
Woodstock Congregational,	2 00
	——— 480 30
DELAWARE.—Milford Presbyterian,	$5 00
Wilmington Christian Endeavor Union,	25 00
Wilmington, Delaware Avenue Baptist,	5 00
	——— 35 00
DISTRICT OF COLUMBIA.—Washington, Covenant Church	$1 00
Washington, Plymouth Congregational,	5 00
Washington, 5th Congregational,	5 00
	——— 11 00
ILLINOIS.—Austin, 1st Presbyterian,	$5 00
Chicago, Hyde Park Presbyterian,	10 00
Chicago, 1st Presbyterian,	50 00
Chicago, Western Avenue,	2 00
Chicago, New England Congregational,	10 00
Chicago, Central Park Presbyterian,	5 00
Chicago, St. Paul's Reformed Episcopal,	20 00
Decatur Christian Endeavor Union,	20 00
Elgin, 1st Congregational,	5 00
Hinsdale Congregational,	2 00
Rushville, 1st Presbyterian,	10 00
Springfield Christian Endeavor Union,	50 00
	——— 189 00
INDIANA.—Evansville, Cumberland Presbyterian,	$5 00

Evansville, Grace Presbyterian,	$10 00
Evansville, Walnut Street Presbyterian,	5 00
Goshen Presbyterian,	5 00
Indianapolis, 2d Presbyterian,	5 00
Indianapolis, 7th Presbyterian,	5 00
Richmond, 1st Presbyterian,	10 00
South Bend, 1st M. E.	5 00
South Bend, 1st Christian.	5 00
South Bend, 1st Presbyterian,	5 00
South Bend, 1st Baptist,	5 00
	$65 00
Iowa.—Burlington Union,	5 00
Des Moines, Central Presbyterian,	10 00
	15 00
Kansas.—Paola M. E.	$5 00
Topeka, Central Congregational,	5 00
Topeka Christian Endeavor Union,	50 00
Wichita, 1st Presbyterian,	10 00
	70 00
Kentucky.—Louisville, 2d Presbyterian,	$5 00
	5 00
Maine.—Augusta Congregational,	$5 00
Augusta, 1st Baptist,	5 00
Brownville Congregational,	5 00
Castine Congregational,	1 00
Kennebunk Congregational,	20 00
North Bridgton Congregational,	2 50
Portland, Williston Congregational,	25 00
Portland, 1st Baptist,	5 00
	68 50
Maryland.—Baltimore, 1st Presbyterian,	$1 00
Baltimore, 1st Congregational,	5 00
Colora, West Nottingham,	5 00
Rising Sun M. E.	1 00
	12 00
Massachusetts, Andover, West Congregational,	$15 00
Attleboro, Second Congregational,	5 00
Auburndale, Congregational,	15 00
Berlin, Congregational,	5 00
Boston, Berkeley Temple,	25 00
Boston, Union Congregational,	100 00
Boston, Dorchester, Pilgrim Congregational,	10 00
Boston, Dorchester, Stoughton Street Baptist,	5 00
Boston, Park Street Congregational,	25 00
Brighton, Evangelical Congregational,	10 00
Brookline, Bethany, Harvard Church,	50 00
Bradford, 1st Congregational,	15 00
Cambridge, O. C. Baptist,	5 00
Cambridgeport, Pilgrim Congregational,	10 00
Charlestown, Trinity M. E.	5 00
Charlestown, Winthrop Congregational,	15 00
Chelsea, Central Congregational.	5 00
Chesterfield Congregational,	5 00
Chicopee, 3d Congregational,	25 00
Concord Congregational,	20 00
Danvers, 1st Congregational,	5 00

Enfield Congregational,	5 00
Fall River, 1st Christian,	3 00
Fall River, Central Congregational,	10 00
Fitchburg, 1st Baptist,	15 00
Fitchburg, Rollstone Congregational,	25 00
Franklin,	1 00
Gardner, 1st Congregational,	35 00
Gloucester, Evangelical Congregational,	10 00
Groton, Congregational,	5 00
Hadley, 1st Congregational,	5 00
Hatfield,	1 00
Haverhill, West Congregational,	10 00
Haverhill, Central Congregational,	100 00
Haverhill, North Congregational,	100 00
Haydenville Congregational,	15 00
Holyoke, 1st Congregational,	15 00
Holyoke, 2d Baptist,	5 00
Hyde Park, 1st Congregational,	10 00
Jamaica Plain, Boylston Congregational,	10 00
Lawrence United Presbyterian,	5 00
Lawrence, South Congregational,	2 00
Lexington, Hancock Congregational,	5 00
Lincoln, Congregational,	25 00
Lowell, High Street Congregational,	15 00
Lowell, Highland Congregational,	25 00
Lowell, Royal Legion,	25 00
Lynn, Central Congregational,	10 00
Lynn, North Congregational,	25 00
Malden, First Church,	25 00
Medford, Mystic Congregational,	100 00
Melrose Congregational,	20 00
Middleboro, Central Congregational,	5 00
Natick, 1st Baptist,	5 00
Natick, 1st Congregational,	10 00
Newburyport, 1st Presbyterian,	5 00
North Brookfield, 1st Congregational,	10 00
North Brookfield M. E.	5 00
North Wilbraham, Grace Union,	10 00
Pittsfield Baptist,	5 00
Princeton Congregational,	5 00
Plymouth, Pilgrimage Congregational,	5 00
Reading Congregational,	25 00
Salem, Crombie Street,	25 00
Shrewsbury Congregational,	3 00
Somerville, 1st M. E.	5 00
South Boston, Phillips' Congregational,	50 00
South Natick,	2 00
Southville Congregational,	2 00
Spencer Congregational,	50 00
Springfield, North Congregational,	25 00
Springfield, 1st Congregational,	50 00
Wakefield Congregational,	25 00
Wellesley Congregational,	5 00
Warren Congregational,	10 00
Westfield, 2d Congregational,	25 00
Westhampton Congregational,	5 00

West Medford Congregational,	$5 00	
West Newton, 2d Congregational,	25 00	
Worcester, Salem Street,	10 00	
		$1,449 00
MICHIGAN.—Benzonia,	$5 00	
Detroit, Central Presbyterian,	5 00	
Detroit, Trumbull Avenue,	1 00	
Reed City, Congregational,	10 00	
Traverse City, Congregational,	10 00	
		31 00
MINNESOTA.—Albert Lea, 1st Presbyterian,	$5 00	
Duluth, Pilgrim Congregational,	10 00	
Minneapolis, Westminster,	15 00	
Minneapolis, Church of Christ,	5 00	
Rochester, 1st Presbyterian,	1 00	
St. Paul, Woodland Park Baptist,	3 00	
St. Paul, House of Hope,	25 00	
St. Paul, 1st M. E.	5 00	
Winona, 1st Congregational,	5 00	
		74 00
MISSOURI.—Hannibal Congregational,	$2 00	
Hannibal, Park M. E.	2 00	
Kansas City, Indiana Avenue M. E.	10 00	
Sedalia, 1st Congregational,	5 00	
St. Joseph, 1st M. E.	10 00	
St. Louis, 2d Presbyterian,	10 00	
St. Louis, Westminster,	5 00	
St. Louis, 1st Christian,	5 00	
St. Louis, Lafayette Park Presbyterian,	10 00	
St. Louis, Soulard Market Mission,	10 00	
St. Louis, Pilgrim Congregational,	10 00	
St. Louis, Central Presbyterian,	25 00	
St. Louis, Cumberland Presbyterian,	5 00	
		109 00
NEBRASKA.—Ashland Congregational,	$5 00	
Lincoln, Plymouth Congregational,	5 00	
Norfolk Congregational,	5 00	
		15 00
NEW HAMPSHIRE.—Concord, So. Congregational,	$50 00	
Concord, 1st Congregational,	35 00	
Exeter, 1st Congregational,	5 00	
Keene, 2d Congregational,	5 00	
Manchester, 1st Congregational,	20 00	
Milford Congregational,	20 00	
Nashua, 1st Congregational,	20 00	
Nashua, 1st Baptist,	10 00	
Penacook, Congregational,	10 00	
Peterborough, Union Evangelical,	10 00	
Reed's Ferry, 1st Congregational,	5 00	
West Concord, West Congregational,	5 00	
		195 00
NEW JERSEY.—Arlington, 1st Presbyterian,	$10 00	
Ashway Presbyterian,	5 00	
Asbury Park, 1st M. E.	5 00	
Belleville Reformed,	15 00	

Beverly Presbyterian,	$25 00
Blackwood Presbyterian,	10 00
Boonton, 1st Presbyterian,	10 00
Bridgeton, No. Pearl Street Baptist Chapel,	3 00
Bridgeton, 1st Presbyterian,	5 00
Bridgeton, Western Presbyterian,	5 00
Bridgewater, Central Methodist,	10 00
Caldwell, Presbyterian,	5 00
Camden, 1st Presbyterian,	10 00
Closter Congregational,	5 00
Colt's Neck Reformed,	5 00
Dover Presbyterian,	10 00
Dunellen, Presbyterian,	5 00
Elizabeth, East Baptist,	5 00
Elizabeth, 3d Presbyterian,	10 00
Flanders Presbyterian,	5 00
Freehold, 1st Reformed,	5 00
Freehold, 2d Reformed,	5 00
Hackensack, 2d Reformed,	10 00
Hackettstown Presbyterian,	5 00
Hightstown Baptist,	5 00
Haddonfield Baptist,	5 00
Jamesbury Presbyterian,	25 00
Jersey City, Westminster Presbyterian,	5 00
Jersey City, Waverly Congregational,	5 00
Jersey City, Bergen Baptist,	10 00
Jersey City, Claremont Presbyterian,	5 00
Merchantsville Presbyterian,	5 00
Metuchen Reformed,	10 00
Millston Reformed,	5 00
Montclair, 1st Presbyterian,	10 00
Newark, Clinton Avenue Reformed,	2 00
Newark, Woodside Reformed,	5 00
Newark, Emanuel Reformed Episcopal,	5 00
Newark, Belleville Avenue Congregational,	5 00
New Brunswick, 1st Reformed,	10 00
Oxford, 2d Presbyterian,	5 00
Perth Amboy Presbyterian,	10 00
Plainfield, 1st Presbyterian,	10 00
Plainfield, Trinity Reformed,	5 00
Plainfield, Warren Mission,	2 00
Princeton, Witherspoon Street Presbyterian,	2 00
Rahway, 2d Presbyterian,	10 00
Readington,	1 00
Ridgewood, 1st Reformed,	5 00
Salem, 1st Baptist,	5 00
South Amboy, Presbyterian,	3 00
Springfield, Presbyterian,	20 00
Tenafly, Presbyterian,	5 00
Trenton, Messiah,	5 00
Vineland, 1st Methodist,	5 00
Vineland, 1st Presbyterian,	5 00
Vineland, Baptist,	5 00
Westfield, Baptist,	5 00
Williamstown Presbyterian,	3 00
Woodbury, 1st Baptist,	10 00
	———$426 00

NEW YORK.—Albany, 1st Reformed, $25 00
Auburn, Central Presbyterian, 10 00
Aquebogue, Congregational, 2 00
Aquebogue, Northville Congregational, 5 00
Bath Presbyterian, 10 00
Binghamton, West Presbyterian, 10 00
Broadalbin Baptist, 3 00
Brooklyn, Kent Street Reformed, 10 00
Brooklyn, Lewis Avenue Congregational, 5 00
Brooklyn, Tompkins Avenue Congregational, 5 00
Brooklyn, 2d Presbyterian, 5 00
Brooklyn, South Reformed, 5 00
Brooklyn, Bedford Reformed, 5 00
Brooklyn, Central Baptist, 5 00
Brooklyn, 1st Baptist, 5 00
Bruynswick, Shawanayunk Reformed, 5 00
Buffalo, 1st Congregational, 10 00
Buffalo, West Avenue Presbyterian, 5 00
Buffalo, Delaware Avenue Baptist, 5 00
Buffalo, Glenwood Avenue Baptist Mission, 5 00
Buffalo, Seneca Street M. E. 5 00
Buffalo, 1st Presbyterian, 5 00
Catskill, Reformed, 5 00
Churchville, Union Congregational, 5 00
Cleveland Methodist, 3 00
Dryden Presbyterian, 5 00
Fairport Congregational, 5 00
Flatbush, Reformed Mission, 1 50
Flushing Reformed, 2 00
Flushing, 1st Baptist, 5 00
Geneseo Presbyterian, 3 00
Glens Falls, 1st Presbyterian, 5 00
Greenport Presbyterian, 10 00
High Falls, 5 00
Huntington, 2d Presbyterian, 3 00
Huntington, 1st Presbyterian, 3 00
Jamaica, 1st Presbyterian, 2 00
Kingston, 1st Baptist, 2 00
Lockport, 1st Congregational, 3 00
Lockport, 1st Presbyterian, 5 00
Lyons Presbyterian, 5 00
Medina, 1st Baptist, 5 00
McGrawsville Presbyterian, 5 00
Mont Moor, Clarkstown Reformed, 5 00
Mt. Vernon Presbyterian, 10 00
Mt. Vernon Reformed, 10 00
New Brighton Union, 5 00
Newark Presbyterian, 5 00
Newark Valley M. E. 2 00
New York, Church of Strangers, 25 00
New York, 1st Baptist, Melrose, 5 00
New York, Morrisania Congregational, 5 00
Newburgh, Calvary Presbyterian, 10 00
Niskayuna Reformed, 5 00
New Paltz Dutch Reformed, 5 00
North Chili M. E. 5 00

Nyack Baptist,	$15 00	
Nyack Reformed,	10 00	
Oneida Baptist,	5 00	
Oswego, Grace,	10 00	
Ovid Presbyterian,	5 00	
Palatine Bridge Reformed,	5 00	
Troy, 3d Presbyterian,	1 00	
Phœnix, 1st Congregational,	2 00	
Portville, 1st Presbyterian,	5 00	
Poughkeepsie, Washington Street M. E.	2 00	
Poughkeepsie, Hedding M. E.	3 00	
Randolph Union,	2 00	
Rochester, Brick Presbyterian,	25 00	
Rochester, 1st Presbyterian,	25 00	
Rochester, St. Peter's Presbyterian	5 00	
Rochester Central,	60 00	
Rochester, 2d Baptist,	5 00	
Rochester, Westminster,	10 00	
Rochester, Cornhill,	5 00	
Saratoga, 1st Baptist,	5 00	
Sauquort Presbyterian,	5 00	
Sodus Presbyterian,	5 00	
Spencer M. E.	1 50	
Staten Island Calvary Presbyterian,	5 00	
Tarrytown, 2d Reformed,	5 00	
Watertown, 1st Presbyterian,	1 00	
Wellsville Congregational,	5 00	
West Brighton Calvary Presbyterian,	1 00	
Yonkers Reformed,	28 00	
		596 00
NOVA SCOTIA.—Yarmouth, St. John's Presbyterian,	$5 00	
		5 00
OHIO.—Central College Presbyterian,	$5 00	
Cincinnati, Walnut Hill Congregational,	5 00	
Cleveland, Willson Avenue Baptist,	2 00	
Cleveland, Euclid Avenue Disciples,	10 00	
Cleveland, Euclid Avenue Congregational,	10 00	
Cleveland, Scranton Avenue Free Baptist,	5 00	
Cleveland, Plymouth,	15 00	
Cleveland, Jennings Avenue Congregational,	5 00	
Columbus, Broad Street Presbyterian,	25 00	
Defiance, 1st Presbyterian,	3 00	
Greenville, United Brethren,	2 00	
Independence, 1st M. E.,	1 00	
Marietta, 1st Congregational,	4 00	
Sandusky Congregational,	5 00	
Tallmadge Congregational,	3 00	
Tiffin, 1st Presbyterian,	3 00	
Warren Presbyterian,	1 00	
Westerville, United Brethren,	2 00	
Westerville Presbyterian,	1 00	
Xenia, 1st Presbyterian,	6 60	
Youngstown, Plymouth Congregational,	5 00	
		118 00
PENNSYLVANIA.—Anselma, St. Paul's Reformed,	$5 00	
Bechtelsville, New Mennonite,	1 00	

Bethlehem Moravian,	$3 00
Columbia Methodist,	1 00
Doylestown Presbyterian,	1 00
Easton, 1st Presbyterian.	30 00
Erie Christian Endeavor Union,	10 00
Faggs Manor,	5 00
Franklin, 1st Presbyterian,	2 00
Gettysburg, St. James,	5 00
Harrisburg, Market Square Presbyterian,	10 00
Hatboro Baptist,	5 00
Lancaster, Duke Street M. E.,	5 00
Linfield Reformed,	1 00
Mauch Chunk, 1st Presbyterian,	10 00
Media Presbyterian,	2 00
Millersville,	5 00
Moosic Presbyterian,	15 00
Mt. Jackson Westfield Presbyterian,	2 00
Norristown, 1st Baptist,	10 00
Norristown Central Presbyterian,	10 00
Norristown. 2d Baptist,	5 00
Oxford M. E.	4 00
Philadelphia, 13th Street M. E.,	10 00
Philadelphia, Central Baptist,	1 00
Philadlphia, Wesley M. E.,	5 00
Philadelphia, West Spruce Street Presbyterian,	25 00
Pittsburg, Mt. Washington Presbyterian,	10 00
Plymouth Christian,	1 00
Reading, 2d Reformed,	5 00
Scranton, Providence Presbyterian,	5 00
Scranton, Washburn Street Presbyterian,	10 00
Scranton, 1st Presbyterian,	5 00
Scranton, Jackson Street Baptist,	5 00
Scranton, Providence.	1 00
Scranton, 2d Presbyterian,	5 00
Slatington Presbyterian,	2 00
Stroudsburg Presbyterian,	1 00
Washington,	1 00
Waynesburg,	5 00
West Pillston, 1st M. E.	2 00
Williamsport, 1st Baptist,	2 50
Zionsville Mennonite,	2 00
	250 50
RHODE ISLAND.—Central Falls, Broad Street Baptist,	$10 00
Central Falls, Congregational,	25 00
North Smithfield, Slatersville Congregational,	10 00
Pawtucket, 1st Free Baptist,	10 00
Providence, Beneficent Congregational,	10 00
Providence, Broad Street Christian.	5 00
Providence, Pilgrim Congregational,	25 00
Providence, Union Congregational,	20 00
Woonsocket, Globe Congregational,	10 00
	125 00
UTAH.—Salt Lake City, State Christian Endeavor Union.	$25 00
	25 00
VERMONT.—Burlington, 1st Congregational,	$20 00
Burlington, College Street,	10 00

Essex Junction, Union,	$5 00	
Rutland Congregational,	10 00	
		$45 00
WISCONSIN.—Chippewa Falls Presbyterian,	$10 00	
Green Bay Presbyterian,	5 00	
Milwaukee, Grand Avenue Congregational,	15 00	
Racine, 1st Congregational,	5 00	
Oshkosh, Algona Street M. E.	5 00	
		40 00

PERSONAL OFFERING.

CALIFORNIA.—San Francisco, Nellie Cole,	$1 00	
		$1.00
CONNECTICUT.—Ansonia, Ida J. Cook,	$ 50	
Bristol, Geo. P. Allyn,	1 00	
Bridgeport, Mary L. Dimond,	1 00	
Canton Center, Daniel B. Lord,	1 00	
Danbury, Alice Treadwell,	1 00	
Fairfield, Mary B. Kippen,	2 00	
Granby, Selden W. Hayes,	50	
Hawinton, F. E. Snow,	1 00	
Hartford, Letta L. Gilbert,	1 00	
Kensington, H. L. Hutchins,	2 00	
Madison, Everett G. Hill,	1 00	
New Haven, Walter M. Davis,	20 00	
North Canaan, Rev. T. H. Baragwanath,	1 00	
North Haven, Mary B. Goodyear,	1 00	
North Canaan, G. Willis Parsons,	2 00	
Norwalk, Chas. A. Haveland,	1 00	
Norwich, Susan C. Hyde,	50	
Preston, R. H. Gidman,	50	
Somers, Annie L. Moore,	1 00	
South Manchester, Annie I. House,	2 50	
South Manchester, C. E. House	3 00	
South Manchester, Emma K. Eldridge,	2 00	
South Norwalk, John Francis,	1 00	
Torringford, Alice E. Birge,	1 00	
Torrington, Emma L. Phippeney,	1 00	
Wallingford, F. M. Cowles,	1 00	
West Norfolk, W. Warland,	1 00	
West Winsted, F. W. Marsh,	1 00	
Winsted, Lella Cook,	50	
Winsted, Abby F. Hull,	50	

Winsted, Chas. B. Moore,	$1 00	
Windsor Locke, A. Bickett,	2 00	
		$57 50
DELAWARE,—Newark, Jas. L. Malone,	$2 00	
		2 00
DISTRICT OF COLUMBIA.—Washington, J. Ralston Fleming,	$1 00	
		1 00
FLORIDA.—Daytonia, Jacob Slough,	$ 50	
Gainsville, Mrs. M. L. Selden,	2 00	
		2 50
INDIANA.—Richmond, Ella S. Harold,	$1 00	
Richmond, J. J. Dickenson,	1 00	
		2 00
IOWA.—Davenport, H. H. Smith,	$5 00	
Muscatine, Ella Mulford,	1 00	
		6 00
KENTUCKY.—Louisville, A. A. Hill,	$2 00	
		2 00
MAINE.—Bath, Lucy P. Cary,	$1 00	
Brewer, W. I. Bunker,	50	
		1 50
MARYLAND.—Baltimore, C. A. Evans,	$1 00	
Baltimore, John McKenzie,	1 00	
Baltimore, A. Gertrude Kaltenbach,	1 00	
		3 00
MASSACHUSETTS.—Amesbury, S. A. Gibson,	$ 75	
Amesbury, Chas. M. Goodale,	1 00	
Andover, Rev. F. W. Greene,	15 00	
Ashland, Ida E. Metcalf,	5 00	
Auburndale, Mrs. F. E. Clark,	10 00	
Auburndale, Maude W. Clark,	2 00	
Auburndale, Julia M. Pickard,	3 00	
Bernardston, Josie E. Fletcher,	5 00	
Boston, W. R. Lamkin,	1 00	
Boston, Lelia A. Smith,	1 00	
Boston, Dwight H. Smith,	2 00	
Cambridgeport, Helen F. Hidden,	1 00	
Cambridgeport, Wm. H. Hidden, Jr.,	1 00	
Charlestown, W. P. Hart,	50	
Chesterfield, Carrie M. Edwards,	50	
Dedham, J. Y. Noyes,	10 00	
Fitchburg, I. A. Burnap,	1 00	
Hinsdale, Rev. J. H. Laird,	1 00	
Lincoln, G. H. Flint,	50	
Lowell, K. L. Ward,	1 00	
Lynn, F. E. Drake,	1 00	
Lynn, James M. Marsh,	5 00	
Lynn, Chas. L. Chamberlain,	1 00	
Lynn, Myra L. Foss,	50	
Marion, M. Louisa Allen,	1 00	
Middletown, Geo. M. Derry,	1 00	
Monson, Edward L. Morris,	3 00	
Monterey, Misses Townsend,	50	
Newton Highlands, W. Bennett,	2 00	
Newtonville, G. W. Auryansen,	1 00	
Princeton, Chas. A. White,	1 00	

Salem, Willard G. Bixby,	$1 00	
Saxonville, A. W. Parmenter,	1 00	
South Boston, Chas. T. James,	2 00	
South Boston, Francis A. Cornish,	5 00	
South Boston, Julia H. Duncan,	2 00	
South Deerfield, H. A. Field,	10 00	
Somerville, Ella Harris and Alice Frye,	50	
South Weymouth, Sadie B. Finett,	2 00	
Springfield, M. E. Garrett,	1 00	
Stoneham, two members,	1 50	
Wakefield, Clara P. Riggs,	3 00	
Wakefield, Chas. Bridge.	2 00	
Whitinsville, A. H. Whipple,	5 00	
Worcester, Marion Smith,	50	
Worcester, G. S. Blakely,	1 00	
Worcester, Emma M. Plympton,	1 00	
Worcester, Susie A. Partridge,	1 00	118 75
MICHIGAN.—Bay City, A. E. Ronech,	$3 00	
St. John, John H. Petrie,	1 00	4 00
MINNESOTA.—Minneapolis, Fred S. Shepherd,	$2 00	
St. Paul, E. B. McClanahan, Jr.,	10 00	
St. Paul, G. Middleton,	1 00	13 00
MISSOURI.—Hannibal, R. J. Egelston,	$ 50	
St. Louis, Rev. B. E. Reed,	5 00	5 50
NEW HAMPSHIRE.—Bennington, J. H. Heald,	$1 00	
Keene, Carrie E. Whitcomb,	3 00	
Nashua, Robert M. Matthews,	2 00	6 00
NEW JERSEY.—Bloomfield, Theodore Herring,	$1 00	
Boonton, Flora C. Woodruff,	1 00	
Boonton, Jessie M. Doremus,	1 00	
Bridgeton, Miss Mulford,	1 00	
Camden, Mrs. Andrew Cline,	1 00	
Dayton, J. W. Osborne.	1 00	
Dennisville, Harry C. Wheaton,	1 00	
Dover, Geo. E. Jenkins,	1 00	
Jersey City, Mrs. L. L. Harvey,	1 00	
Junction, Grace F. Kelly,	50	
Junction, Florence Lewis,	50	
Little Falls, Geo. L. Vanness,	50	
Mt. Freedom, Annie A. Wolfe,	2 00	
Newark, Samuel D. Price,	1 00	
New Brunswick, H. B. Patton,	1 00	
New Brunswick, C. E. Corwin,	1 00	
Ocean Grove, S. S. Assembly, by Rev. B. B. Loomis,	5 00	
Passaic, Lizzie Thorpe,	1 00	
Paterson, James A. Tasney,	50	
Perth Amboy, Mrs. J. H. Owens,	50	
Perth Amboy, John A. Henry,	50	
Perth Amboy, Emma Morris,	50	
Ridgefield Park, J. B. Tukey,	1 00	
Trenton, I. L. Condict,	5 00	

Tenafly, T. L. Masdutyn,	$5 00	
Wenonah, Annie K. McGill,	1 00	
		$35 50
NEW YORK.—Albany, E. M. Dickinson,	$ 50	
Albany, Rev. J. Wilbur Chapman,	25 00	
Brooklyn, James C. Doty,	1 00	
Brooklyn, Augustus V. Heely,	2 00	
Brooklyn, E. M. Spence,	1 00	
Brooklyn, Howard Haviland,	5 00	
Bruynswick, Mrs. P. K. Hageman,	50	
Catskill, Grace Donahue,	1 00	
Clifton Springs, Ellen Johnson,	1 00	
Corona, Rev. W. J. Peck,	2 00	
Glens Falls, Miss A. C. Wing,	2 00	
Glens Falls, S. A. Hays,	1 00	
Greenport, F. L. Terry,	1 00	
Greenport, D. L. Bardwell,	10 00	
Hastings-on-Hudson, J. T. Wheeler,	50	
Ithaca, Lou H. Williams,	10 00	
Jamaica, J. E. Phelps,	50	
Jamesport, Wm. Hedges,	1 00	
Keyswike, Jennie Sahlen,	1 00	
Medina, Mrs. Ida M. Garlock,	1 00	
New Hartford, R. E. Evans,	1 00	
Newburgh, Miss L. Frazier,	50	
Norwich, E. F. Mueson,	1 00	
Morrisania, A. H. Fraser,	50	
Morrisania, E. Griffith,	50	
New York, H. M. Andrews,	5 00	
Oneida, Clara C. Hurd,	50	
Palatine Bridge, H. S. Beach,	2 00	
Rhinebeck, W. A. Chadwick,	1 00	
Rochester, S. L. Munson,	1 00	
Rochester, Carrie McConnell,	3 00	
Sayville, A. P. Comstock,	1 00	
Schenectady, R. Clements,	2 00	
Smyrna, F. W. Avery,	50	
Stockbridge, Rev. Chas. Haynes,	1 00	
Stockbridge, F. G. Schoonmaker,	3 00	
Troy, Geo. T. Lemmon,	2 00	
Utica, A. B. Mitchell,	50	
Utica, Gertrude Penner,	1 00	
Utica, Geo. A. Swentfager,	50	
Walkill, Estella Upright,	50	
		95 00
NOVA SCOTIA.—Canso, F. G. Creed,	$1 00	
		1 00
OHIO.—Cleveland, Isabella J. Stocke,	$1 00	
Cleveland, Frank Piwonka,	1 00	
Cleveland, F. C. Luff,	50	
Cleveland, William E. Luff,	1 00	
Kingston, S. W. Elliott,	50	
Mansfield, Irene Bushnell,	50	
Millersburg, H. H. Grotthouse,	50	
Wooster, E. F. Greene,	1 00	

YOUNG PEOPLE'S SOCIETY

Xenia, John Acherson,	$1 00	
		$7 00
ONTARIO.—Toronto, David J. Howell,	$1 00	
		1 00
PENNSYLVANIA.—Bally, J. B. Bechtel,	5 00	
Cannonsburg, Maggie N. Espy,	50	
Carlisle, Rev. L. L. Mapes,	1 00	
Columbia, F. A. Duttenhofer,	1 00	
Conshohocken, T. A. Lloyd,	5 00	
Delta, Rev. S. C. Ohman,	5 00	
Easton, Fannie Greene,	3 00	
East Smithfield, R. M. Hunsicker,	50	
Gettysburg, H. F. Smart,	50	
Heckton Mills, Carrie W. Heck,	1 00	
Lafayette Hill, Mrs. W. A. Ret,	1 50	
Lafayette Hill, Bertha Staley,	75	
Lebanon, R. D. Smith,	50	
Lebanon, V. R. S. R.,	1 00	
Lebanon, Mildred R. Smith,	1 00	
Lewistown, Anna Mutthersbaugh,	1 00	
Moosic, S. H. Houser,	25 00	
McAllisterville, W. H. Hooper,	1 00	
Norristown, J. Dickerson,	1 00	
Norristown, J. S. Barden,	1 00	
Oxford, Helen Worth,	50	
Philadelphia, Miss D. B. Carpenter,	2 00	
Philadelphia, Rebecca M. Nelson,	50	
Philadelphia, R. J. Sellers,	1 00	
Philadelphia, Kate Meeke,	1 00	
Philadelphia, M. Warner,	50	
Philadelphia, Geo. M. Kibe,	2 00	
Philadelphia, Mary F. Maxfield,	1 00	
Philadelphia, C. R. Williams,	50	
Philadelphia, Maude F. Stone,	1 00	
Philadelphia, Mrs. Emma Bradley,	1 00	
Philadelphia, Duane Wevill,	2 00	
Philadelphia, Wayland Hoyt, D. D.,	25 00	
Philadelphia, Nellie M. Fletcher,	2 00	
Philadelphia, Adele B. Kay,	10 00	
Phœnixville, George Herzel,	1 00	
Pittsburgh, Samuel McKinley,	5 00	
Port Carbon, S. B. McQuade,	1 00	
Pottsville, Belle Simmons,	1 00	
Reading, F. F. Boas,	1 50	
Scranton, A. May Benedict,	1 00	
Scranton, E. Boyd Weitzel,	5 00	
Scranton, Mary McCulloch,	1 00	
Scranton, Nettie Moore,	50	
South Bethlehem, Rev. J. F. Scott,	00	
Stroudsburg, Sallie M. Detrick,	50	
Stroudsburg, Mary Greenwold,	1 00	
Titusville, Minnie L. Benton,	50	
Tyrone, Miss M. M. Lindsay,	50	
Wellsboro, C. U. Caurse,	1 00	
Williamsport, Ida R. Houtz,	1 00	
		129 75

RHODE ISLAND.—Ashaway, Jessie F. Briggs, . . $5 00
 Ashaway, Mrs. I. L. Cottrell, .   1 00
 Auburn, Clara L. Read,   2 00
 Central Falls, Mrs. Wm. N. Angell,   1 00
 East Providence, Rev. J. Stewart,   1 00
 Olneyville, Emma C. Gifford, .   2 00
 Providence, John N. Gardner,   1 00
 Providence, Henry M. Hutchins,   2 00
 Providence, Rev. M. H. Bixby,   2 00
 Providence, W. M. McNair, .   1 00
 Providence, A. S. Abbott, .   1 00
 Westerly, Alice Masson,   1 00
 Westerly, Isaac C. Taylor,   1 00
             $21 00

TURKEY.—Harpoot, A Friend, $9 00
 Harpoot, Emma C. Wheeler, .   10 00
             19 00

VERMONT.—Burlington, Mrs. C. L. Smith, $1 00
 Burlington, A. Abbott, .   50
 Montpelier, E. E. Towner.   1 00
 Windsor, Rev. S. S. Martyn, .   1 00
             3 50

WEST VIRGINIA.—Parkersburg, W. B. McGregor, $1 00
             1 00

WISCONSIN.—Milwaukee, Wm. W. Christie, $5 00
 River Falls, Sarah and Amy Powell,   5 00
             10 00

Cash, . .   102 87

THE ADDRESSES OF WELCOME.

The addresses of welcome this year by Rev. J. T. Beckley, D. D., of the Beth Eden Baptist Church, Philadelphia, in behalf of the Pennsylvania Union, of which he is president; of Bishop Nicholson, of the Reformed Episcopal Church, in behalf of the churches of Philadelphia, and the response by Rev. S. V. Leach, D. D., of the First Methodist Episcopal Church, Albany, New York, in behalf of the Trustees, were all of them of a very high order, because they were not simply greetings, but dealt with principles as well.

ADDRESS OF REV. J. T. BECKLEY, D. D.,
Pastor Beth Eden Baptist Church, Philadelphia, Pa.

It is my pleasure to welcome you to the Commonwealth. I am only an immigrant myself. Following illustrious example, I have turned to the cyclopedia. I find there the astute remark that in Pennsylvania it is cold in winter and sultry in summer, and that the dreaded northeasters of New England lose much of their vigor by the time they reach the Delaware. While you are our guests we can assure you, at least, protection from the dreaded northeasters.

I will say in confidence that I have been asked more than once how we lured you to Philadelphia just when everybody who can is anxious to leave it. I reply, you are here to show the mettle of Christian Endeavor enthusiasm. You can't burn it; you can't melt it; you can't evaporate it. If it can stand Philadelphia in July, it has nothing to fear. Here, where William Penn tried his "holy experiment"—a free colony for all mankind—we celebrate an experiment that is not an experiment. As I look over these assembled thousands, it seems impossible that this is only the eighth anniversary of this movement. In magnitude it seems like the celebration of a centennial.

THE POWER OF CO-OPERATION.

You represent three elements.

First.—The power of co-operation. In the list of men who came to David at Hebron and made him king were the men of Zebulon, 50,000, which could keep rank and were not of double heart. They could stand in order of battle with undivided heart. Such an army, ten times multiplied, you represent.

This is the age of association. Co-operated capital is putting new power into the hand of commerce. It has pierced an isthmus and tunnelled Alps and spanned continents. Co-operation is such a power in the church. We may lament that the sphere of single-handed endeavor has been usurped by the power of organization. There is a romance about the lonely missionary who goes forth to subjugate an empire. A single evangelist, like a Patrick among the Irish, Columba among the Britons, a Boniface among the Germans, an Augustine among the Saxons, winning by persuasive eloquence, may fascinate us, but we do not win our battles in that way. In the days of chivalry battle was a duel. It turned on individual prowess. To-day it turns on organization. If we have "fewer heroes, we have more trained soldiers of the cross."

DISCIPLINED DISCIPLES.

Second.—You represent the force of disciplined discipleship. You are a company of pledged disciples — that pledge, the point of attack on the part of our critics, an object of fear, at first, to ourselves, now recognized as our strength. Our purpose is not to build an organization, but to establish character, to train disciples. Let those who criticise, criticise by offering something better. Pastors all over the land are rejoicing in that it has confirmed and established the young disciple. Stability is worth something in a world like this. And I could come back, after the lapse of months and years, and find these disciples firm as I find the tree under which I rested when a boy, and the same stars shining through its leafy branches. We meet here surrounded by the implements of war. We meet in a hall generously given to our use by the First Regiment of the National Guard of Pennsylvania. These men are in no sense discredited as to their patriotism, because they have confirmed it with an oath, and have solemnly pledged fidelity to their country and their Commonwealth.

It was said at first that we asked too much of our young people. The church has made a mistake in not asking more. It has not expected enough. It has not kept close to the apostolic line and appealed to the soldier-like instinct. The response was a surprise. That was a fatal mistake when the church emphasized unduly, "How shall we amuse and attract young people?" It is not the business of the church to amuse. There are attractions that, in the end, repel and weaken. I say frankly, it were better that the church go to the theatre than bring the theatre into the church.

The Christian Endeavor idea has in some churches worked not simply reform, but revolution. A pastor of one of the strongest churches in the country has given me his experience. The first thought after a solemn service was our next entertainment and the discussion of committees and schemes for its success. A little room that seated fifty was large enough for its devotional meetings. Now it requires a room that holds four hundred. The prayer-meeting is the magnet that attracts. It sends out a company of evangelists every Sunday to wharves and car stables, and rich trophies have been the result.

INFLUENCE OF A SPECIAL TYPE.

Third.—You represent the influence of a special type. It is a joy to welcome you. There are guests whom we endure because they have belonged distinctly to the family. They have nerves and ailments and peculiar temperament, and the children must be suppressed and the household economy readjusted. There are people who are good, but their goodness is trying. But we welcome to our hearts to-day the joy of the household. It has been said the natural man must become spiritual, and then the spiritual man must learn to be natural. Christian Endeavor develops a type near to nature, near to Him who was nature in its perfect state. In all His life was not a morbid note.

We welcome you to our hearts and our home. My soul thrills with a new faith and a new courage as I greet you. Here is a force to hasten the world's regeneration. May He whose we are and whom we serve, preside over our assemblies and get glory to His holy name.

ADDRESS OF BISHOP W. R. NICHOLSON, D. D.,
Reformed Episcopal Church, Philadelphia, Pa.

Mr. President and Brethren of the Society of Christian Endeavor:—Designated the grateful task of representing on this occasion the churches and ministers of Philadelphia, it is with sincerest pleasure that I bid you welcome to this, our goodly city. Your name we regard as itself a benediction.

"Endeavor" is the consolidation of purpose and effort, is the walking forth of interest and energy, the enlightenment and the marshaling of human forces, the process of achievement, the life of civilization. That is endeavor. Christian Endeavor is all this as turned in the direction of Gospel truth and Gospel blessing.

Rightly understood, comprehensively considered, Christian Endeavor is, perhaps, the greatest of all God's grand causes for the accomplishment of His redemptive plan. A mighty force, moving grandly, working effectually, pointing with an unerring finger of light to the destined consummation of the kingdom of Heaven.

So, brethren, your name we regard as a benediction, reminding us thus, as it does, of God's bountiful provisions of mercy, and telling us of glorious possibilities.

We are glad to believe that this beautiful name is no misnomer. Abigail said of Nabal, "As his name is, so is he." Brethren, as your name is, so would we fain trust are you; originated in that love for souls which the Gospel of our Lord ever enkindles; conceived, fostered and developed by a true minister of Christ, whose presence with us to-day does us honor.

EVANGELICAL TRUTH.

Your society has thus far prosecuted its work along the lines of evangelical truth: the warm, precious love embodying the doctrine of the Holy Trinity; the substitutional sacrifice of the Lord Jesus Christ for us guilty, helpless sinners, the blood that redeemeth, the righteousness imputed; the gracious ministries of the personal Spirit of God wakening, enlightening, sanctifying, comforting; salvation simply by faith in the Son of God; the interest of Christian growth and of an ever increasing power of personal consecration to God. These are the truths constituting that Gospel under whose auspices your society was born, and which, ever since, have sheltered and magnified your work.

You have thus far taken and kept the holy position of antagonism to the scepticism and irreverence and the godlessness of the world. You have gathered together the young, fresh energies of the church of Christ in one grand, brave battle for God and His truth, and under the magnetism of numbers, the glow of sympathy, the stimulus of union, have placed yourselves in serried ranks coming up to the help of the Lord against the mighty.

No, brethren, your beautiful name of Christian Endeavor is no misnomer.

Is not there a cause? Shall we ministers and churches of Philadelphia not do honor to this mighty host in the army of God's elect? May we not reasonably hope that you are fast becoming one of the strong armies of the church of Christ?

Often have we been asked, "What shall we do with our young people?" What pastor has not asked the question, "How shall we give them a sufficient interest in the church, and guard and save them from the contamination of the world? How shall we set them upon and secure them in the earnest work of a personal Christianity? How shall we train them so that when, subsequently, they come to manhood and womanhood, they shall fall easily into their proper places in the great work of the church? How shall we encourage and make strong within them a genuine love for souls, for whom Christ died? How shall we inspire our young people in the church with an appreciation of Christian brotherhood?" My young brethren of the Christian Endeavor, these are the problems that you yourselves are now helping us to solve.

A GREAT UPRISING.

It is a grand thing, this uprising of the young people of the church of Christ. Here they come to-day by thousands from so many parts of our broad land, and what is so remarkable is, they come solely in the interest of evangelical truth and piety. It is one of the phenomena of these closing years of this nineteenth century; it is one of God's great revivals of His religion, and a revival itself of the very best sort.

Brethren of the Christian Endeavor, guard well your important trust, but be faithful, be humble, be loyal. Let the eye be kept single; be strong in the Lord and in the power of His might.

In the name of those for whom I stand to-day, I greet you on this occasion. Welcome, thrice welcome, to our hearts and our homes.

RESPONSE BY REV. S. V. LEACH, D. D.,

Pastor First Methodist Episcopal Church, Albany, New York.

Mr. President and Friends:—The time of this splendid convention is of such superlative value that I shall occupy but a few minutes in responding, by request of the trustees, to the eloquent addresses of welcome just delivered by eminent representatives of our societies and of the Protestant churches of this magnificent city. I esteem it no ordinary honor to voice the gratitude of this vast national body for the ardent and felicitous reception we have received to-day.

None of us are strangers to the factors constituting the celebrity of this metropolis of one of the most enterprising and loyal States of the Federal Union. We have long been familiar with the fair fame of this "City of Brotherly Love" from such standpoints as its commercial greatness, its multiplied churches, its renowned hospitals, its great schools of medicine, its benevolent institutions, and its extensive libraries. Nor have we forgotten the fact that in the heart of Philadelphia stands the sacred edifice in which our patriotic forefathers, at one of the darkest periods in our country's history, signed that immortal decree that gave to us our civil independence. Thirteen years ago many of us were privileged to spend some days among those wonderful buildings in Fairmount Park, where the foremost nations of the civilized world displayed, in bewildering splendor, their marvels of machinery, their wealth of manufactures, and their costly creations of painting and sculpture.

A TRIBUTE TO WANAMAKER.

Nor do we fail to remember that it was Philadelphia that presented to President Harrison the first officer or member of a Christian Endeavor Society who has ever graced a cabinet office — our upright, munificent and tireless trustee, the present Postmaster-General of the United States. We regard it as fortunate that we are here, warm as is the atmosphere to-day, and we are grateful for the sentiments of the addresses of greeting.

Permit me, as appropriate to this introductory session, to say that within eight years the 8,000 societies and 500,000 members have all enlisted under our banners. Thousands of the delegates who will be present with us, bear on their brows the freshness of early manly Christian culture, or on their fair faces the beauty and purity of young womanhood in supreme devotion to Christ and the varied work of His church. Each of our societies is as intensely loyal to its own local church and communion as if it alone constituted the entire organization we represent. There cannot possibly exist a true Christian Endeavor Society that is not as thoroughly subject to local church supervision as any purely denominational association can be. We train our members, under the arch of a solemn covenant, daily to read the Scriptures and pray in secret to God, and weekly either to offer public prayer, or to bear public testimony in honor of Jesus Christ their only Redeemer. Our pledge is as vitally related to our work as the Koh-i-noor is related to its setting, or the plume of light to the Argand Lamp.

NO FORMULATED CREED.

And while we have every safeguard for church loyalty that any denominational association of young Christians ought to have, we are so non-sectarian as to have no elaborate formulated creed, and so inter-denominational as to encourage the young people of our various churches to assemble in local unions, district conventions, state conferences and national convocations, for mutual acquaintance and the discussion of the wisest methods for doing God's work.

In view of eternity I stand in this august presence and declare that I am not less loyal to the great denomination in whose pulpit I have stood for thirty years because I enter an earnest protest against the transfiguration of *our* existing societies into denominational organizations under new names. I would consider it dishonorable to attempt to transfer, by a pastor's influential pressure, to any one of our State associations, any purely denominational society contented with its name and sectarian relationship; and before this great and intelligent body of cultivated young men and women, I publicly declare that it is equally as unjust for any pastor to determine to transform into a denominational association a Christian Endeavor Society in defiance of the general sentiments of its members. I have vigilantly watched the practical operations of the Christian Endeavor movement in congregations under my own pastoral oversight, and can assure our bishops, editors and general secretaries, as I said to my honored guest, Bishop Andrews, yesterday, that it has not impaired the affection of the young people for Methodism; but it has amazingly widened and deepened their appreciation of the young people of other branches of the one church of Christ. During none of my pastorates have I had associations of young Christians that have proven as popular, magnetic, laborious and helpful to me, as a pastor, as our societies of Christian Endeavor.

THANKS FOR COURTESIES EXTENDED.

At this introductory session it is also appropriate that I should also publicly express the thanks of the trustees to our thousands of societies for three things: first, for the manifold courtesies extended throughout the country to our beloved and laborious president, Rev. F. E. Clark, D.D., on whom a celebrated college last month, honoring itself as well as our chief representative, conferred the degree of *Doctor Divinitatis;* second, for the innumerable hearty welcomes, in every part of our work, accorded to our gifted and inexhaustible general secretary, Mr. George M. Ward; and third, for the marvellous patronage bestowed on our handsome and ably-edited weekly journal, THE GOLDEN RULE.

The sessions of this largest-delegated congress in the history of Christianity will flash with interest and blaze with privilege. The young people of Philadelphia will have the gratification of listening to many speakers of eminence and success in Christian work from other states. May we all earnestly strive to lay here more broadly and massively the foundations of future spiritual achievement among the young. May we return to our homes crowned with the benedictions of the citizens of this historical metropolis. And may we so have improved these occasions of address, discussion, song and supplication, as to leave behind us memories and influences that shall prove as fragrant and permeating as the ointment from the broken alabaster box with which the woman of sacred story anointed her divine Lord. Let us, in all of our plans for the future, bear in mind the words of Jesus, "Without me ye can do nothing;" nor forget the imperial statement of Paul, "Our sufficiency is of God." In the name of the general officers and trustees, and voicing the universal sentiment of our Eighth National Convention, I bring to the churches of Philadelphia, so fitly represented in the person and loving words of Bishop Nicholson, and to the Christian Endeavor Union of Philadelphia, so ably represented by the Rev. Dr. Beckley, Paul's words: "The God of peace, that brought again from the dead our Lord Jesus, that great shepherd of the sheep, through the blood of the everlasting covenant, make you perfect in every good work to do His will, working in you that which is well-pleasing in his sight through Jesus Christ; to whom be glory forever and ever."

TREASURER'S REPORT.

By *William Shaw*, *Treas.*

The Treasurer's report covers a period of eleven months only, as by vote of the Society the beginning of the financial year was changed from July 1st to June 1st.

In presenting his report your Treasurer would respectfully call your attention to the rapid growth of the printing and publishing business of the Society. During the past year our sales have amounted to $7,942.74, on which was a fair margin of profit, which has been used in the spread of the work. Some months ago it became evident to the Trustees that the bills for printing, stock, labor, etc., in this department had no place by right in the report of the Missionary work of the Society, as they increased the total of expenditures without showing the profit derived from the work. The Trustees therefore voted to organize a separate department March 1st, in order that the work might be pushed with more vigor, and the publishing and missionary accounts be kept distinct and separate. As you will see by the report, the total contribution received from societies and individuals, including the balance from last year's account, was $9,742.18. The publishing department was the largest contributor to the funds of the Society during the past year, and with the same hearty co-operation of the local societies in sending us their orders for printing, etc., we hope to largely increase our contribution the coming year. We feel justified in pressing this matter upon your attention, as no private individual is enriched or benefited by it, but every cent of profit is used in advancing the great cause of Christian Endeavor. I feel that we ought to be profoundly thankful to God for the large measure of blessing that has attended our work the past year. During the year nearly as many new societies have been reported as were formed in the previous seven years of our history. The call for information from all parts of this and foreign lands; the tens of thousands of letters that had to be answered, and all the other expenses that this growing work entailed upon us have been met by the *free will* offering of the societies, and the profit from publishing. No appeal has been made to the societies for funds for our own use, but every society was urged to make a thank offering on the National Christian Endeavor day in February, to the missionary work of their several denominations. This suggestion met with a hearty and generous response and thousands of dollars, accompanied by the prayers of the young people, were given to missionary objects at home and abroad.

Large contributions were also made by societies in all parts of the country to the sufferers by the terrible flood in the Conemaugh Valley, May 31st. In these and many other ways our young people are showing their loyalty to Christ, and to the motto given them last year by our beloved President.

"Not to be ministered unto, but to minister."

Dr. William Shaw, Treasurer, in *Account with the* United Society of Christian Endeavor. *Cr.*

To cash on hand July 1, 1888,		$2,034 19	By Cash paid as follows:	
To cash received from convention,	$192 48		Convention Expenses, 1888,	$1,558 82
To cash received from sales at convention,	38 88		Office expenses, rent 11 mos. Repairs,	$389 62
To cash received from sundries,	18 50			10 74
To cash received from sales of reports,	139 75		Supplies, expressage, etc.	1,614 47
To cash received from sales of hymn books, badges, literature, etc.,	7,745 61	$8,135 22	Badges,	2,014 83
			Hymn Books,	1,430 97
			Golden Rule Publishing Co.	1,396 59
			Advertising in newspapers,	1,500 00
			Mailing and postage,	244 90
				1,109 73
				1,354 63
To cash received from contributions,	7,417 51		Travelling Expenses: Trustees, Treasurer, Secretary,	122 10
To cash received from annual fees,	98 00	$7,515 51		62 80
				1,275 00
				1,459 90
			Salaries: Office Clerks, Secretary, 10 months,	1,241 75
				1,666 67
				2,908 42
			Printing: Literature, etc.,	2,930 57
			Copyright,	3 00
			Paper,	424 66
		$15,650 73	Work on report,	124 00
		$17,684 92	Binding,	52 75
			Certificates,	27 25
				3,562 23
				$17,186 39
			Cash to balance,	498 53
				$17,684 92

The above is a condensed statement of the Treasurer's books, which I find correctly cast, and properly vouched.
Lowell, Mass., *June* 12, 1889.
Albert W. Burnham, *Auditor.*

PUBLISHING DEPARTMENT.

Dr. Wm. Shaw, Agent, *in account with* The United Society of Christian Endeavor. **Cr.**

To Sales and Payments From Feb. 25 to June 1, 1889,	$4,513 31			
		4,513 31		

June 1, 1889, By Cash Paid as Follows :—				
Office Expenses, Stamps,	$476 71			
Repairs,	17 70			
Expressage,	87 82			
Money Refunded,	12 47			
		594 70		
Stock, Badges,	$386 35			
Paper Stock,	301 59			
Record Books, Cards, Envelopes, Electros, Lithos, etc.,	276 98			
		964 92		
Salaries, 3 months,		591 04		
Printing Literature, etc.,	$1,082 55			
Copyright,	1 00			
		1,083 55		
Cash to balance,		$1,279 10		
		$4,513 31		

Assets:
Stock, ... $947 50
Bills Receivable, ... 1,754 74
Cash, ... 1,279 10
                    3,981 34

Liabilities:
Bills Payable, ... $710 05

The above is a condensed statement of the Publication Agent's books showing business from February 25 to June 1, which I find correctly cast and properly vouched. *June* 29, 1889.   Albert W. Burnham, *Auditor*.

GENERAL SECRETARY'S REPORT.

Annual Report of the General Secretary of the United Society of Christian Endeavor, George M. Ward, Esq.

My friends, members of this Eighth National Convention, I have been trying ever since I first realized the dimensions to which this conference has grown, to comprehend that this great gathering represents the workers in the same cause of Christian Endeavor which six years ago held its third annual conference, in 1884, in my native city of Lowell. The themes you are here to discuss are the same, yet different; the same in their first principles, yet so much broader are they in the field to which they are applied, that they seem hardly alike. As on that earlier occasion, your speakers are drawn from all the regions where the cause has spread; but at that early day a Christian Endeavor worker from California, or a speaker from Canada, or that other extreme, Florida, would have been set up on a pedestal to be looked at; and yet here, these friends of ours from the West and North and South, to-night, make a very large portion of our audience. It is not that you are strangers to me, for you know, you who are Westerners, that I claim to be a Westerner also; and you who are from the South, that I too claim a relationship with you; in fact, wherever Christian Endeavor finds a home, there I also claim a place. You are none of you strangers; hundreds of you I have met on your native heath, and the rest of you I know by reputation. It is not the strangeness of your faces, but the coincidence of seeing you all together, that would make your audience a puzzle to me, were I with you. If I looked in one direction I might see one well-known and beloved face, and say to myself, that is my dear friend from California, and that next neighbor is another kind friend from St Louis; the next, unless I am mistaken, is from Montana or the far Northwest; while all around me are the many home friends, and those from the familiar old state of Pennsylvania. They, to-night, are acting as kind hosts; the good people of the beautiful Lehigh Valley are entertaining strangers from Florida or Utah, or some other distant point, and if these guests are sharing the good fortune which has been mine on many an occasion in time past, they are finding that their lines have fallen in extremely pleasant places. The whole State delegation, I have no doubt, is overflowing with a desire to welcome to their side the young people of this country; while the members of the local Endeavor societies seem like the patrons of some great social gathering whose duty it is to keep a general oversight of all the workings.

DISADVANTAGES OF A WANDERER.

I look it all over, and I say, the whole Christian Endeavor world is here. My mind goes back to a time when I was given as a theme for my speech at a convention not far from here, "The World, the Christian Endeavor Field." Now I wish that topic were mine, for I would only have to turn to your vast audience and say, The whole world is here! Look at her! Here is my topic illustrated, let it speak for itself. I find there is a disadvantage in being a wanderer; for example: I go out from my home, and spend close upon a year or two wandering around in the Endeavor cause, then I return, and, behold, every one has changed! I meet my friend walking down street, and I say, "Whose boy is that with you?" and he looks hurt, and says, "It's mine, of course." I stammer, try to smooth matters over, and proceed on my way. The next person I meet is smiling and seems very happy, and announces that he is sorry I was not at home for his wedding. I ask whom he has married, and he looks surprised that the whole world does not know the full particulars of this important event, and tells me Miss So-and-So; again surprise overcomes my wisdom, and I say, "What, that child?" and my friend draws himself up and magnificently informs me that that child has grown considerably since I went away, and if I will come and see them he will show me the lady in question, no longer a mere child, but at the head of her household.

THE GROWTH OF THE WORK.

I undergo exactly the same experience in my Christian Endeavor work. When I first went West, three years ago, I stopped at a great many little meetings, — some held in the vestry, some held in the body of the church, with plenty of room to spare for those who did not come; and then, as I happen into the same town or city, a year or two after, I find a union meeting, and a hall hired, or the largest church in town, and I say, "What's all this for?" and am told it is necessary to accommodate all who are sure to come from the neighboring societies. They explain to me that all this growth is from that little original society, and I look over the crowd that gathers, and I say, " What, that little child grown to such magnitude!" I stop in Chicago, and I talk with Mr. Howell, or Mr. Holdrege, or Mr. Chase, or some of these workers, and they tell me of their hundred societies, and I say, "What, is that the child that I met in the Union Park Vestry less than three years ago!" I stop in St. Louis, and learn that the little infant there has grown to be a man, with descendants of his own; and so it goes on, till I feel sure I have, during my illness of the winter, indulged in a Rip Van Winkle sleep, and waked to find the cause of Christian Endeavor not eight, but twenty-eight years of age. I wonder if you realize, my friends, what the growth has really been. Had I indeed indulged in a Rip Van Winkle pastime, I should have found on awakening an advancement made which would warrant the supposition that a period of at least twenty years had passed since the cause had its birth. In 1881, one society; in 1889, seven thousand six hundred and seventy. Yes, friends, God has been very good to us, and a vast band of nearly five hundred thousand young people now marches under our banner in regularly enlisted, united service. Last year we told you how it had spread geographically; to-day we can add nothing in territory, for twelve months ago it had encircled the globe. Everywhere along this road it has gained in numbers; single societies of last year have multiplied and increased, till now an entire neighborhood enjoys what last year was confined to a single church.

England has made a great advance, and to-day sends greeting from thirty-seven Societies of Christian Endeavor. The foreign mission field is also awakening, and about fifty societies are aiding the hard-working missionary in all his foreign fields. In our own country, New York still holds the banner with one thousand three hundred and eighty-seven societies; as many societies in a single state as the whole world could show a few years ago. Next comes Massachusetts with her seven hundred and forty-two; than that land of the Holdreges and the Howells, the "far away western" land of last year's convention, Illinois, with five hundred and forty-one societies.

EFFECT OF A NATIONAL CONFERENCE.

My friends, will you notice here the effect of a national conference on a state's growth in this respect. New York, with two national gatherings, has held the lead for two years, and now Illinois, from the effect of last year's convention, jumps up to five hundred and forty-one. Pennsylvania, we look to you next year to leave us all in the rear and mount up with New York.

One of the most noticeable growths of the year past is that of Ohio, where good management and hard work on the part of State officers has swelled her ranks from about two hundred to four hundred and sixty-five societies.

California, also, has doubled her lists, and all the Western field is fast rivalling the longer established Eastern societies.

Look out, my home friends, we had four or five years start of the West, but their soil is wonderfully prolific.

In the more blessed record of the number of young people, who, during the past year, have come out on the Lord's side and left the ranks of the world to join the church to which they owed allegiance, the report is equally encouraging; two thousand one hundred and forty-one societies report that there have been fifteen thousand six hundred and seventy-two young people who have come from their associate membership to acknowledge Christ.

Do you realize, friends, that this is less than one-third, about one-fourth, of all these societies? And should the same average hold true of those who did not report on this topic, it would give us about fifty thousand young people to whom the last year was the most critical and blessed of their lives, since in that year they had confessed their Master.

Does Christian Endeavor need any future endorsement? Answer, my friends, has not a cause with such a record *come to stay?*

A SHORT REST.

In rendering an account of my stewardship for the year past, it is my unpleasant duty to acknowledge a period of time not spent in actual labor. The Providence to which we all must yield, laid its restraining hand upon me, with so positive a gesture, this past winter, that, for a time, I feared that all work, not only for Christian Endeavor, but for all else, was past. A rest from labor and the kind assistance of loving friends have, however, given me much to be thankful for. In consequence, the report for this year does not show the same number or miles travelled, or work done, as indicated in the corresponding report of last year. I have, however, covered twenty-five thousand miles or territory, and presented your cause on about one hundred and sixty different occasions. The most important trip made, was through our great and growing Northwest; I wish I could take you with me for a few moments up through that glorious country; we would start from the great twin cities, St. Paul and Minneapolis (I am not brave enough to single out one as the greater). Only last fall the largest church in Minneapolis was found too small to contain the young people who gathered to hear reports of the Chicago Convention. I could not agree with them up there in their enthusiasm for their cold weather, though I found their climate only an introduction, in a very mild form, for what was to follow in Dakota; but I could thoroughly understand their enthusiasm for Christian Endeavor.

ENTHUSIASM.

Those of my acquaintance in this audience will, possibly, remember that I have at times been accused of allowing my youth to excite me to enthusiasm in this cause of ours; I hope I may never have a worse complaint. I heard one Christian worker, whose name is a household word, say, some time since, "Unless one can bring enthusiasm to the work, he cannot expect to convince others," and thus I felt acquitted. The very definition of the word, "God in us," would apply it directly to our case; and so up there in that gate-way of the Northwest, they literally have God in their work; and if we may go farther, and use the definition I have somewhere found of the word, "The zeal of credulity," then, indeed, in that far Northwest, they have zeal in a cause in which they thoroughly believe. Years ago, in 1871, at a time when a grant of land was sought by the Northern Pacific Railroad for a terminus on Lake Superior, at the site of the city of Duluth, the Hon. Proctor Knott, of Kentucky, then one of the most noted wits of the United States Senate, made a most telling and sarcastic speech against such grant. He described that northern country as given up entirely to Pigeon and Creek Indians, and inhabited only by buffaloes and elks. He described those who had travelled into those regions as "men who had been so reckless of their personal safety as to venture away in those awful regions where Duluth is supposed to be," and spoke of the proposed stockyards as only useful for herding the buffaloes driven in by the Indians. To-day a city of forty or fifty thousand people marks this much abused spot, and your secretary, after being "so reckless of his personal safety as to venture" away off up there, found one beautiful night (beautifully cold night), a union meeting of all denominations filling the Presbyterian Church. I looked in vain for the Indians; I looked in vain for buffaloes (though I did find a bear, shot in the suburbs, a few day previous); but I found, in plenty, loyal Christian Endeavor young people, whose honesty and fidelity to our cause would put some of us to shame.

DAKOTA.

I lost by my absence last fall my right to cast a presidential vote, but Providence was kind to me in locating me in Dakota. I did not feel the loss, I was out of the voting world; I tell you I felt for those people; I was one of them. We could read the papers and listen to the reports, but we were outsiders, citizens of a Territory, and so not voters. I wish you could have seen their elation when they learned that Statehood would probably fall to their lot; it was not a party issue, but it meant representation. On the evening of election day, when everything was excitement here, we held a Christian Endeavor meeting in a small Dakota town. I do not think the question of politics was unpleasantly introduced, but one good friend of mine about that time, in his public prayer, said, "O Lord, we don't want to talk politics to Thee, even if we are Westerners, but, O Lord, give us Statehood, and how we will serve Thee!" On a Sunday not many days separated from the above date, it was my fortune to fill the pulpit in a little home missionary church in that Territory; never have I had a stronger impression made upon me of the work which Christian Endeavor may do than here. The pastor was away, and his hard-working wife, a lovely Eastern woman of cultivated tastes and delicate, careful rearing, had upon her shoulders, not only the burden of a large family, but also the cares of a pastorate. Do you realize what a pastorate under such circumstances means? It is not the preaching, not the pastoral visits and work alone, but it is the arousing even of the sentiment which is necessary to induce the people to even come to church and place themselves under religious influence. You can imagine my pleasure when she said to me, "It is to my Society of Christian Endeavor that I look for all my help; its members are all I can rely upon. The training which they receive seems to bring out in them a feeling of responsibility that makes them of help to me in a way which their parents, with their lax ideas, can never be." God bless those hard-working missionaries, and God bless and prosper the young people who are working and toiling under our banner, fitting themselves to fill places which you and I could not fill were we in their locality, and training them up to live as Christians, in those regions where the sentiment is all the other way.

NORTHERN DAKOTA.

Away up in Northern Dakota, where the cold is so intense that the citizens proudly tell you, " One can freeze without knowing or feeling it," lies a great territory, now known as Northern Dakota, just opening up, and destined, ere long, through the virtue of its rich wheat crops, to be an intensely rich region. If one is in doubt as to the theory that stern climate develops sturdy men, let him visit Northern Dakota. At some of the district conventions held there, the young people travelled as far as did most of you to this national gathering, coming sometimes on freight-trains, or, for distances in wagons, to attend the gathering. There they take the constitution *as it is written*, no variations, no questioning as to pledge, but taking it *as it is;* pledging their whole time and loyal service to the cause of Christ. I would I could fire you all with some of their zeal. They can never attend such gatherings as these, never without great expense, even the State meeting (and money is not plenty with those emigrant youths) but day after day is spent in loyal work in their church society, and in making their society felt as a power in their neighborhood and vicinity. But I am keeping you all too long in Dakota.

MONTANA.

There is one other region yet to be traversed, ere we reach the Pacific slope, the mining regions of Montana. If there is one section of country more than another that demands the work of our young Christians, it is there. One has only to visit the great mining centres of Helena or Butte, to walk along their streets and read the flaming advertisements of *licensed* gambling-houses, grog-shops, and even places of lower and meaner vices, without realizing what must be the prevailing sentiment of a region that can openly put its seal upon such dens of iniquity, and throw them open under the sanction of law to serve as a constant temptation to every young man or woman who goes out from our Eastern homes to seek a living in the Western mining country. I shall never forget the face of one young man, almost a boy, as he came up to me as I stepped down from the platform of a public hall, where the meeting had been held in one of those mining centres. Putting out his hand he took mine and said, " Is it really true that young people in some places are really as earnest as that in religious things? Do they really put the church first?" I told him I had told the truth. "Ah, well," he said, "they don't live in the mines. Tell them they don't know what temptation is, but ask them to pray for those of us who do." My friends, I know no nobler work than that being done by the devoted pastors and missionaries on those Rocky Mountains that constitute the backbone of our continent geographically, but whose people seem to think that because they possess an empire's spinal column that personally and morally none is needed.

UTAH AND THE PACIFIC SLOPE.

You have here to-day delegates from two other regions of which I would say a word or two, namely, Utah and the Pacific Slope. It was my fortune to eat my Thanksgiving dinner with kind friends in Salt Lake City, and to attend a three days' Territorial meeting of Christian Endeavor. Utah is not ready to be admitted as a State, nor can she have representation in a national Congress, but she does deserve a front seat in a national Christian Endeavor convention. Out there they realize that their only hope is for the youth. "Save our youth and you save Utah, lose them and you lose Utah." I believe that in the Providence of God, Christian Endeavor was raised up, in part, to solve the great problem that overhangs that stricken country. The young people believe in it; its honest and outspoken methods appeal to them as the subterfuge of the Mormon Church did not, and we have only to see the hold which the society has upon its members to realize what it may yet accomplish. One kind teacher pointed out a little girl who was taking part in a children's prayer-meeting and told me that, a child of Mormon parents, she had been put out to work in a Mormon family. By some means she was drawn into the Society of Endeavor, but when the time came for meeting, she was always given extra work to prevent her attendance. She was true, however, and by rising earlier than ever and working late, she had, by promising to repay a portion of the small pittance of her wages, earned the right to the half-hour's leave which enabled her to attend the meeting and take her part. Have we no lessons to learn from Utah, and can we not in some way, out of our abundance, aid them?

WASHINGTON TERRITORY AND OREGON.

We have heard a great deal lately about Washington Territory and Oregon; just at present it is the Mecca toward which the entire restless, roving, emigrant portion of our country is turning its face. One has no adequate idea of the vast herd of strangers that constantly pour into the cities of that new region. For illustration: I walked from my hotel one night, in search of the telegraph office; it was late, the evening service was over, and I had returned to my room to read and answer some mail matter which I found awaiting me. As I walked down the streets, instead of finding them deserted — as we would expect at the dead of night — I found little knots of men grouped together here and there, apparently without shelter or abiding place. Partly from curiosity, I inquired of the first group the way to the telegraph office. None can tell me, and each explains his ignorance on the ground of his being a stranger in town. The same inquiry is made of four distinct groups, and each time with the same answer, "We are all strangers." Imagine, if you can, this state of affairs. Nearly all of these persons were young men, and no restraining influences whatever exerted. Think you there is no place here for Christian Endeavor?

In another city of Washington Territory a gentleman interested in our work said to me, "Yes, Mr. Ward, this work is exactly fitted to this region; it appeals to us. We are very busy in the rush and boom, as you know, and everything with us must be business, and your work makes a *business* of Christianity." The work there is gaining a strong-hold, although it is yet in its infancy. I do not know when the cause has had a more general bearing as regards all classes of listeners than it received in Tacoma. Here the Opera House was engaged for the occasion. The fact that all the churches in town, regardless of denomination, had given up their weekly prayer-meeting, ensured us a gathering of church people, while the selection of a hall and its location attracted many from the streets. The theatre was full, and a more attentive audience never listened to the claims of our cause.

GENERALLY KNOWN.

There are few to-day, my friends, that have not heard the claims of Christian Endeavor. That there are a few, I must acknowledge. I was one day seated upon the deck of a steamer away up in Puget Sound, when a gentleman sitting beside me produced a copy of a paper which gave an account of one of our meetings in Seattle. Turning to me, he asked me if I knew anything of this new movement. I said yes, I had heard of it. He asked me if I had ever seen such a society. I told him yes, several. Then he wanted to know if it was a sort of Y. M. C. A. for both sexes. No, I told him, it was not, and attempted to explain. "Oh," he said, "a sort of prayer-meeting for young people." I explained that it included that, but was wider; that it was a training school for church work. "Oh," said he, "does a man need that? does he need a training to know how to go to church on Sunday, and take his seat in the pew?" Perhaps it is just as well that that man does not know of our methods, but ignorance of that sort is to-day rare. I wish that I could continue to take you with me to the region of last year's travels through Oregon and California to Colorado, Missouri, Iowa and Wisconsin, to the provinces where our English cousins are doing so much to arouse their young people; but time does not permit. May I sum it all up in saying, the whole English-speaking world knows of Christian Endeavor. Everywhere its fame has gone, and its methods are to-day being put to the test. For years our cry has been, "Further this cause, give to those who have not yet learned of its helpfulness the means of gaining such knowledge." God has answered our prayer in part, and to-day all of this continent has learned of its workings. What is now our opportunity? What is our mission? Not to relax in any degree the missionary efforts that are being put forth to further the cause, but in addition to remember that now that the cause is known it must speak for itself. That, I believe, as one who has travelled over the whole field, and presented the cause in every State and territory over which our government holds sway, is the great labor of this convention, the great labor of every Christian Endeavor worker, to hold what we have gained, and to raise our standard and that of those around us. That be our mission! That *is* the mission of to-day. Even the same mission is that of all His followers since first He sent His disciples forth from His presence, to do the will of the Father and uphold His Cross throughout the world.

OUR PRESENT DUTY.

We need not look back to the labors of the past. Only in the lessons to be learned of loyalty to God and principle, need we study the stories of the old crusaders, when men left home and families to carry the cross into other lands, and to win at the point of the sword the tomb of the dead Christ. Not for our following is the example of those devoted men and women of the fourth and fifth centuries, those "Athletes of Penitence," as they have been called, who fled from the wickedness of the world to enter a spiritual warfare in the desert, and as hermits to pass their lives in solitude. Our duty will not be found in any of their examples; each had its place, each played a part in working out God's plans, but since that time many years have passed, and in this nineteenth century we realize that it is not by deserting this beautiful world of ours that we can best serve Him, nor by carrying the Cross to the gates of the City of Jerusalem, that we can show the greatest honor, but by taking the place He assigns us in the world of to-day, and upholding the Cross in our midst to teach those about us the beautiful story of its atoning power, and pointing them to this blessed standard to lead them onward and upward to the Heavenly Jerusalem.

OUR INSPIRATION.

Let us keep ever before us this thought : The standard of truth and righteousness is in our hands. Raise it till all the world shall see and recognize the beauty of its story. Show to the world about you that the one inspiring aim of our lives, the one principle of all our actions is the love of the crucified Christ, whose Cross is our standard. Let that love be the one great inducement for all our devotions, for all our service. At the thought of that love, let all else sink into insignificance. With such an inspiration our tasks will become easy. Then, indeed, we may set any aim before us and never fear defeat. We all know the power there is in love like this. Look at the love of parent and child. I have sometimes feared, in the great eagerness with which I looked forward to being re-united with the dearly loved mother, whom God saw fit to take from me, that I might be in danger of losing sight of the other great influences that should draw me heavenward. If, then, the love of one even so dear can thus influence us, how gladly should our lives yield their whole influence, their entire sway, to the all-controlling power of Him who is both father and mother to us, and whose great love sent His son into the world, to leave all power and splendor, to suffer and die the ignominious death of the Cross for us.

> "Do what thou dost as if the stake were heaven,
> And this thy last day ere the judgment day."

This be our inspiration! And thus inspired, my friends, members of these societies of Christian Endeavor, keep up your standard, and show to the whole world what it means to be a consecrated Christian Endeavorer, and prove the truth of our two mottoes, that our lives are spent, "not to be ministered unto, but to minister," and ere long our early motto will prove true, and in addition to "A Church in every hamlet, and a society in every church," we shall see the dawning of the day when all the world shall serve Him with noble Christian Endeavor.

WHAT GOD HATH WROUGHT.

ADDRESS OF REV. FRANCIS E. CLARK, D. D.,
President of the United Society of Christian Endeavor.

The sight of this vast audience, of this sea of faces, of this crowded platform, recalls another Christian Endeavor Convention that assembled some eight years ago. The moderate-sized church in which it met was, perhaps, a quarter part filled. I see here not more than two or three whom I saw there. Instead of being in this great metropolis, the second city of America, it was in the small but beautiful city, the birthplace of the movement. When we think of the larger audience represented by these two audiences the contrast is still more striking. Then there were, so far as I know, seven, possibly eight, Societies of Christian Endeavor in the world; now there are 7,586 recorded Societies of Christian Endeavor in America alone. Then there were, by a liberal estimate, four hundred members in all the societies; now, by a moderate estimate, there are nearly 500,000. This audience is twenty-five times as large as that first audience; those whom we represent are a thousand times as many. I mention these facts simply to make forcible and significant the exclamation, "What hath God wrought!" This is the only exclamation which to-night expresses our emotions! If the growth of the work had been less marvellous, it any one could have predicted it and expected it, if any one had planned for it and foreseen it, vain human nature might be tempted to take to itself some credit; but so unexpected and unforeseen and unlabored for has it all been, that all ground for self-gratulation is taken from any of the hundreds who have been used of Providence in this work, and no one is tempted to say aught except, "This is the Lord's doing."

AT THE BEGINNING.

Let me confess, if it is proper for one to speak a single personal word, that all that was done in forming the first society was done with a very inadequate faith, and with no confidence that it would result in any far-reaching movement, and every succeeding development has been a rebuke to the little faith that began it. The first newspaper article, which, after six months' of trial, told about the society, was entitled, "How One Church Cares for Its Young People," and was written with very little thought that any other church would care for its young people in the same way. The first constitution was printed upon a home-made hectograph-pad, thinking that it was not worth while to waste printers' ink upon any such evanescent matter; since then the printing-presses have been kept busy, striking off at least a million copies in many different languages. Such, too, has been the development of the work, in the later years, in every line. This convention itself is a striking illustration of what I seek to prove. It was, in the first place, a simple coming together of Christians interested in common methods of work; that it has been ever since, but what conventions have they been! From the early prayer-meeting, which has given its tone of sweet devotion to the service, to the late consecration-meeting, which has gathered up in itself the blessed impressions of all the hours, these conventions have filled for us with new meaning the threadbare phrase about "sitting together in heavenly places in Christ Jesus."

THE PROVIDENTIAL ELEMENT.

These meetings have been full of the spontaneous element. Each one has been carefully planned for, the speakers have been engaged, but the numbers, the enthusiasm, the spirit of devotion could not be planned for by human wisdom. This is the providential element, and this is what has made the meetings so wide-reaching in their influence.

Then, too, consider the state conventions, scarcely inferior in enthusiasm, power and influence. Who foresaw them eight years ago or five years ago? Who was wise enough to predict them? Think of the United Society that keeps half a dozen printing-presses busy, and which, through the mail, reaches out its hands to the ends of the earth. It was not dreamed of until 1885, and then only because the correspondence had become so large that it could not be answered by men busy about other things. What it was at the beginning it is now, simply a bureau of information, and it will always be that and nothing more. No one seeks honor or emolument through it. It is no snug berth for men who have failed in other employments. Its work is done in large measure gratuitously, for love of the cause it represents. It is very largely self-supporting already, and no authority or government of the local societies has been for a moment dreamed of. From the beginning to the present day it is a conspicuous example of the providential aspects of the whole movement. It came because of God's call. It had to come. Consider also the later developments of the work. Who started the first Junior Society? Do you know? I must confess that I am in the dark on this subject, and I doubt very much if the person himself or herself who was used by God in this way knows it even. The little pledge which has been used as the basis of most Junior Societies, beginning, "Trusting in the Lord Jesus Christ for strength," etc., was used by a pastor down in Maine, in his church preparation class, for at least two years before the first Christian Endeavor Society was formed, but when or by whom the first full-fledged Junior Endeavor Society was formed, I doubt if any one will ever know. So it is with the development of the local union and the district convention and the state convention. The first local union was formed in New Haven, in the Dwight Place Church, at the suggestion of the honored pastor, Dr. J. E. Twitchell, but it was started, I presume, with no thought beyond New Haven and the immediate need which seemed to make such a movement desirable. But the same need existed elsewhere, and the same methods, when the way was once shown, prevailed, for the very simple and sufficient reason that it was a good way.

The Providence that began this work and continued it and has made it what it is, is as plain as the sun in the July heavens. He would be monumental in his conceit, or else afflicted with mental and spiritual strabismus of the very worst kind, who should for a moment doubt this.

GRATITUDE, HUMILITY, CONFIDENCE.

And now let me ask what should be the effect on us here assembled, and upon all whom we represent, of these repeated and unmistakable signs of providential guidance? Most obviously it is a cause for gratitude and humility; for gratitude, that God, in such a signal manner, has shown His approval of these methods of training the young; humility, since the administration has been so largely taken out of the control of individuals. No men have done this. No individual can say, "See this great Babylon which I have builded." It is not of human foresight or wisdom. It is God who has given the increase. With profound sincerity and humility and gratitude we will all cry: "Not unto us, O Lord, not unto us, but unto Thy Name be all the glory!"

Another effect of this review of the providential aspects of this work should be to inspire us with a certain confidence in the methods which God has approved. A noted magnate of the church saw, or thought he saw, a blazing cross in the sky. He took the vision as a sign of the Divine favor, and emblazoned the cross on his banners, and encircled it with the legend "*In hoc signo vinces*," and went on to the victory which he thought he saw presaged in the sky. Skobeloff, the Russian General, aroused himself from his couch in the army wagon long enough to ask his aids from which side the new moon, whose crescent had just been seen in the west, appeared, and, when told from the right, he sank down again to contented slumber, taking it, with the Eastern superstition, as an omen of victory. In this modern crusade of the young people of America, let us too look up at the sky. We, too, are guided by the cross, yet it is no *imaginary* cross or new-moon superstition, but by actual indications of the favor of God in the quickening of churches, in the inspiration of new life, in the conversion of souls; and the confidence thus engendered should inspire us with hope and zeal, and unbounded trust that He who has begun a good work will continue it.

If these theories in which we believe were the theories of visionaries and doctrinaires, if the prayer-meeting pledge and the consecration meeting and the due proportion and balance of work, through the committees, to confession in the prayer-meeting, existed only on a paper constitution, untried and not sealed by the Divine favor, we might well have little confidence in the future of our work, and go forward with little hope; but now, with humility, gratitude and confidence, we can evidently go forward along these providential lines to better and better service.

A PLAIN PROPOSITION.

Once more we find here a supreme reason for following out carefully and conscientiously the methods which Providence has approved, or, in other words, which experience has shown are most efficient in attaining the highest aims. The proposition is very simple. Certain plans, adopted at first as a mere experiment, have proved remarkably efficient in building up Christian character and quickening the enthusiasm of the young disciple. This very fact shows that they are of God. When we are convinced that a thing is of God, let us beware how we despise or ignore it. There is a Christian utilitarianism that should not be lightly treated. One proof of every doctrine of revealed religion is that it is a useful doctrine, that it has a good effect on the lives of men. The great proof for any method of practical Christianity is that it is useful in growing Christian characters. This proof we honestly believe has been vouchsafed to the Christian Endeavor movement. Then it remains for us, while we perfect details and strengthen weak places, to follow the general lines indicated by God's favor as correct. These lines, if I apprehend them correctly, are, *The Exaltation of Duty*, *The Exaltation of Loyalty and The Exaltation of Fellowship among Young Christians*.

THE EXALTATION OF DUTY.

A weak and nebulous notion has gained currency in our modern religious life, that, in some way, duty is an unworthy, or, at least, a paltry motive for service; springing, very likely, from a perversion of the thought that love is the supreme motive, the fact is forgotten that the pathway to the table-lands of loving, joyous service is always over the stern and rugged path of duty; this perversion of a great idea has unconsciously crept into the religious life of many, and has done untold mischief. Love for Christ is too often confounded with a sentimental "feeling like" serving Him, and when the Christian does not " feel right " he takes altogether too little pains to act right. The consequence too often is that feeling rules the day, and a sentiment is substituted for an unfaltering purpose. Christians go to the prayer-meeting when they feel like it, and two-thirds of them do not usually feel like it. The remaining third confess Christ when they feel like it (when they are in the right mood), and two-thirds of them never feel like it; so it comes about that only a third of a third, which, if my arithmetic does not fail me, is one-ninth, of professing Christians are confessing Christians. The same reasoning applies to all Christian service and often emasculates every effort. Too many go to church when they feel like it, *i.e.*, when it is neither too hot nor too cold, too wet nor too dry, and when there is no other possible excuse. Too many speak to the unconverted friend when they feel like it, *i. e.*, never. Too many others give only what they "feel like" giving, and the contribution-box rattles with pennies and nickels instead of silver and gold.

THE WATCHWORD, "DUTY."

Now the Christian Endeavor Society has sounded out to half a million young Christians the bugle-note, "*Duty, duty.*" Go to the meeting whether you feel like it or not, because it is a duty. Confess your Lord, whether you are in the mood or not, because it is a duty. Sustain your church whether the weather is moist or dry, or cold or hot, because it is your duty. Give to the cause of God at home and abroad, because it is your duty. This is the real meaning of the prayer-meeting pledge, of the consecration meeting, of the "cast-iron" rules, as they have been opprobriously called, of the provision for dropping unfaithful members, and of the distinguishing marks of the work of the committees. I say it reverently, I believe Providence has put the seal of divine approval on this distinguishing characteristic of our society, and I believe we shall be terribly unwise, yea, we shall be false to what God has taught us, if we ever recede from the high standard of the past. The prayer-meeting pledge is not a whim, it is not a mere ear-mark which distinguishes the Christian Endeavor Society from other organizations of young people; it is embodied in an eternal principle, and has its roots in the thought that duty alone leads to the table-lands of God. The Christian Endeavor Society, then, that leaves this idea out, or tampers with it, or ignores it, or fails to enforce it, *is false to a principle*, which, in this work, Providence has shown us to be essential. Such a society cannot hope for any large measure of success; and, so far as I know, such a society has never had any large measure of success in gaining the spiritual results which alone are worthy of such an organization.

The fact that, during the last year, hundreds of societies that started wrong have reorganized, and greatly to their gain, is proof of this; were further proof needed, I could summon out of this audience, I have no hesitation in saying, thousands who, from their own experience, would corroborate my words.

THE EXALTATION OF LOYALTY.

Another principle for which the society has come to stand, and for which experience has proved that Providence intended it should stand, is the Exaltation of Loyalty. Loyalty to Christ first; loyalty to Christ's Church next; loyalty to both Christ and the Church always.

It has never, so far as I know, uttered an uncertain sound on this subject. It has never failed to exalt loyalty to the individual local church with which any society might be connected. It was begun in one church for that one church; every subsequent society has been started in just the same way and for the very same purpose. There has never been an individual who has evinced any desire to become rich or famous, or to use the society as a stepping-stone. No one has ever desired to make a living out of the society. I could give you no better proof of this than to refer you once more to the way in which the United Society and the State Unions have been managed.

WHAT THE UNITED SOCIETY IS FOR.

Here was a chance, some might have said, to build up a great institution, to have many officers and fine buildings and a large pay-roll. The young people are generous, they will support it. But the United Society said: "No, we will be nothing of this sort. We will exist to give information, and when our work is done we will go out of existence. We will levy no taxes, we will ask for no recognition, we will claim no authority over any local society, but each one shall manage its affairs just as its church chooses, with no possibility of outside interference. If a society does not like the constitution we furnish, it can furnish its own; one or two fundamental ideas give it a right to the name Christian Endeavor, and, if the societies deem best, every constitution may differ from every other. Our annual conventions shall be for fellowship and inspiration, not for legislation. We will have only one secretary for the whole land; for the whole world, for that matter, and his duty shall be to give information when required, not to form new societies; and, as to expenses, they shall be reduced to the lowest possible limit, and, as soon as possible, the society shall support itself through the sales of its literature." So in state work it was decided at the beginning and has been consistently held to ever since, that it was not wise to have paid state officers. The necessary work could be done by the voluntary efforts of busy men.

NO BUREAU OF AUTHORITY.

We would afford no excuse to furnish and equip a bureau of authority in any State, or anything that might grow into that. We would have nothing that might be a temptation to officious persons to establish or foster societies where pastors and churches did not ask for them. And all this because we wished to guard so jealously and underscore so emphatically the principle that each society was in and of and for its own local church. Its business as a Christian Endeavor Society was there and nowhere else. I know of no one who would any sooner think of interfering with a local Endeavor society than with the church of which it is a part. If the pastor and church wish it to come into existence, it exists; if they wish it to wait, it waits; if they wish it to die, as, through prejudice, occasionally happens, it dies, as promptly and gracefully as possible. In all these ways has loyalty to the church of Christ been fostered, and to the particular church of which each society is a part, until I believe, in thousands of societies and tens of thousands of our members, loyalty to Christ has become a prevailing passion. The Church Service, the Church Prayer-meeting, the Church Sunday School are supreme; the Christian Endeavor meeting, though important, is but preparatory to them. This is the theory and almost universally the practice of our societies.

THE EXALTATION OF FELLOWSHIP.

Once more, our society stands for the Exaltation of Christian Fellowship, and providentially it has come to stand for this. There was no thought, in the first place, that it would extend into all denominations. There was no premonition of such a convention gathering within its ample walls young Christians of a dozen creeds. This, I say, is one of the providential leadings, for which no man is responsible. Shall we despise this indication and refuse to follow? We do not weaken or sever denominational ties; in short, we intensify our love for our mother's faith and our father's church; but we also remember on such occasions as this that the church of God embraces us all, and that "all we are brethren." Shall we, by dividing into strictly denominational clans, give up such fellowship? I think I know your answer. But we need not give up either the benefits which come from hearty loyalty to our own denomination, or the benefits which come from the broad fellowship of such a gathering as this. The genius of our society provides for them both.

In some quarters, I regret to say, through a misunderstanding of what the Christian Endeavor Society really is, a vigorous and what seems to be a systematic effort has been made to crowd out Christian Endeavor Societies and crowd in strictly denominational societies, not because the Christian Endeavor Society was not doing an admittedly good work, but because it did not belong exclusively to a single denomination. By all means let us have the best. If any denomination or individual church has a better society, let us all have that; if the Christian Endeavor Society is good for all, why should not all have it?

IS THIS HONEST?

In other quarters I have heard of societies that have adopted every distinguishing feature of the Christian Endeavor Society—the pledge, the consecration meeting, the roll-call, the Lookout committee, the dropping of the name for three consecutive absences, our motto even, "For Christ and the Church," and have called it by some other name, and have refused all fellowship with and acknowledgment of the Christian Endeavor movement, but have rather striven to weaken and destroy it. Is this right? Is this honest? But these are unpleasant things to mention. Our fellowship as a whole is unbroken, and, I say without hesitation, we shall be false to the leadings of Providence if, in the future, as in the past, we do not make the Society of Christian Endeavor stand for the Exaltation of Fellowship between Evangelical Christians as well as for the Exaltation of Loyalty to the individual.

Joshua made the sun to stand still, and for Hezekiah the shadow went back upon the dial; but we do not believe that in these days the rising sun of denominational comity and fellowship will stand still, or that the shadows of suspicion and distrust among Christians will return upon the dial that marks the advance of fraternity and brotherly love. It is too late in the nineteenth century to fear that.

THE CONCLUSION OF THE WHOLE MATTER.

There remains but one thing for us to do in the coming year and in the coming years as Christian Endeavor Societies—to find out what God would have us do, and do it. The Jew would not tread on the smallest piece of printed paper, fearing lest it might have the name of God upon it. Here is a movement over every part of which we reverently and humbly can say is written the name of "God." "God" everywhere. Let us in the future, in view of what we have seen, not despise these indications, but seek reverently to carry out God's evident plan.

We will not set up our own wisdom as the guide. We will not follow our own inclinations, unless we can see that our inclination is God's will. We will look both ways; backward, to see the way God has led us; upward, to see how He would lead us; forward, to see how He may lead us. As some one has amplified the famous and admirable motto of the Ten Times One Club, "We will look forward, and sometimes backward, outward, and occasionally inward; but, at the same time, always upward, and we will lend both hands."

A MOTTO.

Two years ago it was my pleasant duty to propose a motto for our societies. Its virtue lay not in the motto simply, but in the way you adopted it and put life into it: "For Christ and the Church." Everywhere have I seen this motto. We do not want any better motto, I am confident. It will always be stamped upon the great seal of the society. A year ago, with heartiness and unanimity, while not forgetting or setting aside the first, you accepted another motto to go with it and to supplement it for that year: "Not to be ministered unto, but to minister." This motto, too, I have seen on your programmes, on your badges, on your banners, even in the costly stained "Christian Endeavor window" of a beautiful church. For this year, in view of the thoughts of the providential character of the work, may I propose this motto, in which, perhaps, until we come together again for another International Convention, we may find something of inspiration? "*We are laborers together with God.*" Let us in our thoughts dwell upon each weighty word. "We." It is comprehensive, and embraces every one of our army of a half million in every denomination. "Laborers," not idlers, nor drones, but "active members" either now or, we pray, soon to be. "Together"—there is fellowship and brotherly love and true Christian union in that word. "With God." There is our encouragement, our strength, our confidence. For the exaltation of duty, for the exaltation of loyalty, for the exaltation of Christian fellowship in all our Christian Endeavor Societies throughout the world, *we are laborers together with God.*

REPORTS FROM STATES.

MAINE.

Rev. E. M. Cousins.

I want to say to this Convention that the State of Maine is not ashamed of that little child she sent out from her borders eight years ago. It was planted in rugged soil, it was planted in a rigorous climate. You have taken it into the milder latitudes, and you have improved a great deal upon the original plan; still we take credit to ourselves, and we rejoice that we were permitted to send out thus another Maine idea to the world. We remember that we have also sent other ideas. There is one more idea that you have not altogether got yet that we are holding in Maine, and I want to ask you to come to the Prohibition line that we have held forth as well as the Christian Endeavor line.

The motto which you will find on our State Shield is "Dirigo," which being translated modestly and freely, means that we do not take any back steps. So we have taken no back steps in regard to our interest in the Christian Endeavor movement. To-day Maine has an interest that is growing deeper and broader. The prophet is not without honor save in his own country, and there has been a time when this Society had to fight somewhat for its standing in the State of Maine, but that time has passed by. It is due in a large measure to the services of the President of our State Union, Mr. V. Richard Foss, who ought to speak to you to-day, but whose modesty prevents him.

We have given you different ideas; we have given you more than thoughts; we have given you many of the men that come here from the other states. That is what Maine does. She knows the blessedness of giving, and she gives young men and young women to fill up these other states, and with the aid of the Christian Endeavor movement we are going to send you better young men and better young women than we have ever sent before, because they are going to be trained in Christian work in larger measure as they start out from us. And so we rejoice in this movement for what it is doing for us at home, taking our young men earlier and giving them to Christ's service, and for what it is going to do as it goes out in this land of ours and into the world doing God's work.

UTAH.
Mr. C. H. Parsons.

Dear brethren and sisters, I bring you greeting to-day from one of the furthest territories that is represented here. We are very glad that we can say to you that since your last meeting in Chicago the number of Societies in our territory has just exactly doubled. I do not know whether any other state can make such a report as that or not, but our Societies have doubled in number and far more than doubled in the membership in the last year.

You might wonder perhaps whether we find the Christian Endeavor Society what we need in that dark place in our nation, and I am glad to say to you to-day that we find, it has filled a place that needed to be filled there perhaps more than any other place in the Union.

Our young people there have had no training of any kind in Christian work, and we find that this Society trains them for the Sunday School and for the Church. I believe that there is no place where we need that training as much as we do there. I wish you could have seen our Convention held last November, the first gathering of the young people of the territory that was ever held. They came from the mountains and valleys into Salt Lake City, and we had one of the grandest meetings that I ever attended in my life.

I am very sure that we may say the Spirit of God was with us, and our young people went forth from that meeting more fully determined than ever before that they would come up to the help of the Lord against the mighty. You know, dear friends, the need we have for workers in that territory. There is probably no place in the Union where darkness reigns as it does in our Territory of Utah.

MARYLAND.
Rev. Alexander Proudfit.

I suppose the greatest wonder of the members of the Convention this afternoon will be that one so young should represent a Young People's Society of Christian Endeavor, but I assure my friends I entered very early and very young into the work. I was pastor in the northern part of New Jersey when this good idea of Father Endeavor Clark was started out in Portland, and I promptly started it up in the mountains of New Jersey.

I think our society up there ranked about fifth on the list, and there are three delegates here from New Jersey to-day to testify that the society is still alive and vigorous.

I now come from Maryland and am more or less like Benjamin among the houses of the Israelites, one of the little ones. I suppose this is the reason the Maryland delegation called upon me to represent it, because I was the means of starting the very first society in Maryland. I believe the first society was started in the Second Presbyterian Church in Maryland, of which I have the honor to be the pastor.

The society has grown now and covers some fifteen different churches in the state of Maryland. We know of fifteen, but we think there are a few more that have not been reported to us.

The society has grown very rapidly within the last two years. I believe it has doubled since the last state convention. We sent two delegates to Chicago to represent our state, and they came back so brim full of the enthusiasm of the Chicago convention, that they inspired our society with fresh life.

Within eight weeks we have organized the State Union, covering about fifteen societies we know of, and we expect to go to work in the fall and try to get Father Endeavor Clark down there to give us a good stirring up, so we may spread out over the whole state.

CALIFORNIA.

Rev. John A. Cruzan.

I am glad you put California's banner at the front. She never takes a back seat. I am glad that so many of our friends find the California seats so comfortable. I look down there with pride, and I see thronging there delegates from the sunny South and even from the foreign shores of New Jersey. They like our California seats. So I could say with Elijah, "I only am left" of the California delegation. I have been hunting for the other members all morning, but I fail to find them. I stand here a delegate myself.

Five years ago it was my privilege to organize the Western Pacific Coast and the Hawaiian Islands with Christian Endeavor. I bear you testimony that it works as well on heathen ground as it does on Christian soil.

In California we regard Brother Clark not only as a father, but as a great-grandfather. He was the father of the Christian Endeavor Society; out of that has grown our Junior Christian Endeavor Societies, and in my own church we have the Primary Christian Endeavor Society; so of course that makes him a great-grandfather.

We find that it works well all along the line. If it is good for the young man of twenty-five, why is it not good for the little boy of eight? In my church we have that threefold organization: the senior, the junior, and the primary. We have fifty-three little boys and girls under eight years of age. Why not make him a great-grandfather at once and put on this threefold organization all along the line.

(Inasmuch as Mr. Cruzan represented the Hawaiian Islands as well as California, two minutes more were granted him.)

Mr. Crusan:—You do me proud when you give me two minutes more of your valuable time.

In California we believe in great things and we recognize a great thing when we see it. We deal in climate very largely as you do here in Philadelphia, but ours is a different climate; we are wearing overcoats now in the City of San Francisco. One would not be very comfortable here this afternoon.

We recognize at once, we who believe in great things, in this Society of Christian Endeavor a great thing. There we have the battle between the world, the flesh and the devil, a little hotter I think than any other place, except it may be in Utah, and we regard this Christian Endeavor Society, not only to be a means through which our young people may work, but it may be the loving hands of the Lord Jesus Christ to hold our young people in the midst of that great whirlpool of iniquity where they are planted.

Allow me to say for the California delegation, that our headquarters are at the Aldine House, and we send greeting, especially to Nova Scotia, the easternmost outfield, and we want to say that our headquarters are open and we are holding receptions all the time, and I am the reception, and we want especially to see Nova Scotia and all the delegations that call at our headquarters at the Aldine Hotel at any time. The house is always open.

NOVA SCOTIA.

Rev. J. M. Fisher.

I am already known as the long delegate from little Nova Scotia, a country it is said a number of you Americans want, but a country about which the most of you perhaps know very little. We are just a peninsular speck on the coast of North America; we have an area of two hundred and forty miles long and one hundred miles broad, and a population of four hundred and eighty thousand, and we have the oldest European settlement that was ever made on the Continent of North America, and the first ship railway.

About Christian Endeavor Societies I have not any very definite statistics, but on the 11th of May last we had fifty-one societies. We really have about sixty. The first Christian Endeavor Society in Nova Scotia was organized in the town of Yarmouth, where I am now stationed. I am a Methodist minister, and I am half sorry to say the first Society was started in the Presbyterian Church about a year before the other one was organized, but we have swelled up now to about sixty.

In my town, Yarmouth, we have four societies and we have a Christian Endeavor Union. In my own church we are thoroughly organized; all the committees are at work, and I may say, as indicating the influence of Christian Endeavor on Nova Scotia, that about a year and a half ago I found my older church members with their heads down, saying, " When we are gone who will take hold of the work?" About three weeks ago I had to send out some of my young people to stir up the old ones. That is the way it is working in Nova Scotia. We are expecting grand things for the future.

COLORADO.
Mr. E. B. Clark.

Colorado, as a State organization, is your infant to-day. We organized last May. We have enrolled one hundred and twenty-five societies of Christian Endeavor in that State, a gain of fifty since the 1st of July, last year. As a city Denver has twenty-five societies, with over 1,000 members enrolled. We have been the means, in God's hands, of bringing fifty-seven out of the associate membership into the active membership of the society.

Pueblo has nine, Colorado Springs has six, and to-day I bring greetings from Colorado to this Convention, greetings from the State Association and greetings from the Denver Union, and I bring an invitation from the Societies, the Governor of the State and Mayor of the city, soliciting that the next convention be held in Denver.

VERMONT.
Mr. E. E. Towner.

We have about one hundred and thirty-five societies in the State of Vermont, and some local unions, all of which I believe are doing good work. A few weeks ago probably many of you read about the little society up in Woodford, composed of five young ladies, in a lumber camp. They were called a little handful of corn, and I am sure that the Lord Jesus is going to bless that little handful of corn, and it is my desire that the delegation will go home and impart some of this enthusiasm to our brothers and sisters, that we may increase the number and influence of our societies.

ILLINOIS.
Mr. C. B. Holdredge.

In regard to Illinois, I bring you greeting. We feel very grateful for having had the national convention at Chicago last year, and the fruits of it have been shown in local and state work. Our members have increased from 12,000 to 24,000, and best of all, we have the record of over seven hundred young people who have come into our churches through the membership.

Our state work has never been in as good shape as it is now. Our young men are thoroughly loyal and our young ladies are more loyal still, and we are grateful for all the impetus that was left upon us by the great gathering in Chicago last year. Our motto is to go forward. Our increase has been so great in the past that we feel encouraged to go forward and do more for Christ and the Church than we have ever done before.

NEW HAMPSHIRE.

Mr. Tom C. Baldwin.

We read that when Christ sat in the Temple over against the Treasury and the widow came in bringing her mite she received his commendation, because out of her small resources she was willing to give so much. We from New Hampshire have small resources, but I think we will receive the commendation of the Master because we are permeated with that same spirit of Christian Endeavor which you will find in the large organizations of other States.

Our numbers are far smaller than those of Illinois, Massachusetts, or New York, but we are enabled to report to-day instead of the one hundred societies which we could report last year, one hundred and thirty, with a total membership of about 4,000.

It has been said of New Hampshire that whatever she could or could not raise, she could raise men, and we are raising men in New Hampshire to-day, and, through the providence of God and the Christian Endeavor Society, we propose that they shall be Christian men and Christian women.

Since we stood one of the thirteen, shoulder to shoulder under the flag of Liberty, beside the representatives of Massachusetts and New York and those other States, I think New Hampshire has not failed to furnish men when called upon, and to-day we propose, through the grace of God, that our record, as we stand under this banner of Christian Endeavor, loyal to the same Leader as yourselves, we shall not be unworthy, and we shall fittingly have a place beside these other societies in Christian Endeavor work.

INDIANA.

Mr. J. M. McCoy.

I am very proud indeed to meet you here, and as the good brother has suggested, I come from the state where we have recently made a good President. We did not come to talk politics to-day; we come to talk about Christian Endeavor work. Indiana has doubled her membership since the convention in Chicago. I think Pennsylvania will do the same. We can never tell what these conventions will do until we have seen their effect. We have now one hundred and sixty societies, with a membership of 7,000. This is rather a remarkable number when the first society is not quite five years old. The first society organized in our state was up in the northern part of the state. I do not know that they have a delegate here to-day. Being so far away, there were only eighteen of us able to get here. We are glad to see so many. This is the largest prayer meeting I ever was at in my life.

WASHINGTON.

Mr. E. W. Willey.

I am sorry that I am compelled to say that I cannot give a detailed account of the societies of the territory, as my appointment to the convention was unexpected and merely incidental to my being in the city. Consequently, I shall confine my report to Walla Walla, the city from which I come, and I think this can be credited with the average work of the state.

Three years ago two societies were organized in Walla Walla, and one started with eighteen active members and it now has one hundred and thirty. About twenty of our members have joined the different churches. There is also another society of about equal size and importance and doing equal work, and just recently there has been a junior society started in connection with it that bids fair to supplement successfully the work of the older society.

ONTARIO.

Rev. G. H. Cobblebeck.

I greet you to-day in the name of Ontario, the fairest province in all the confederation, which you have honored by placing at the very first of the list of all the Canadian Provinces to-day, and in the name of the Province of Ontario I have to report that we have managed, following your bright example set on this side of the line, to organize about one hundred societies, comprising about seven thousand members. The chief centres of local unions are in Toronto, Hamilton, London and Guelph. The work is going to be prosecuted more thoroughly during the coming year than heretofore. We are now organizing an Ontario Union, and we expect to do some aggressive work during the next twelve months. We are catching the inspiration of the Americans. They are a go-ahead people, but I must tell you, since you applaud that so vigorously, that I was taken for an American since dinner time, and in fact, in Guelph, where I live, I have been taken for that about half a dozen times in the last twelve months, so you see there is not so very much difference between the American and the Esquimaux of Canada. I do not know what idea the American people have generally of Canada, but I know this, that you have some good ideas over here, and we are not above learning from anybody that has a good idea to give us.

CONNECTICUT.

Mr. Eli Manchester, Jr.

Connecticut greets you to-day with three hundred and thirty-five societies. We estimate our membership at about twenty-three thousand. We cannot tell you the exact numbers. You know in Connecticut we like union. We have a number of unions. Besides the flourishing state union, we have thirty-three local unions.

The junior work is taking a good firm foothold amongst our societies, and our secretary reports to-day that he is looking for grand results from that work.

Six years ago Connecticut was present at one of these gatherings by one delegate. To-day we come to you with about five hundred. I have very little more to say, only that next year we will try to do better; we will try to bring more than five hundred.

We wish you God-speed all over this broad land for Christian Endeavor. It is doing and has done for us in Connecticut grand things. Our churches feel it, our pastors feel it in their work, and the young people themselves feel it, and we all feel that it has been a great help to us.

NEW YORK.
Mr. Henry D. Jackson.

New York the Banner State, organized July, 1886, with ninety societies, and in one year later there were four hundred and thirty-eight societies, and in July, 1888, nine hundred and forty-nine societies, and to-day finds us with nearly fifteen hundred societies. During the spring of this year we have held twenty-one conventions in our state. Our state has at the present time very nearly eighty thousand members, or about one-sixth of the membership of the Christian Endeavor in the world.

Our growth for the past twelve months has been five hundred societies, and nearly twenty-five thousand members,—enough new members during this period to equal a city the size of Elmira. In other words, in New York State a new member has been added for every ten minutes of every day and night for the past twelve months. Our State will show fully six thousand conversions during the year. Think of it, through Endeavor in part at least, more souls brought to Jesus in this Empire State than the number of this vast congregation here to-day.

Sister States, we ask your prayers, we ask your earnest petition before God for a blessing upon us.

MICHIGAN.
Mr. Robert Murray.

I am sorry that I cannot give you as full a report of Michigan as I would have liked to have done. I did not know when I left home that I was to speak for Michigan. What I gleaned I have got from the delegates.

In Grand Rapids there are eleven societies numbering one thousand members. We are spoken of in the highest terms in the Sunday Schools and among the young. In Detroit we have sixteen societies numbering from about eight hundred to one thousand members. I cannot give you a full account of the state work, but I will say, as my time is limited, that in Detroit the work done among the young people is very highly commended as the most encouraging institution in connection with the church, and we feel greatly encouraged. The pastor, when he comes down to our church on Friday night, seems to look brighter and happier than any time we see him, and the members of the society, although we have such intense heat, say they do not want to give up the meetings for the hot months.

NEW JERSEY.
Mr. F. B. Everett.

You have already heard from the doubtful States of Connecticut, New York and Indiana, and now New Jersey also comes. We can assure you that she is not doubtful in Christian Endeavor, if she is in some other things, for the tide from that territory the last few days has been so strong that it has carried over the border line into this state at least five hundred delegates, representing two hundred and seventy-six societies, an increase of fifty-seven per cent during the last year.

We yield to only one society west of the Hudson in priority of organization, and of course Ohio had to steal that, because their society was organized as the second one west of that river, in 1882. For five years the growth was slow, but since that time it has been exceedingly rapid, and at our convention in Newark, in 1887, we had ninety-two, and the next year at Trenton, in 1888, we had one hundred and ninety, and now we have two hundred and seventy-six societies. These societies will approximate fifteen thousand members, and are found in all denominations, the Presbyterian leading with ninety-seven, and the Baptists closely following with seventy-one, thus giving these two, at least, over one-half of the societies in the state.

Young people of New Jersey, remember this, that if there is any society near you that is, so to speak, dead, it is your duty, each and every delegate here appointed, to try to revive and quicken every society in this state. Remember our motto is, "Every society shall be as a fountain of running water."

NEBRASKA.
Rev. E. S. Ralston.

I bring you the greetings of Nebraska. We stand related to the great new West very much as our friends of Massachusetts do to the great Northeast, and somewhat like them, we are always modest in our claims and always reasonable in our demands. The State of Nebraska for the past two years has increased fifteen hundred per cent in membership of its Christian Endeavor societies. In my own city we have increased seven hundred per cent. In the city of Omaha we have increased three hundred per cent.

We take your saplings from down East and we make pillars of the church of them in the West. We take your boys and your girls and we are all boys and girls out there together. It is well to see gray heads in our missions. We are all Christian people there, and we are making the societies a mighty force in the Church of Christ in the State of Nebraska.

So I bring you greetings in the name of the present membership. We wish to make Christians of your boys and your girls and your young people who go West and grow up—and they do grow up. Young men grow there until they are like our corn, only not so green. Girls grow there until they are as fair as our bright beautiful sunflowers, only not quite so red in the centre.

MISSOURI.

Mr. A. H. Fredericks.

I report for the State of Missouri that we have gained one hundred and seventy-seven societies, an increase of nearly sixty per cent over a year ago. Our membership is six thousand five hundred and eighty-seven of the active and associate members, and five hundred and seven of the junior societies, thus making a total of seven thousand and ninety-four, an increase of over two thousand since last year.

We have union societies in all the largest cities in the state. The total conversions reported since the 1st of May, 1888, have been five hundred and forty-seven.

There are just two things that we want in Missouri; one is, we are working to bring every young man and woman, all of the young people in the state, to Christ, into the Young People's Society of Christian Endeavor and into the Church; and the second thing we are working for is that the next Christian Endeavor National Convention will be held in the city of St. Louis.

MINNESOTA.

Mr. E. B. McClanahan.

We are glad to be called the New England of the Northwest, and we want to say to our brother of the State of Connecticut, that while they can report the organization of the first Union, we can report the formation of one since the organization of this Convention, in Mankato, Minn., so we are not standing still there waiting for our delegates to return, but are working, and we are also working for the Convention of 1890. Minnesota has two hundred societies of Christian Endeavor. At the Chicago Convention they reported one hundred societies. We have four city unions; one in the city of St. Paul, one in the city of Minneapolis, one in the city of Rochester and one in the city of Mankato, and I think there will very soon be one in the city of Winona and one in the city of Duluth.

St. Paul and Minneapolis are working for the entire Northwest, for around these two cities centres the great work of Christian Endeavor. You must know that through our cities pass hundreds and thousands of those who are without homes and who are seeking homes in the far Northwest, and it remains to St. Paul and Minneapolis, as the great populous centres, to educate and to refine and to christianize these vast crowds of people.

PENNSYLVANIA.

Mr. E. Boyd Weitzel.

There is a young married lady in a Society in Pennsylvania whose husband was an infidel two months ago. She tried to get him to attend the Christian Endeavor prayer-meetings with her. It was impossible. One stormy evening she was afraid to go alone and she persuaded him to come. What was the result of his coming? He was so impressed by the earnestness of the young people that he had no peace until the following Saturday, when he gave his heart to the Lord Jesus.

Another society, with the co-operation of their pastor, have during the past year brought from the ranks of the associate members thirty-four to active membership, all of whom have united with the church.

The prayer-meeting committee of another society made up their minds that their society should do something. They made it a point at one meeting to pray for a certain object, and what was the result? Eight of those for whom they prayed that night were converted to Christ. I wish you could have heard those young people afterwards as they offered up their own prayers to the Lord Jesus.

Pennsylvania has not done the work in the past that she had hoped, but we expect from now on to do more. During the past year we have been able to get down to some systematic work as a State Union. We have now thirty-one secretaries working in thirty-seven counties, and we hope to have a secretary in every county. We have about five hundred societies with a membership between twenty-five and thirty thousand. We hope with God's blessing, by next year that we can double that through the influence of this Convention here during the past three days.

IOWA.

Mr. J. E. Mershon.

Prohibition Iowa sends greeting. We are workers out in Iowa, 9,000 strong, shoulders to the wheel, representing two hundred and sixty societies and ten local unions. The past year we brought eight hundred members into Christian fellowship with the Church through our society. We have grown greatly in the missionary work in the past year, largely through the efforts of our State Secretary. Our young people are also working in the prohibition line.

DELAWARE.

Mr. Harry J. Guthrie.

We cannot make as large a report in Christian Endeavor as our sister States, and we cannot make as large a report as we would like to, but we can report something.

Our first society was organized in Wilmington, Delaware, October, 1886, about three years ago. At the present time there are twenty-one societies in the state, with an active membership of eight hundred and fifty, with eighty-two associate members and thirty-six honorary members, or a total membership of nine hundred and seventy-eight.

We also have one local union in Wilmington to which nine societies belong, and it contains about five hundred and seventy-five members. The prayer-meetings throughout the state are well attended and there is much interest shown in the work. I find in our city that in the regular prayer-meeting, and in fact in all the other meetings in the different churches since we have had the Christian Endeavor movement in Delaware the attendance has increased at least fifty per cent. We might at the present time have more members: we might run up to two thousand members, no doubt, but we have stuck to our pledge. Some say, "You have an iron-clad pledge." Our pledge, however, is not too strong, and we would rather have quality than quantity.

WISCONSIN.

Mr. H. W. Nickerson.

Four or five years ago when I first came back from the west to my old home in Ohio, a good old lady called me over to her house to tell her about Wisconsin. After I had talked for some little time about the state she said, "Well, Wisconsin must be a grand state, but I should think you would be afraid of the Indians out there." Although we have 10,000 Indians in Wisconsin we have a little more than that number of white people, and we have one hundred and sixty-two Christian Endeavor societies, with a total membership reported of 6,152. We have four local unions in the state and three or four district conventions which meet quarterly. Our growth in Wisconsin has been retarded in two or three of the strong denominations on account of the pronounced hostility toward the movement on the part of a few of the so-called prominent ministers of those denominations. In the city of Milwaukee, the largest city in the state, the strongest denomination has not a solitary society. They have one so-called young people's meeting led by young people, but their pastor has to sit on the platform to bolster up the leader to give him the necessary amount of courage.

OHIO.

Mr. J. C. Beecham.

I am proud to say to you that I not only represent the home of a good many Presidents of the United States, but the homes of a good many Christian Endeavor members. I find them here from almost every state in the Union. In reply to our brother as to stealing the first society west of the Hudson from them I want to say we are alive out there in Christian Endeavor work as well as in getting Presidents of the United States. With a membership of about two hundred societies last year we now have four hundred and sixty-five.

Our President, Mr. Clark, in his talk, and as he comes before us through the columns of *The Golden Rule*, has spoken about "ideal societies." I want to read you about it.

"The Society of Christian Endeavor of Dr. Hubbell's church, Mansfield, Ohio, wish to publicly thank President Clark for the wonderful principles given us in the *The Golden Rule* two weeks ago; we do not deserve it, for we are by no means the ideal society. Still, it made us very humble and his kind words have sent us joyfully forward, conquering and to conquer."

MASSACHUSETTS.

Mr. H. A. Field.

Massachusetts was one of the first to adopt the Christian Endeavor idea, and after eight years' experience is more enthusiastic than ever in the cause of Christian Endeavor. Massachusetts has contributed both men and money to the cause. Since the United Society was organized at Old Orchard in 1885, she has contributed nearly one-third of all the money used in advancing the work. Massachusetts has shown her appreciation both by her words and her works. God's blessing has rested upon our work, and hundreds have united with the different churches during the year. We come before you to-day with a delegation five hundred strong. We have seven hundred and forty-two societies in the state with a membership of about fifty thousand. We hope by October to have strong district organizations all over our state, and next year when we come to St. Louis to the State Convention, to tell you that we have seventy-five thousand members.

KANSAS.

Mr. Olin S. Davis.

I have the honor and very great pleasure of representing and bringing to you the greetings of the young people of a state whose virgin soil drank the first blood for freedom in this country, the freedom of the slaves, and of a state that long since joined with her sister state of Maine in proving to the world that prohibition does prohibit if the people want it to. Of a state that has gone a step further and is proving to the world that the question of municipal administration can be solved and is being solved by giving to woman her inherent right of suffrage, and by electing to the mayoralty and to the council women to administer our affairs, and she has made it a success.

In 1886 the first society in Kansas was organized. The following year the first superintendent was appointed at Saratoga. In the year following that, 1888, we held our first state convention, and now we have two hundred and forty societies. In one hundred and fifteen there are three thousand six hundred and fifty-two active members and nine hundred and sixty-four associate members. One hundred and eleven of these societies have reported three thousand one hundred and eighty-seven members, and fifty-four societies have reported three hundred and sixteen young people as having joined the church within a year from these societies. The societies reported are to be found in forty-seven of our counties and in seventy-four of our cities. We raised at our last state convention $400 in twenty minutes for our state work. We are going to work the districts and start an organization and local union and junior societies, and push the work throughout the state.

FLORIDA.
Mrs. M. L. Selden.

I think it would pay our state to send a delegation to a Christian Endeavor convention as an advertisement. Otherwise, you will think I am the only person in the state. Our superintendent has gone away to London, our corresponding secretary could not come, so as the state secretary I have to represent again our state, but there is another delegate here to-day, so Florida has two inhabitants.

Last year we organized Christian Endeavor work, and we held our first convention and organized a state union. There are only twenty-five societies in our state now, but I am happy to say they are well scattered through the state, and you know what that means. To be near a Christian Endeavor Society means another or several Christian Endeavor Societies. So, from the Georgia line to the Coral Reefs, and from the Atlantic Ocean to the Gulf of Mexico, Christian Endeavor is represented. This year we hold another convention, when we hope to do even better work.

RHODE ISLAND.
Mr. H. E. Thurston.

With grand old Massachusetts and Connecticut on the other side it would be impossible for Rhode Island to be out of the ranks of Christian Endeavor, and we are, although very small in numbers, I believe very enthusiastic as regards Christian Endeavor. We have in the state about seventy societies, with a membership of about 3,500. We have five local unions, each one of which holds quarterly, and sometimes oftener, meetings, and we enjoy not only the fellowship of those in our own state, but we have had the pleasure of hearing from those from other states as well. I believe that Christian Endeavor stands at the front in Rhode Island as far as good honest practical Christian work is concerned. Nor is this confined to our young people, but we have in the ranks those older in years who are very ready and very willing to do the work which Christian Endeavor calls for, and that I understand to be to live a good, honest, Christian life, and that, it seems to me, is what we all strive to do.

It seems to me, my Christian friends, that although Rhode Island is so very small, still we have a part in this work, and we ask your prayers that we may be more useful, more influential, and may have an influence in reaching those that are not members and who have not as yet accepted the Lord Jesus, that he may bring them out upon His side.

QUEBEC.

Rev. Dr. Wells, of Montreal, being unable to be present, President Clark, who had been requested to speak for him, stated: "We heard from Quebec most eloquently last night, and I am sure that with such a representation and with such a sermon as we heard we need know nothing more about those who come from that province."

KENTUCKY.

Mr. A. H. Hill.

Two years ago we had no Christian Endeavor society in our state at all. About that time the young people of the First English Lutheran Church formed a society, and other churches soon followed, and to-day, under the blessing of the Almighty God, we have twenty-two societies in the city of Louisville, having a membership of about six hundred and twenty-five, or an average of thirty-two to each society.

We have twenty-two societies in other parts of the state, with an average membership of about thirty, making in all, forty-three societies, and about 1,000 members in the whole state.

TEN MINUTE TOPICS.

HAND-SHAKING.

Address of Rev. H. C. Farrar, D.D., Pastor of the Trinity M. E. Church, of Albany, N. Y.

This is the "Young People's Age.' The phrase sounds revolutionary; the reality is, if possible, more so. Wise revolution is better than protracted stagnation. Everywhere and in every way it touches society, and it touches it with electric purpose. The "children's crusade" of the mediæval ages, with its weird and aggressive mission, is reproduced in our day by this "young people's movement"—with a difference. That represented the unenlightened zeal of the youth of the thirteenth century. This is the Christian embodiment of intelligent enthusiasm so typical of the closing decades of this nineteenth century.

This young people's movement is surely struggling to meet the demands of the age intellectually, socially and religiously. These demands are equally positive and peremptory. The church of the Lord Jesus should be the originator and defender and promoter of whatever is healthful and helpful in its effect upon society. The church is for man as he is really, and not ideally. It should touch and teach and train him in every department of his being. Cultivate the physical only and you have the athlete, cultivate only the intellectual and you have a monstrosity, cultivate the social and you have flippant and fickle fools, cultivate the religious and you have the ascetic. The Christianity of to-day demands the perfect man in Christ Jesus. Sociology is rapidly coming to be as important a study as theology. The ministry for the times deals with the livest issues. Many of the stirring theological issues of the past are dead and buried; *requiescat in pace.*

CHRISTIAN SOCIABILITY NEEDED.

I know of no one issue that comes so positively to the very forefront in our churches and in all our Gospel work as "Christian sociability."

Society will never purify itself. It has no Decalogue, no Gospel, no Pentecost! Reformation and regeneration must be introduced, however undesired. The Christ must enter society through His disciples and infuse the leavening power of His life. Society must be purified, elevated and saved. This is the problem confronting this young people's movement to-day. There is a gospel of the tongue; the truth must be preached. There is a gospel of the character; the truth must be lived. There is a gospel of the hand, and the world must feel the warm, cordial grasp of compassionate love. The hand is the "biggest human power"; it is the symbol and type of sociability. The hands are not dumb — they speak as distinctly as lips. With our hands we invite, we repel, we invoke, we entreat; we wring them in grief, or clap them in joy, or spread them abroad in benediction. How often in the ministry of Jesus it is recorded, "And He took him by the hand." He loved to exercise His Divine power through personal contact, as though He would teach us that if we would help our fellows we must come into some sort of vital closeness with them and make them feel that our relation is of the heart, and not a mere patronizing and dainty compassion.

It is no use to mount lofty pedestals and draw one's skirts about one's self, and toss fine maxims at the weak. The world will never consent to be haughtily lectured into morality. There must be a face to face, hand to hand, heart to heart touch. Even lepers we must not shun. The blind must be led, the overburdened must feel our magnetic influence. Our love sympathies must be transmitted by touch. Personal contact is the very and only point of His inspiration. There must be genuine gospel hand-shaking. Across cradles and dying beds and graves shake hands. With your enemies, who have done all in their power to defame you, but whom you can afford to forgive, shake hands. At the door of churches, where people come in and go out, shake hands. At prayer-meeting and all social meetings, both before and after, shake hands. On the streets, in the store, at the markets, in public and in private, everywhere, let the spirit of our Christian sociability express itself in sincere and hearty hand-shaking. In some way we must bring the world to confess, as they did in the first century, "Behold, how these Christians love."

THE TIE OF CHURCH-FELLOWSHIP.

Every church member ought to recognize his interest in and show his regard for every other church member. No tie of blood, or of affection, or of patriotism, or of social companionship, or of business relation, or of political affiliation, ought to be counted dearer or stronger in its proper sphere, than the tie of Christian or church fellowship. Those who have fellowship with the Lord Jesus at the communion table have no right to be as strangers one to the other.

The duty of promoting Christian sociability is a personal duty, incumbent alike on each member of the church. Theoretically, everybody concedes this. But to operate it and illustrate it in reality is one of the distinct responsibilities that Providence has put on the Society of Christian Endeavor. A besetting peril of our times is that of trusting too much to organizations. Organizations are good, aye, indispensable. To do any good and effective work there must be plan and system. The house, the school, the mill, the store, the bank must have an orderly movement. Nor is it otherwise with the church. There must be method in work, division in labor.

But the danger is of laying too much stress on organization, over-emphasizing fine plans, and thus throwing off personal responsibility.

In all schemes of church activity the thing is to set men face to face, side by side, and hand to hand with their fellow-men. In the last analysis this business of helping and saving men all turns on the outgo of personal force, through personal touch. And personal obligation for service is one of the things most strongly insisted upon in the Society of Christian Endeavor.

HOW REACH THE MASSES?

Not by beating wildly on the old drums of theological speculation; not by any acrobatic pulpit feats, nor yet by any dexterous sacerdotal legerdemain. Make your church warm and cosy with human love that has been touched by divine love, and shivering souls will somehow surely find their way into it for warmth; make your church a real shelter and covert, and the storm-smitten will be glad of a housing under its hospitable roof; make your church a genuine brotherhood, and the circle of fraternity will enlarge. Men are not measured in squares, nor built up in cubes, nor told off in circles, nor aggregated together like a pile of cannon balls, but rather knit together or cemented like the myriad lives in the coral rock. They form societies, their lives interlace and interlock and interweave, and are in every way interdependent. There is a positive social correlation of forces. Companionship is more than natural; it is a divine endowment, and from the Christ won divine endorsement. Society is man's place, physical, moral and spiritual. Here he evolves his forces and glorifies his nature.

The church is pre-eminently social. This is its history in the past, this is its life to-day. Its law is one and irrepealable, "Thou shalt love thy neighbor." Hence the church is a kingdom and at once establishes a community of interest. The Lord Himself was in society. He was at the wedding, the feast, and the funeral; these all found a responsive chord of sympathy in His great heart.

RELIGION AND SOCIETY NOT ANTAGONISTIC.

There is never any antagonism between the religious and social. How, then, may we blend them in our church life that they may work beautifully and blessedly? How carry the true religious spirit into society, so that it shall prove winsome and regenerative? Many attempt and fail. In becoming spiritual they become ascetic, or, in endeavoring to hold liberal notions in regard to society, degenerate into mere slaves of its fashions, or, holding most careful watch, become legalists, and so fall out of liberty. „Let your light so shine before men that they may see your good works and glorify your Father which is in Heaven."

Society needs the social Christian — not his pocket-book, not his patronage, but his recognition, his cheery "good morning," as well as his devout "God bless you." It needs his example of refined, courteous godliness, his cheerfulness without frivolity, his piety without sanctimoniousness, his conversation without cant. It needs to see illustrations that the Christian religion is not a cloak, but an easy, delightful and natural life — a life that does more, enjoys more, and is more than any other life; that there is a wide difference between it and a worldly life; that its motives and methods, its aims and accomplishments, its temper and spirit, are in every way better, higher and diviner.

How shall we promote this social spirit? Have a thorough conviction of its feasibility. Many teach that the social spirit ever antagonizes the religious, and that in proportion as you cultivate the social, in that proportion you lose the religious. Such teaching is flatly unbiblical. It makes a breach between the social and religious nature, and in God's economy there is none. I grant a soul godliness has no affinity with an amiable sociability, nor a frivolous sociability with a godly spirit. Life is a Mosaic, patterned after the heavenly; its colors should be positive and bright, and so give a cheerful picture.

THE LIFE MAN SHOULD LEAD.

Man was not made for the social, nor for the civil, nor for the intellectual, nor yet for the spiritual, but for all combined. Blessed is he who grasps the unity of his being and cultivates assiduously all its powers in harmony therewith.

The religious should dominate. This is God's order. Grace should be triumphant. Leadership and rulership belong to it. No argument is needed. The best surety for forces and faculties is that they be grounded in love. Then our pleasures and amusements will be taken as Daniel took his prayers—with his windows open; pleasures which need never cause a blush on an ingenuous cheek;. pleasures which will ever and only give an additional zest to the devotional spirit. The greatest contribution one can make to the solution of this "social religious question" is to be just what in theory he holds possible. "Myself" was the contribution of a young lad in his church on missionary day. Every member of the Society of Christian Endeavor ought consciously and intelligently to say, in the practical solution of this question, "myself," and then blend in himself or herself the two things most needed—social and religious. On this social line we must reach souls. This conviction grows in me.

There are members in almost every church who illustrate the beauty and purity of the religious spirit, and who are at the same time among the most sunny and social, who delight in the means of grace and mingle freely in society, and ever give but one impresssion. Blessed is the church that has in it at least one such sweet, sunny, social, spiritual saint!

THE VALUE OF TIME.

By Miss Ella Reinking, Des Moines, Iowa.

The value of time! who can estimate it? Who can place a proper valuation upon these golden moments which are so precious that in all the immense expanse of creation there are never two in existence at the same time, and when one is lost, it is lost forever. Moments which are silently speeding away, even as we speak, and hastening up to heaven with the record of every mortal indelibly written upon them, an unerring record which is registered above, and at the day of reckoning will either justify or condemn, will bring us either the tender "well done, good and faithful servant, (she hath done what she could") or the stern and terrible "depart from me!" Moments are sacred trusts committed to us by God; but do we regard them as such? and are we making the best use of them? Are we filling them with deeds of kindness and works of love? or, are they ushered into God's presence all blotted and stained, and disfigured with the record of squandered time, neglected duties and wasted opportunities? Not one of us but would recoil from the very thought of appropriating for self one penny belonging to another, yet we squander with impunity the time belonging to our Master, time which is far more precious than silver or gold. Well might He say to us, even as He said to His people of old, "Ye have robbed me!" For have we brought the *tithes* of time into His store-house? have we each made our life sacred by devoting it all to God? It is said that Agassiz, in reproving an indolent student for an unprepared exercise, was answered with the excuse, "I did not have time, sir;" the aged professor quietly replied, "You had all the time that was going, young man; you had all the time that was going." Lack of time can never be pleaded at the bar of heaven, for God never gives us work to do without also giving plenty of time in which to do it. We, indeed, have all the time that is going, and yet how often we devote only the *fragments* to God. We can always find time to do that which we really desire to do, and even make personal sacrifices that it may be accomplished, but how easy to plead want of time when some unpleasant or difficult duty presents itself. When we look about us and see the different uses men make of their time, we cannot realize that each possesses exactly the same amount—that he who always has leisure for every God-sent duty, whose every moment is sacredly consecrated to service, possesses no more, and the sluggard, or the idle, selfish pleasure seeker no less than every other mortal. It is the way we employ our moments which stamps our lives with either success or failure.

Oh, could we but realize that the one object of our life is to *glorify God!* could we but comprehend that He has a purpose in everything. That when He leads us into the mournful shades of life's Gethsemanes, and holds the bitter cup of suffering to our lips, it is not because he loves to chide, nor finds pleasure in our pain, but it is that *He may be glorified;* and when some great and sacred joy sweeps majestically into the life, illuminating it from horizon to zenith, the divine purpose is still the same, the *glory of God*, and not the simple object of our own pleasure. A great and mighty purpose underlies everything. There are no *trifles*, as there are no accidents in the purposes of God. It is said that the weaver of the beautiful Cashmere shawl, works upon the wrong side and sees not the right with its perfect design, until his labor is completed; so it is with us, we see only the wrong side of life, — the tangles, the knots and the meaningless ends, unconscious many times that we are weaving a design of beauty, as we obediently take up, now the golden thread of joy, now the somber one of sorrow, mixed with the continuous gray-hued thread of duty, but in the beyond we will understand it all, and gazing upon the finished design will know that every knot, and snarl, and confusing end, and every thread of various shades was necessary for the perfection of the wonderful design. "What I do thou knowest not now but thou shalt know hereafter."

Dear Endeavorer, let us weave no threads into our lives but those given by our Divine Master. Let no thread of disobedience mar its beauty; none of selfishness; none of wilful sin. Let us make this beautiful consecration prayer of the order of the King's Daughters our own, not only praying but living it. "Take me, Lord, and use me to-day as thou wilt. Whatever work thou hast for me to do give it into my hands. If there are those thou wouldst have me to help in any way, send them to me. Take my *time*, and *use it as thou wilt*. Let me be a vessel close to thy hand and meet for thy service, to be employed only for thee and for ministry to others In His Name." Oh, let us give our time to God; let us use it for him wherever we are, and whatever we may be doing. This whole-hearted consecration gives dignity to the homeliest toil, and renders every employment sacred. Let us so live that we shall never be surprised into betraying our Lord, but shall, by our daily life, in the home, the school-room, the shop or the office, convince all who see us that we have been with Jesus, and are taught of him. Winning souls to Christ is the work of the Christian —the Christian's aim in life. We sometimes think our efforts are wasted, and precious time but thrown away, but there will be many surprises in heaven, for what we in blindness call failure, God in his mercy calls success. Time used for self may be wasted, but that employed for Christ is never lost, for it passes on to eternity and awaits us there. Would we *save* our time? Then let us use it freely for Christ. Truly, "he that winneth souls is wise." The time is short; souls are hastening down to death; souls which we might save, and for whom God will hold us accountable. "That thou doest, do quickly," is the Lord's command to each; the past is gone, the future may never come, the present alone is ours, and even *it* is speeding rapidly away. Who of us could stand by with healing balm in his hand and see the life-blood oozing away from a fallen brother's side without attempting to close the gaping wound? Yet this is what we each are doing if we make not every effort within our power to " rescue the perishing." Fiery darts taken from the quiver of death and hurled by the hand of the arch-fiend, rankle in too many hearts, some, perhaps, which are throbbing only for us. We know this, but we do not realize it, else our lives would not be what they are, for we could not sit at ease in Zion and know that souls were dying just without its walls. Moments are indeed precious trusts; may we regard them as such, and be made to realize that "as it is a solemn thing to die, so it is to live; but he to whom living is Christ, is sure to find that dying is gain."

Dear Endeavorers, brothers and sisters in Christ, do we realize the work God has for us to do? Do we realize that upon the use we make of our time depends the eternal fate of an immense army of souls! God forbid! that we, the young disciples of Christ, " should glory save in the cross of the Lord Jesus Christ," unless we fully realize all this.

ST. PAUL'S ADVICE TO THE SISTERS.

By Miss Emily Wheeler, Harpoot, Turkey.

I thank you very much for your applause, but I do not think it is quite fair to take my time, do you? I wish St. Paul were here to-day; oh, I wish he could see you. I wish he could have gone with me around this magnificent country, even the small portion of it that I have been over —Massachusetts, Connecticut and a little bit of New Hampshire—and could have seen the things that I have seen and could have heard the ladies and gentlemen speak, could have noted the spirit of your meetings, — I do not think he would have given you the advice to be silent.

It is a blessed thing to come back from Turkey, after being absent ten years, and see this great assembly of the young people of Christian Endeavor Societies. I could talk to you six hours about it. I should not tell you you were frivolous, and advise you to be more passive. Keep close to Christ, no matter if they *do* talk about you, no matter if they *do* criticize you. "Woe unto you when all men speak well of you." Only let the evil be spoken falsely.

I thank Dr. Hoyt and our good friends, Dr. Deems and Dr. Chapman, who have helped me in this subject of St. Paul's advice to the sisters. I will not have to say very much about it. They have explained its meaning and saved me the trouble. You see how it has been misunderstood. Come with me out to Turkey; come to the very land where Paul gave his famous advice. I wish you could attend the Commencement of Euphrates College at Harpoot this very morning and could hear some of the female graduates read their essays. There are not more than five hundred men and women to hear them because we dare not let the public in to hear girls speak — only the select few. My last mail brought the news that twenty little girls had taken part in a Sabbath School concert in a church in the Garden of Eden. I never expected to live to see such a sight as that, but I have, and am going back to see still more radical changes. Therefore, Paul's advice right there in the place where he gave it is being disobeyed. I wish you could see what kind of women there are out there in the Orient, and compare these Nineteenth Century girls with the girls of long ago in Corinth—with the uneducated village girls of to-day in Turkey. What a difference you would find. There our girls are married when they are twelve or fourteen years old, and must be ruled over with a rod of iron by the mother-in-law, lest in the patriarchal families of twenty or thirty sons the brides quarrel. Therefore a bride may not speak aloud to an older member of her husband's family, much less in a church. See them go about with two veils, one tied over the mouth and one covering the eyes. Would you change places with them? Does not St. Paul say a woman's head must be covered? A bonnet or a hat is not sufficient covering for the head in the Orient, and if you keep St. Paul's advice in one particular why not in this? Come out there and see how degraded some of these women are. When we ask them to learn to read they say, "A woman is a squash-head; a woman has no brains; the seeds are few in the squash-head and they rattle." Hear them say, "A woman is a donkey; a woman cannot read; donkeys we come and donkeys we go; ashes on our heads." Do you agree with them? It used to be an open question whether a woman had a soul. Ah, my sisters, you do not know the privilege you enjoy in living in a Christian instead of a Mohammedan country. But the Bible is conquering, and to-day thousands of women in Turkey are reading and studying. How about St. Paul's advice there? I would not speak to a mixed audience in a church in Turkey for anything. It would create a scandal. We are not ready for such changes. But the question in America is a totally different one. Why not speak here? What is the trouble? We women are weak creatures; we cry sometimes, you know, and very often we go into personalities. We say foolish things; we *are* weak and foolish, but I read here in I. Corinthians that "God hath chosen the foolish things of the world to confound the wise, and God hath chosen the weak things of the world to confound the things which are mighty." I am glad I am foolish; I am glad I am weak, so that God can use me.

"When I am weak, then I am strong," says St. Paul. Oh, dear sisters; oh, dear brothers; what is the trouble? We women are leaders in other things. Go to the history of France; go to Boston, New York, and everywhere, and see how women lead in evil. Sisters, why may we not lead in good things? We need not speak in the churches, but in our Father's family, in the prayer-meeting, shall we not bear our part? Can we not talk in the family? Can we not talk about bonnets, and can we not talk about dresses, and can we not even talk about politics? In our Father's family can you not tell what he has done for you? If we would only *communicate* in private, if we would only "*pray without ceasing*" in private, we should be happy to communicate in public, and we should gladly pray in chapels; and does not St. Paul say: "To do good and to communicate, forget not;" "Let him that is taught in the word communicate to him that teacheth;" also, "Pray without ceasing."

It has been said here that the word *brethren* includes the sisters. Very well, then surely all St. Paul's advice to "the saints" and "the churches" *must* include the sisters. Are you communicating in private? Are you "praying without ceasing" for your friends, your church, for this poor, sin-sick world of ours?

Go to St. Paul's advice, my sister, and see *many* things he says. Look over *all* his advice if you are going to keep any. If you are a sister that does not believe in speaking in the churches, keep every other bit of advice also. We want women to "pray everywhere,"

When you sit down in a horse car, do you pray for the people in that horse car? When you go in a railway car, do you pray for the people in that railway car? Are you speaking to your sister, to your brother, to your pupils in the Sabbath school or the day school about the Lord Jesus Christ? My friends, if you are not, you had better look up Paul's advice. I wish he were here to talk to you instead of me. What is the difficulty? We are so proud, my sisters; we are so full of self. I am sorry to confess it, for it does not seem quite right, but in our missionary meetings, where there are only women, only the sisters, no brethren to alarm us, it is exceedingly hard to get anybody to make a prayer, exceedingly hard to get anybody to give us information. The ladies must *read* a paper and the old stand-bys must pray. No new voices are heard. It is simply pride. We are afraid we shall not speak or pray properly. Let us get rid of self. Breathe out self and breathe in Christ, and then your pride will not keep you from speaking or praying in meeting. Let us pray for that prayer-meeting that we are going to; as we go along the street let us mention the name of the leader to God; many times a day before we go to it let us pray for it; then write the name of your Christian Endeavor Society opposite your favorite verse, your favorite chapter, and when you see that verse or chapter in turning over your Bible, mention the name to God, and when you go to its meeting you will be so full of prayer and longing that it will bubble right straight out. You cannot keep from praying, from speaking, and thus helping to bless your society.

Some one has said people know the difference between a bashful attempt to do your duty and a spring of life within welling out. If the love of Christ is within, if you are full of Christ's spirit, and are praying for those around you, you cannot be silent. You *must* help them. If you really know Christ, you will long to let others know how grand and beautiful a thing it is to have Christ for an intimate friend. "They that loved the Lord spake often one to another." Do you speak of Christ to your friends in private? do you pray with them in private? Then you can not keep still in public.

You need not speak to a convention; you need not speak from the pulpit; but you *may* speak in the prayer meeting—your Father's church family circle. You may not believe it wise for a weak and feeble woman—a physically, mentally, and spiritually feeble woman—to get up and talk at a convention.

I wonder if we understand *who* is to do this speaking and praying. *We* are not to speak. What does our Lord and Master say? "I am glorified in them," and His word is with power. Oh, that is what we want. Not to let self speak, but to let Christ speak right out of us. Find out what that means, and see how your life will glow and shine. He says, "Who art thou that art afraid of the Son of Man? I have put my words in thy mouth." Get God's word in your mouth and then speak, and let Him speak through you. I cannot teach you how to do that. I did not come here to teach you, but to commend you to a teacher—the Holy Spirit. "The Comforter which is the Holy Ghost, He shall teach you all things." Go home and write Y. P. S. C. E. Convention, '89, opposite that verse in the fourteenth of John, and pray that we may all be willing to learn what the Spirit would teach us. Dear brothers and sisters, if you do not know what to do about this matter, if you do not believe in women speaking in meeting, if you do not know what to say in meeting yourself, go into your closets and, taking your Bibles, read that verse and pray. "We know not what we should pray for as we ought," but "the Spirit also helpeth our infirmities." The Spirit will help you. Pray to the Holy Spirit to "open Thou mine eyes that I may see wondrous things out of Thy law." Teach me how to pray; teach me how to speak; teach me all about St. Paul's advice, not only to the sisters, but to the brothers.

I am going out to Turkey to form societies of Christian Endeavor. Will you not pray for us? We need your prayers sorely. Dear sisters, if you can pray for nothing else in your meetings, will you not pray for your sisters in Africa and Asia? Dear brothers, will you not pray that God may send laborers into the harvest fields, that we may all work harder, and give more for God's glorious kingdom, that we may emulate St. Paul and work for the world. Do not forget the fourteenth chapter of John, the twenty-sixth verse.

"The Comforter which is the Holy Ghost, whom the Father will send in My name, He shall teach you all things." May He teach you how to pray and give for missions. May He teach you how to be missionaries, for Christ says, "As the Father hath sent me, even so send I you." Good-bye, I am going back to my work. God bless you, and the Spirit guide you into all truth.

THE SOCIETY OF CHRISTIAN ENDEAVOR INTERDENOMINATIONAL, NOT UNDENOMINATIONAL.

By Rev. W. H. York, Pastor of the Furman Street M. E. Church, Syracuse, N. Y.

Most of you who are here to-day would not have to turn the "wheels of time" back very much to find yourselves once more as pupils in the public school. No branch of study which you pursued in those days made any deeper impression on your mind than mathematics. With what enthusiasm you started out with the simple number table, and how proudly you assaulted other difficulties when that one was mastered, until at length you came to fractions. Then it seemed almost as though you had reached something insurmountable. How long it took you to get clearly in your mind the difference between numerator and denominator! You were taught that the denominator told the denomination of the fraction. It was the divider of the unit into different parts. It was difficult for you to comprehend how the larger the numeral in the denominator, the less the real value of the fraction. Confusion often came to you, as it once did to a minister who was urging his congregation to give one-tenth of their income to the Lord, when he said, "Brethren, if any of you do not feel able to give one-tenth, then give one-fifth."

In the many times that you have met the word denomination since those school days, you have wondered if there was any relation between fractions and the different church denominations. Let me tell you that the words have the same meaning now that they did in the school days, viz: a part of a divided whole. As the Jones family is a part of the human family, so the Baptist, Presbyterian or Methodist denomination is a part of the great family of the redeemed.

IS OUR SOCIETY UNDENOMINATIONAL?

Un means not; therefore, undenominational means not denominational. An undenominational organization is one that is not distinguished by any particular church doctrine, and usually works independent of the church.

Undenominationalism is carefully guarded against by our society. The first proposition from the "platform of principles" reads like this: "The Society of Christian Endeavor is not, and is not to be, an organization independent of the church. It is the church at work for and with the young, and the young at work for and with the church. In all that we do or say let us bear this in mind and seek for the fullest cooperation of pastors, church officers and members in carrying on our work. The society can always afford to wait, rather than to force itself on an unwilling church." If our society were undenominational, it would seek to advance its own interests regardless of the interests of any branch of the church of Christ. But it is not so.

Everywhere and always it seeks to build up the local church. It may be that for a time, under peculiar circumstances, a society may be formed that is undenominational, just as a man may go into a new country without a family, but when he neglects to plan for a home of his own, suspicion is aroused, and his standing in a community is seriously affected. Thus it may be that, as a pioneer, a society may be formed as an undenominational society, but sooner or later its greatest usefulness and its best influence will require that it have a denominational home of its own.

IS OUR SOCIETY INTERDENOMINATIONAL?

Inter means among; therefore, interdenominational means among the denominations. A good example of this idea would be the Sunday school. This is an organization which, while it is common to all denominations, is strongly characterized by the denomination where it is employed. The second proposition from the "platform of principles" very clearly answers this question. It says, "Since the societies exist in every evangelical denomination, the basis of the union of the societies is of common loyalty to Christ, common methods of service for Him, and mutual Christian affection, rather than a doctrinal and ecclesiastical basis. In such a union all evangelical Christians can unite without repudiating or being disloyal to any denominational custom or tenet." The Christian Endeavor is among us as a handmaiden of the church, and just as the employment of servants is not the exclusive right of any one family, so this method of work may be employed by any branch of the church of Christ.

REASONS FOR INTERDENOMINATIONALISM.

We firmly believe that the best thing for a young people's society is that it shall be interdenominational, and for the following reasons:

First, interdenominationalism enables the hosts of Israel to present a solid front to the enemy. Long ago it was remarked by a leading Romanist: "The reason that the Protestants don't get on faster is that they consume so much time and strength combating each other."

Second, interdenominationalism exalts Christ above creed.

What is more bewildering to a young convert, when first brought to Christ, than to be confronted with a long array of dogmatic propositions? It would be like trying to teach an infant one month old the propositions of geometry. Or what more harmful for one just giving up "fighting against God," and who is feeling that the lion nature is giving place to the lamb nature, than to witness a wrangling between experienced church-members over denominational tenets? As well might you take a Sunday school scholar to witness a prize-fight.

Observation teaches us the sad lesson that whenever denominationalism is made more prominent than the salvation of the soul, the convert very soon loses his spiritual power and Christian usefulness. As we learn in fractions, so we learn in the Master's cause—that the higher the denominationalism, the less is the real value.

Third, interdenominationalism admits of many methods of cooperation, such as state, district and local unions.

IMPORTANCE OF THESE UNIONS.

As the convention has become a great power in political affairs, so these unions have become a great power in advancing the Redeemer's kingdom in the world. We need them for counsel, for wise deliberation, and for the awakening of enthusiasm.

Nature plainly shows her abhorrence of exclusiveness. When any one family becomes so exclusive that it will not associate or marry with any other family, it does not take many generations before it will become imbecile. So abhorrent is nature of this exclusiveness that she withholds the mental endowment, and the exclusiveness is broken up.

Fourth, interdenominationalism is in harmony with the spirit of the times. This is an age of large enterprises. Young people feel instinctively that they live in a large and busy world. They think and read about interests that reach beyond their neighborhood. Their sympathies, hopes and ambitions are expanded by this broad view of life. Unconsciously this enterprising spirit permeates their religious life, and they become intensely interested in advancing the kingdom of God. They covet souls for Christ; they eagerly desire to rescue the perishing.

What more fitting organization or method of work for them than the Young People's Society of Christian Endeavor?

May the blessing of God be with our society in the future, as in the past.

By Rev. J. B. Helwig, D. D., Pastor First Lutheran Church, Springfield, Ohio.

In the history of the centuries gone by we read of *a golden* age—an age that was so-called by reason of the perfection of the thought and the literature which it produced. Shall there not be a still brighter and a still better *golden* age in the years to come—the golden age of the perfection of Christian association? In the Divine revelation such an age is certainly predicted, and *it* may, therefore, also be confidently hoped for and prayed for. And is not this vast audience itself one of the *good* omens pointing to that golden age? Is not this great gathering in the interests of Christian Endeavor a most impressive outline, yea, may *it* not be called *a great, living sermon* on one of the sweetest earthly utterances of our Saviour—"That they all *may be* one as Thou, Father, art in me, and I in Thee, that they also may *be one* in Us; that the *world* may believe that Thou hast sent me—I in them and Thou in me, that they may be made perfect in one; that the world may know that Thou hast sent me and hast loved them as Thou hast loved me." John 17, 21-23. The utterances of our Saviour are, indeed, worthy of applause. There is the basis for a Christian unity—for a Christian interdenominationalism, such as is still somewhat rare, and, therefore, precious among the children of God. And when we inquire for the permanent basis of Christian interdenominationalism, such as the world now needs, we may reply that so long as there remains not only the visible organization, but so long as there remains the invisible church of the Lord Jesus Christ—a church in and through all our churches—a people of God in and through all the people of God; so long as there remains that invisible church of Christ so long will there also remain a permanent basis for Christian union—a lasting bond for interdenominational Christian work. And my inquiry must also be how far are the societies of Christian Endeavor in harmony with the spirit of Christian unity taught in the word of God.

BY THEIR FRUITS.

While they are denominational how far are they also interdenominational? The answer of the Bible to that inquiry would be: "By their fruits ye shall know them." The reply of the Saviour Himself would be, "Believe me for the very work's sake." And here we may also add that the Saviour's plans for His work never conflict. All things which He ordains work *together* for good, so long as they are carried forward in the spirit which He designs. Like the wheels in the prophet's vision—the four had but one likeness and they went, every one, straight forward, for the Spirit of the Living Creature was in the wheels, and there was no conflict. And so with these Societies of Christian Endeavor. They are in the churches, they are by the churches and they are for the churches. And so again is there no conflict. They are denominational and they are not undenominational; yet they are just undenominational enough to be interdenominational. They are interdenominational for Christ and for the individual church in which they are, and they are also interdenominational for Christ and for Christianity throughout the world. And in its eight initial years this society has already belted the solid surface of the globe. And so while *it* may also be called "diverse as the waves" *it* is, nevertheless, "one as the sea" that encircles that globe; and never before in the history of Christendom has there been just such an exemplification of Christian one-ness. Here, for instance, we find the Mennonite, the religious descendant of Menno Simon, the persecuted pioneers of your own Germantown six years and two centuries ago, but still with the regulation hooks and eyes, the flowing beard and the broad brim. And whilst it was never so seen in Israel, yet in this Christian Endeavor movement we find him also side by side with the Methodist, the Congregationalist, the Baptist, the Presbyterian, the General Synod Lutheran, the Reformed, the Protestant Episcopalian, the Reformed Episcopalian, the Friend, thy United Brethren, and so on to the end. And so we say again, " Be their fruits ye shall know them," and, then, what also of the interdenominational adaptation of these societies to the various churches in which we find them.

PRIMITIVE CHRISTIANITY.

Do we not here find the prayer-meeting, the experience meeting, the consecration meeting, the conference meeting, the class meeting, the covenant meeting, the Bible study meeting, and so on, and all in one. In every well-organized and well-conducted Christian endeavor society are found all these meetings, as also all those features of Christian duty, of Christian exercise, and of Christian development. And in that do we not also find a revival of primitive Christianity—a revival of one of the *lost Christian arts?* And we call it one of the lost Christian arts for the reason that the Apostle Paul, already more than eighteen centuries ago, wrote to the Corinthian Christians saying —" How is it, then, brethren, when ye come together, every one of you hath a psalm, hath a doctrine—or, as in the revision, hath a teaching, hath a revelation, hath a tongue, hath an interpretation." And whilst the Apostle's language carried with it a rebuke for any unbecoming confusion in their meetings, his language nevertheless implies that those who were present also took part in the meetings—women and all —for he says, every one of you, and hence quite in contrast to not a few modern prayer-meetings, where, in some cases at least, the leader prays twice in order that the meeting may have the usual number of prayers. But not what has been done by those societies in proof of their interdenominational adaptation everywhere, but what is also the testimony of experience on the part of ministers and churches throughout all our denominational diversity. The pastor of a congregational church in the East says : The society of Christian endeavor connected with this church has gathered in and developed the Christian life of the young. And those who are the most active in the society are among the most constant and ready in other church services. A Presbyterian pastor in the west says : I am prepared to give the society of Christian endeavor my unqualified approval, and I heartily recommend it as the best form of a pastor's aid society. The pastor of a Baptist church on the Pacific Coast says : A society of Christian endeavor was organized in my church two years ago, and most excellent results immediately followed, promotive of the general interest and prosperity of the church. Then he says : God bless the society of Christian endeavor. The pastor of the Trinity Methodist Episcopal Church of Sandusky, Ohio, says: The young people's society of Christian endeavor is the latest and the best organization for the conserving of the fruits of a revival—the building of Christian character, and the training of skilled workmen for future use. It has done all this and more.

A POWER FOR GOOD.

The pastor of the First English Lutheran Church, of Louisville, Kentucky, says: The Society of Christian Endeavor needs only to be fairly tried, and its plans faithfully observed, to prove a power for good in any church. And once more. The pastor of one of the Reformed churches in New York City, says: Among all the good omens that cheer the Christian's heart in our day, there is none more significant than the *generous rally of youth* around the Christian endeavor standard. We yet add, God bless the great movement. And in these times, morally so destructive of the youth of our land, too much cannot be done for the young people, and by the young people, also, in order that they may save themselves in the doing of a work for Christ and for His Church, such as will enable them to be instrumental in saving others also. Let the societies of Christian endeavor maintain the spirit of their name and a great and a glorious future is assured for them.

THE NEW PRAYER-MEETING.

By Rev. Wayland Hoyt, D.D., Pastor Memorial Baptist Church, Philadelphia, Pa.

The New Prayer-Meeting is the prayer-meeting of Christian Endeavor, and the reason why the new prayer-meeting of Christian Endeavor is the best is because it is a reversion to the old typical prayer-meeting of the New Testament.

In the gallery at Bergamo there is a fascinating picture of the Virgin Mother and the Holy Child, by Raphael. That picture has a history. When Napoleon the Great was conquering Italy, Milan fell before him and with it Bergamo. Napoleon was taking all the rare and precious pictures and sending them to adorn Paris. Lest this picture should be seized and lost to Italy, some one painted on its face a coarse and ugly picture, which, of course, Napoleon, not knowing the treasure underneath, did not desire. When he was dethroned, the rifled pictures were sent back to Bergamo, and among them hung this treasure of Raphael, but, in the painter's hurry, there had been no mark left upon it and so it could not be identified, and where it hung among the other great and beautiful pictures no one could tell. At last, in the year 1868, the daub began to scale away, and then reverent hands set about to clean the picture, and at last the long lost treasure shone forth again.

DISFIGURATIONS OF THE IDEAL PRAYER-MEETING.

Now over the fair ideal of a real prayer-meeting presented to us in the New Testament, have come many disfigurations; long prayers that take in the Jews and the uttermost parts of the earth, and stiff routine and hard formalism and awfully long pauses, and only now and then a new voice, too much bench and too little people. These things, and things like these, have made too often the sad simile, "As dull as a prayer-meeting," too full of the miserable truth, and have frequently generated the idea that such fervor and enjoyment as are in the typical New Testament prayer-meeting was something that could not be seen and were impossible to obtain. All these things have been blotting the fair vision, in the New Testament, of a genuine prayer-meeting. Thank God, in these days of ours, these hindering blotches are made to scale away through powerful influences, and among the instruments working toward this end, Christian Endeavor has had and is having a very supreme part.

Consider a little that typical New Testament prayer-meeting, that we may see how closely the new prayer-meeting of Christian Endeavor is approximating it, and that we may also be stirred with holy and enthusiastic zeal, every one of us, to bring our Christian Endeavor new prayer-meeting into the exact likeness of that New Testament ideal, for we wish no other ideal than that of the New Testament. There is no deeper purpose in our hearts than the purpose of, so far as possible, making that ideal actual.

A painter was once toiling at a picture; wearied, he left his brush and his color for a little; the picture remained on the easel. When he returned he saw swept around that picture a perfect circle, the most difficult thing to do in art, and the pupil, beholding, could only exclaim: "The Master has been here! The Master has been here!" We wish no higher and no nobler ideal than the touch and sweep of the Holy Ghost.

THE TYPICAL PRAYER-MEETING.

Consider, then, that typical New Testament prayer-meeting. Remember the first few verses of the second chapter of the Acts, and you have it before you. It was an attended prayer-meeting; they were all with one accord, in one place. Peter was not absent because it happened to be a little hot, and James was not away because it happened to be a little cool, and Bartholomew was not away because it happened to be a little wet, and Matthew was not away because his toga was a little worn, and Mary was not absent because her veil had gotten to be a little out of style, and Salome and Bartholomew did not refuse to fill their places because just then there happened to be a party in Jerusalem, and James the Less was not away because he thought that Peter was taking a little too much on himself and was just a little officious. Not for any reasons like these or for any other reasons imaginable was any one away. It was an attended prayer-meeting. They were all with one accord, in one place. Oh, the enthusiasm of numbers! Oh, the holy contagion of religious elbow touch! Oh, the power of presence! And this typical prayer-meeting had all these. It was an attended prayer-meeting.

THE PLEDGE.

How does the new prayer-meeting of Christian Endeavor conform to the old type? Very closely I think, for Christian Endeavor lays steady insistence on attendance. That is the meaning of the pledge. Christian Endeavor makes a sacrament of attendance in the true sense of sacrament.

When a Roman soldier swore fealty to the Senate and people of Rome, he lifted up his right hand and took the pledge, the sacramentum, and Christian Endeavor makes a sacrament of attendance. That is the first thing it does. Whether anybody else is there or not, Christian Endeavor must be there. Not feeling, duty; not convenience, duty; not another engagement, but an engagement with the Lord.

Somebody asked an old Waterloo soldier, who at the battle of

Waterloo was in charge of a gun holding an important summit, what he could see when the battle was going on. "See!" he said, "nothing but dust and smoke." "What did you do?" "Do! I stood by my gun." What a Christian Endeavorer says is, "Whether you can see anything going on or not, whether you know the day is against you or for you, whether this thing is true or that other thing is true, stand by your gun of attendance anyhow."

A MEETING ACCORDANT.

Also, this typical prayer-meeting was a meeting accordant, and they were all with one accord, in one place.

I have no time to go into the philosophy of the matter. It is enough to say that our Lord Jesus tells us that accordant prayer is prevailing prayer. "Wherever two or three are gathered together in my name, there am I in the midst of them." If two of you agree on earth in regard to anything, it shall be done unto you; and a new Christian Endeavor prayer-meeting is also an accordant prayer-meeting, because it takes upon itself the pledge and promise of attendance and participation. Nothing is more philosophical than the Constitution of Christian Endeavor toward securing the feeling of accord, for feeling always follows action and does not precede it. Why, when a man rises to speak to such an assembly as this, if he is at all any sort of a man, he is pretty badly scared. Suppose that man indulges himself in a scared gesture, suppose he means to get scared, suppose he stands every which way and trembles about; he will be scared worse and worse. The feeling of scare will come on with surprising increment, and pretty soon he will have to sit down. But suppose the man scared determines to act as if he were not, puts on the gesture of self-control, stands firmly, maintains, so far as he may, his self centre, it does not take very long before the feeling of not being scared comes, and the man, before he knows it, is master of himself, and perhaps, to some extent, master of those who are listening to him.

It is always action that precedes feeling and never feeling that precedes action, and when Christian Endeavor sets before young Christian people the action of taking of a definite pledge for prayer and service, it does not take very long before the action draws after itself a train of appropriate accordant feeling. So again, Christian Endeavor is in accord with the old type. Its prayer-meeting is a prayer-meeting accordant.

A MEETING OF PROMISE-PLEADING.

Also, that old typical New Testament prayer-meeting was a prayer-meeting of promise-pleading. Thus our Lord told the Disciples that in a little time the power of the Spirit should come upon them, and those Disciples were all of one accord, in one place, to plead that promise. There is a mighty principle there, which I leave you to think through. There are all sorts of wonders in it, this mediating place which prayer holds between promise on the one hand and fulfilment on the other. Pray for what God has promised to give you and you will get what God has promised to give you, for prayer is a condition of fulfilment. This typical prayer-meeting was a prayer-meeting of promise-pleading. They said; "O Thou Risen and Ascended Christ, Thou hast promised. Be true to Thy promise." How in this regard does the new prayer-meeting of Christian Endeavor find accordance with the old type? Ah, how delightful it is! Ah, how spiritually comforting it is in the new prayer-meeting of Christian Endeavor to hear one and another and another and another rise and utter another and another and another of the unchangeable promises of our God in Holy Scriptures!

THE PRAYER OF FAITH.

Do you know that service has deeper relation than you, perhaps, think, for it makes possible the prayer of faith? What is the prayer of faith? A prayer of strain? A prayer of wrestling, misinterpreting utterly a famous passage of Scripture? A prayer of rapture? A seeking to pull one's self up or to push one's self up into a kind of ecstacy? What is the prayer of faith? The prayer of faith is a prayer springing out of great grip on the promises and pleading the promises. That is the prayer of faith.

I asked Mr. Spurgeon once how he prayed, and he said to me: "I always find a promise appropriate to the need, and then in the name of the Lord Jesus, and for His sake, I simply plead that promise."

The old, typical, New Testament prayer-meeting was a prayer-meeting of promise-pleading, and the new prayer-meeting of Christian Endeavor is a prayer-meeting of promise-pleading, too. They repeat the promises and then they present the promises as arguments before the Throne.

GIVING HOLY SPEECH TO WOMEN.

Also, that old, typical, New Testament prayer-meeting was a prayer-meeting which gave holy speech to woman. Look there! What is that? That shining, that strong, celestial, wavering, gleaming tongue of flame! Behold it! It is on the head of Peter. Yes. It is on the head of James. Yes. It is on the head of Matthew. Yes. It is on the head of the son of Alpheus. Yes. It is on the head of Mary. Yes. It is on the head of Salome. Yes. It is on the head of Mary Magdalene. Yes, yes. In all that company there is not a single head unmitered with the celestial flame, as much on women's heads as on the heads of men.

Unmitered in the prayer-meeting women prayed for the gift, or they would not have received the gift, and when the gift came, it came to woman just as much as to man, for the shining, wavering flame was on the heads of all of them.

Paul says: "Let the women keep silence in the churches." Yes; Paul does say that, and if I believed that Paul meant, when he said that, what is the common interpretation of his meaning, I would submit to the apostle; I would not say that the world has outgrown the apostle. I believe in implicit and accurate and abundant submission to inspired authority; but because I am sure that the usual interpretation of that Scripture has been a huge misconception and blunder, I declare that the new prayer-meeting of Christian Endeavor is in close accord with the old typical prayer-meeting of the New Testament, because it gives to woman holy speech; for do you know what the meaning of the words "keep silence" is? Paul says, "Do not let the women lall, lall, lall." Don't you see what he means? That is the Greek word *lalein*, which means to chatter, make a disturbance and a contention. Paul says never let women do that. The men had better take that to themselves as well. But Paul does distinctly say: "When a woman prayeth or prophesieth, let her do it with her head covered." That is, according to the custom of the times, in decent fashion. Why, a woman may pray in the church. Why, prophesying is simply forth-saying your faith in Jesus and your love for Him and exhorting others to come to Him, and Paul distinctly allows that women find tongue for praying and for prophesying in the meetings of the church.

THE HEART OF CHRISTIAN ENDEAVOR.

Therefore, I declare that the new prayer-meeting of Christian Endeavor is in exact accord with the old typical prayer-meeting of the New Testament, because it does give to woman, and insists on giving to woman, and God grant it may forever and continually insist on giving to woman, holy speech. These miserable padlocks on the gracious lips of woman ought to be unlocked and broken off and flung away forever.

I had other points to speak on, but my time is up and I will stop. God bless you. Hold to the prayer-meeting. The hearth and heart of Christian Endeavor is the new old prayer-meeting.

THE COMPLETE CHRISTIAN.

By Major-General O. O. Howard.

Christian Endeavor! These are two words happily chosen.

A Christian has a trinity of phases—an active, a passive and a completer side. In this nineteenth century we are accustomed to place the active in the front rank, and we are so zealous, in our theories at least, that we sometimes even deny the existence of a passive Christianity. But if we look back a century or so, we will find plenty of passivity touching all sorts of Christian work, *e. g.*, in Sunday schools, foreign missions, and other progressive societies; also touching human bondage and other social evils. "Let them alone!" was the common conservative cry. "In God's own time He will convert the young; He will reach the heathen; He will abolish slavery if that be best; and He will Himself purge human society." It was the ascriptive meaning to the Scripture, "Stand still and see the salvation of our God!"

One can often rightly study groups of people in the individual. The sincere follower of Christ passes through different epochs of heart-experience. When the light of God's truth first breaks in upon a man, and he realizes that his sins, which were many, are actually forgiven him, he is full of ardor, and no obstacles appall him. He is active in some line of Christian effort. He is brave; he is aggressive; he penetrates the by-ways, the jails, the poor-farms, and the destitute quarters of the city. He distributes circulars, tracts and leaves of Holy Writ at every corner. He speaks to every sinner that he meets, tells him of a Saviour's love, and invites him to give up his sins and follow Christ. Often this early ardor blinds his vision, so that, though this Christian's effort is great, the fruitage is comparatively small. Older men understand the case. The sapling is not the oak, the young steer has not the strength of the ox, nor has the youthful soul the wisdom of age.

The want of fruitage correspondent to effort soon produces in the young heart a strong reaction. But a little later, after having been chastened by sickness or some fell disaster, much of his old spirit returns, and with it a noticeable judiciousness. He had first the zeal that consumed him, next a sense of great weakness and dependence amid discouragement; or, perhaps, was flooded with a worldliness that for a time engulfed him almost in despair; but at last his Master brought him into better conditions, when again his hope became strong like an anchor, and his fewer efforts, to his astonishment, brought forth more frequent and more abundant fruits. All along our Master was his powerful partner, and was moulding him into fellowship—yes, into a more complete unity with Himself.

Then, to re-state my thought, I would say that *this Christian* was first active, then passive, then more complete.

We have watched our Young Men's Christian Associations throughout these three periods. One most intensely active, with precious little of judiciousness in many places. Then followed the period of great depression, when individual associations were so passive as hardly to be able to hold their own. Oh, the disasters that came here and there, the enormous debts, the failures, the disgrace through false brethren, and what not. At last set in a solid reaction and improvement. Now they revive—they develop again and girdle the world, perfected in organized strength, without perplexing and paralyzing debts; strong in purpose, judicious in management, and really more abundant in fruitage than ever before. When a Young Men's Christian Association, in 1884, paid a visit to Emperor William, of Germany, and was permitted to sing for him some of their sweet hymns, he was much affected, and said, "Young gentlemen, could you not take into your company an old young man!" With a like sympathetic disposition, may not I, who listen to your songs, ask you of the Christian Endeavor to consider the words of " an old young man," and to study carefully the three phases thus presented.

Christian observers have watched the rise and progress of this youngest association luminary, the Society of Christian Endeavor, with much interest and no little anxiety. The missions in the churches were pressed forward, but they needed more money. The churches grew, but the vast majorities were still outside; the prayer-meetings kept alive, but old people said the same prayers, grieved over the same old sins, and the seats were mostly empty. Pastors of flocks said to themselves: "How can we fill up our churches? How can we keep with us the boys and girls who are entering manhood and womanhood? How can we press out the missions at home and abroad? How can we give life to our home meetings for prayer and transform them into places of power and attainment?" To train the young for this service Rev. F. E. Clark proposed a new organization—a society of youth to be an aid to the pastor in each church, and happily named it significantly, "Society of Christian Endeavor." It is to be composed of young men and young women, pledged to work, pledged to take part in the meetings, and pledged to efforts for the gathering in of other young people; pledged to make further efforts for their reformation and Christian training.

I glory in the young. Alexander was a young man and he conquered the world, but his acquired territories could not long be kept together. He had ambition, energy and abundant enterprise, but lacked the true wisdom.

In plain words, I would say in closing, keep close as you have in the past to each individual church, and let the individual church expand by your increasing help. Keep constantly in mind your motto, "For Christ and the Church."

ADDRESS BY HON. JOHN WANAMAKER,

Postmaster-General.

Mr. Wanamaker arrived just before the close of the Thursday morning session, and was most warmly received. He spoke as follows:—

"I am overwhelmed by the beautiful reception you have given me and which I do not deserve at your hands. I think the warmth of it is an illustration of what Christian Endeavor means. The moment you put your touch upon a man, you put him to work. I could not resist the great desire I had to get my eyes upon the sight which is now before me, and to feel in my heart the impulse that throbs in the bosom of this great gathering, the proceedings of which, through the medium of the great newspapers, are being spread all over the country.

"Your work is a blessing because of the prominence you have given to the simple thought underlying the framework of your organization, and because you have shown the people it is not a line set out in the pages of annual reports, a mere subject of reference, but that this blessed work of God has filled you, and best of all, so conspicuously that it seems that you have His blessing while you are doing it. This is God's way. If He calls us, we may be doing a very little; some old thing that church people did in years gone by, some lines of work that have grown old-fashioned, and then He lays His hand of blessing upon it, and it becomes a thing of mighty power.

"I came only to salute you, as one working with you, as one in sympathy with you, and as one honored to be associated with you in the Board of Trustees of your organization, and as one who firmly believes that through this organized church work the world will be brought to the feet of the King. Whatever scepticism of the day may say, there is power in the gospel of the Lord Jesus Christ. Keep uppermost the profound conviction that it is the gospel that is to win the heart and convert the world.

"The things that were sweet dreams to us in our childhood are now being worked out. The procession is being made longer and longer, the letters of Christ's name are becoming larger and larger. God bless you! The sweet fragrance of your presence here will linger after these doors are closed and you have gone away with your good-byes. My greatest hope is that in a few years this work will be trebled and quadrupled, and that the progress which this gathering to-day represents may be only a little thing in comparison with what they who have the heart and the faith will surely bring. God bless you and make you warm-hearted, strong-hearted and full believers in the blessed promises of God."

FOR WHAT DOES THE CHRISTIAN ENDEAVOR MOVEMENT STAND?

LOYALTY TO DUTY.

By Rev. J. Wilbur Chapman, Pastor First Reformed Church, Albany, N. Y.

The time has passed, if ever it existed, when one must needs apologize for an enthusiastic interest in the cause of Christian Endeavor. The time is now upon us when one must needs apologize for lack of interest. The very name is now a synonym for success, not only because its influence is world-wide, nor because its followers are numbered by the hundred thousand—that may or may not be an evidence of true success—but because it is, we believe, the answer sent from God to the question that has rested like a burden on many an anxious pastor's heart, "How shall I reach and hold and train my young people?" and because it is a solution likewise of one of the greatest problems before the church of Christ, for if the young people of this generation be trained in the principles of Christian Endeavor, the masses, through them, will be reached and won. The cause has not been without opposition, and that, too, from sources where one would least expect it. But in this, as in other cases, the opposition has been the prophecy of success.

I am embarrassed at the very beginning by the fact that the society has advanced beyond the scope of my subject. The very fact that a society is genuinely Christian Endeavor is a promise and pledge that it is *loyal to duty always and everywhere*, and yet it is an inspiration to have such a subject in the interests of such a cause. That word duty has two aspects. If preferred, it is a delight and gives us music in the night; if neglected, it is like a goad and only exasperates. The path of duty is like the roads of the South; it is hedged with ever-bloom, pure and white as snow. Keep straight ahead and the fragrance gains. It is only when we turn to the right hand or to the left that we are lacerated by piercing thorns and concealed dangers. So I would speak for a little while on *duty*. Cicero was right when he said, "There is not a moment without some duty." This is true of every individual, true of every community, true of every nation, and certainly true of our society. There is only one stimulant that never fails and yet never intoxicates—duty. Duty puts a blue sky over every man, or in his heart, perhaps, into which the skylark happiness ever goes singing. Even when it is a delusion, as in the case of the Crusaders, under the direction of Louis IX. of France, it has power. How much more when enlisted in such a cause as ours.

LOYALTY TO THE END.

When Lord Nelson was bearing down upon the French and Spanish fleets off Cape Trafalgar with his men-of-war, he said to Captain Blackwood, "Do we not need a signal to inspire the men?" Blackwood answered, "The English navy needs but one signal," and up it went, conveying the immortal words: "England expects every man to do his duty," and even then the victory was won. Here we stand, five hundred thousand strong, against the enemy. The United Society expects that we will do our duty; the Church expects it; Christ expects it. When the sacramentum, or oath, was given to the Roman army by the senate, the leader of the soldiers read the oath, and, lifting up his hand, swore that he would die for Rome if need be. The man upon his right lifted up his hand until every soldier stood, with hand erect, and shouted every man: "That for me! That for me!" Christian Endeavor calls us to duty. The field is white, the need is great. Let us stand and say, "Loyal to the end," and let the interest spread until five hundred thousand, with uplifted hands, shall shout, "That for me!"

Loyal, like Milton with his constant headaches, his late study concurring to weaken his eyes. The left eye at last was gone. The doctor told him if he continued his study the other eye would go, and Milton said: "The choice lay between dereliction of a supreme duty and loss of eyesight, and I could not listen to the physician. I could not but obey that inward voice that spake to me from heaven." Loyal, like the men of Bryan, who, learning that the battle was going against their country, although they were in the hospital, said: "We are too weak to stand, but drive stakes into the ground and carry us out and fasten us to them, and we will fight;" and those old warriors, fastened so that only one arm was free, fought to desperation and to death. Loyal, like Joan of Arc. It was in vain that her father, when he heard her purpose, swore to drown her ere she should go to the field with the men at arms. It was in vain that the priest and her friends doubted and refused to aid her. "I must go to the king," persisted the peasant girl, "for this is no work of my choosing, but I must go and do it, for my Lord wills it," and, pleading with touching pathos, she won the rough captain at last, and he took her by the hand and swore to lead her to the king. Loyalty like this will give the cause we love such increasing power, that naught shall be able to stand against us.

THE FIELD OF DUTY.

What is the field of duty set before the Society of Christian Endeavor, and to which we are pledged to loyalty?

Duty the first. To obey the command of Christ, and as young people, let our lights shine, and also by our lives, our consecration and zeal, to constrain others to come to Him. There is an argument in such a life that infidelity cannot answer nor unbelief ignore. I have read that in 1838, Father Sarrai, of the Soledad Mission in Mexico, refused to leave his work, though famine threatened and the people were too poor to support him. He and his handful of Indians remained, though growing poorer and poorer. One Sunday morning, when saying mass at the crumbling altar, he fainted, fell forward and died in their arms, of starvation. Are we loyal to this?

Duty the second. To carry forward the work of the church. Any influence that would take us from our church, draw one particle of strength from the household of faith with which we have cast our lot, whatever its name, is not born of Christian Endeavor and savors not of it. First, the church; second, our own church and every interest of the bride of Christ. This is Christian Endeavor always. Are we thus loyal?

Duty the third. To aid the pastor in his work. It has been said if we had one hundred consistent followers of Christ, we could bind them together in a living volume and with them make the world believe. The Society of Christian Endeavor, pledged to duty, will meet this want, and every pastor may have his hundred lives and more. This society is to make incarnate, to put into practice the pulpit's message of truth. It is to be the "Amen" to the pastor's speech; it is to be on the lookout for souls that, during the service, have been touched by the truth, and lead them, by the help of God, into the clearer light of Christ; and I speak that I do know and testify that I have seen when I say, all this and more the Society of Christian Endeavor can do. Any pastor may be weak without it, or girded with strength with it.

NEGLECT NO GIFTS.

The fourth duty is: "To neglect not the gift that is within." There is talent enough of speech and prayer in the young people of the church, but like the gold and silver, brass and iron of the Israelites, it has been buried beneath the hills, and just now is coming out into the light. Young men are learning how to speak and to pray, and who that has travelled much in the round of prayer-meetings but has been impressed with the need of training? A man, not far from the Hudson River, was heard to pray again and again with greatest fervor: "O Lord, help us to grow up like calves in the stall and become meet for the kingdom of heaven." And in the art of expressing petitions to God in a short, intelligent and faithful manner, this society unconsciously gives instruction.

And the young women are being trained. I have the honor to represent a denomination that has looked with fear upon women. "speaking in meeting," a church, some of the members of which said, "If you have women speak at your meetings, we will not come," and they did not for a little while. There is a something about a woman's speech—the intonation of her voice, together with what she has to say —when she is consecrated to God, that carries force when man has failed. The number of fanatics is not greater than among the men. Henry Ward Beecher was an advocate of women taking part in his meetings, but was much troubled by one woman, who would wait until the last, and then speak at great length, and not to the edification, always, of her hearers. One evening it lacked five minutes of the close of the hour, and she rose to speak, and kept on for twenty minutes, Mr. Beecher squirmed about in his chair, with that feeling so familiar to a pastor's heart, and when she finished he rose, with the perspiration standing on his brow, and said, with that peculiar expression upon his face: "Nevertheless, I believe in women speaking in meeting." So say we all.

LOYALTY TO THE PLEDGE.

The fifth duty: Loyalty to the pledge—the much-talked-of pledge, the iron-clad pledge. It is no more than you take upon you when entering into the church. It is the life of the society, and the strength of your Christian character. We have had an experience ourselves in forming young people's societies. First, with the name of Christian Endeavor, and without its principles. Then with some of the principles, minus the pledge. But something was lacking always. Finally, in desperation, we said we will have the whole society—name, constitution, by-laws, pledge and all, and many said: "You will kill your society; it will surely die." But we felt like the old negro minister down South, who had to beg every Sunday for some money. His people finally grew tired of it and said: "If you keep on this way you will kill the church." He only replied: "Brethren, I will keep right on. Does not de good Book say, 'Blessed are de dead dat die in de Lord'?" And we felt that the society had better die with the pledge, and be buried decently and in order, than to live without it and be a cripple. But it has lived, and the pledge is its life.

After all, what is it but a pledge to Christ, and who would not do more than that for Him? Think of His life, His humiliation, His death, and it is the very least we can do for Him. King Clovis, of France, sat under the preaching of one of the saints, who was telling, with passionate pathos, the story of Christ's suffering and death, when the monarch suddenly sprang from his throne, and grasping his spear, cried, "Had I been there with my brave Franks, I would have avenged his wrongs." A pledge to him—increase its strength a thousandfold—and then it would be little enough to do for Him. Are we loyal to this duty? Christians, we are on the winning side. Young people, we are enlisted in one of the grandest armies the world has ever seen. Let the fire that is in your heart make its way into another heart and yet another, and by the shining of our light the darkness will flee away.

THE PENTECOSTAL MIRACLE.

A friend told me that one of the most imposing of the ceremonies of the Easter week at Jerusalem was the supposed lighting of the torch in the Church of the Holy Sepulchre the Saturday night before Easter, by the descent of the Holy Spirit—the annual renewal of the Pentecostal miracle. The people throng the temple. All are eager to secure the sacred flame; great sums are paid for the privilege of bearing it first away; the spaces are packed with an eager throng, holding aloft the unlit torches. The Greek Patriarch, followed by the clergy, clad in gorgeous robes, holding their banners, chanting their litanies, moving with slow step to the sound of music, circle three times around the temple.

Then the lights are extinguished, the Patriarch enters the sacred tomb and bows in prayer, the people, meanwhile, waiting in breathless silence.

Suddenly a faint glimmer is seen. As the Patriarch comes forth, torch in hand, eager hands seize it and flash it in the faces of the multitude. The fiery tongues leap from torch to torch until floor and gallery are one sea of flame, and racers take the light and bear it through the streets of the waking city, beyond the gates, over hill and valley to the most distant homes in Judea. This is the parable of the way in which the darkness of sin must flee away; the Holy Ghost must descend upon a waiting people, and every man must light his neighbor's torch.

So let us wait, and so let us run, swift in the performance of duty, until the continents, every one, and the islands of the sea, every one, shall be rejoicing in the light and glory of God.

LOYALTY TO THE CHURCH.

By Rev. Charles F. Deems, D.D., LL.D., Pastor Church of the Strangers, New York City.

[It is due to Dr. Deems to say that nothing of his address was written; that it was delivered with fervor and rapidity; that he has been too closely engaged since the convention to prepare anything, and that all that is reproduced here are some extracts from a stenographer's report.]

When I made my first Christian endeavor, fifty years ago, by going from my father's house sixty miles to plead the cause of temperance, there was a common question amongst young people when they met, and in regard to young people when they were spoken of. That question was this: "To what church do you belong?" When it was uncertain that the man was a professor of religion at all, Christian anxiety about him asked this question: Does he belong to the church? Now, in that day, and certainly before that day, that phrase was not cant; that is to say, it was not a fine phrase out of which the meaning had wholly evaporated; for *cant* is to rational thought what the shell is to the whole nut; very useful when the kernel is there, and very worthless when it is missing. Sometimes phrases had lost their meaning and their power, and when it came to be asked, to what church does a man belong, it was simply meant in what denomination of Christians is his name enrolled. Now, the intent of the Christian Endeavor is to put the kernel back into the shell, is to make the nut full and sweet, and rich and nutritious and fruitful again, when it is asked of each man or woman to what church does he or she belong. The point I wish to make in the few minutes which I will be able to speak to you this morning is this, that when a man becomes a communicant he *belongs* to his church. I am emphasizing first of all the word "belong," and I wish to make it as emphatic as I shall have power to do. It is one thing to be married to a woman, and it is another thing to belong to her. I trust every married man here knows what it is to belong to his wife, in the sweetest sense of being possessed by her. It is one thing for a man to have been born in England, and it is another thing to be loyal to the Queen. It is one thing for a man to have been born in America, and it is another to be ready to die for America. It is the *belonging* after all, which makes the virtue in the service.

When we come to look at the institutions which God has made among men, they are, first of all, the family, the one real and most divine institution existing among men. For the family everything else exists, because the family was God's first divine institution; after the family came God's divine institution of the state, and the state is no longer by Christian people to be considered a sort of compact among men who have come together to help each other out of savagery; it is God's institution. The Son hath ordained the State. Then there is another. There is the Church of the living God. It is not a human institution, but is a divine institution. The Protestant Episcopal Church is a human institution; the Methodist Episcopal Church is a human institution; the Reformed Church even is a human institution; the Presbyterian Church is a human institution; and the Baptist Church is a human institution. All those are human institutions that have been formed by men touched with the spirit and power of God; who have organized themselves together for the purpose of extending the perpetuity and pushing the progress of the one Holy Catholic Church, which consists of the communion of saints in heaven and in earth.

Just precisely so, the Young Men's Christian Association is a human institution, the Christian Endeavor Society is a human institution, but the Church of the Living God is a divine institution.

I came to talk to you of the relation which the Christian Endeavor movement has to the Church of the Living God, which is the pillar and the ground of the truth, and to emphasize that relation. Devotion to that Church! That is what the Christian Endeavor Society exists for, and in order to do that, each member of each society in each church must be made to know that he belongs to the Church of the Living God, and because he belongs to the Church of the Living God he has given his adhesion to some one of the organized churches. There is no other way for men to know whether I belong to the Church of the Living God or not; God may know; I may be a sanctified Christian; I may be ripe for heaven and yet not be in any branch of the Church Visible upon the face of the earth; but how is the world to know that I am for Christ? I have a friend, who, off and on for fourteen years, I have been endeavoring to influence to bring to an open confession of Christ. When I met him we would come to that point. He made the confession that he had been trying to live a saintly life. Last Sunday week it came upon him with power while the sermon was going along, and he said, "I cannot make the world know that I belong to the Invisible Church of Christ until I become a member of the Visible Church." He could hardly wait until the service was done; he felt that he must come out at once and belong to some branch of the Christian church.

BELONG TO THE CHURCH.

This "belonging" means what? Paul said: "I am a bondservant of Jesus; I am a slave of Jesus." He was not ashamed of the word "slave." He used the identical word which was understood in every Roman court and in all the Greek circles when he used it to imply that he belonged altogether, body and soul, to the Lord Jesus. My friends, that is the way Christian people are to belong to the church. Belonging means this: doing for that to which I belong what it needs for its perpetuity and its progress, and what it has a right to demand of me. I belong to my family; I belong to my country; I belong to the Church of the living God in this way; my church, my state, my family have certain claims upon me, to the extent of my abilities and limitations, for the perpetuity of the Church, for the perpetuity of the state, for the perpetuity of the family. Now, then, I belong to each of those in this way; that each has a right to come up and claim my help, and before the claim is made, I am bound to be there with the offering—"Here I am; ask me."

I am very glad that my eloquent young brother had to do the hefty work to-day. I have only come to give you a sort of paternal benediction. I have not come to make much of a speech, but just to say that I love you, and you know there is a great deal in that. So I thought I would come, and if I fainted, as I did in my own pulpit, I would faint with a smile of love on my face, and you could say, "he did love us." I love the Christian Endeavor Society because it is doing precisely what Dr. Chapman has pointed out; it is urging every man to hold himself ready for every claim of duty. What has been the trouble with the young people in the former generations? Just this. In the first place, they had to be hunted out. In the second place, they had to be enthused before anything could be done. What does the Christian Endeavor Society do? It goes out and enthuses persons to be workers in the church, and says, "Here they are ready to be offered up; ready to work," and in that sense, every man and every woman that comes into the society must work for his church.

DOES YOUR PASTOR KNOW YOU?

I think that every man in a church ought to be known to his pastor. I know and have known a great many pastors who did not know their members. It is a very bad thing.

I want to ask you one question. When your pastor meets you, does he know you immediately and call you "Miss Myers," or "Mr. Brown" the moment he sees you? Let me ask you to dwell upon that. Does your pastor know you as quickly as he knows his own child? I insist upon it in my church, that every member of my church must be so well known to me that when I meet a lady I do not hesitate upon her name any more than I do upon the name of Mrs. Deems. I insist every woman shall be known to me as I know either of my daughters. I must know each one of them. No man should be three months in a church and his pastor not know him if he should meet him in China or Philadelphia, or any other "foreign" land. When I look over my roll and find the name of a man whom I do not know, I feel there is something wrong, if he has been in our church three months and I do not know him! The Society of Christian Endeavor is to remedy all that so far as the young people are concerned. You must feel to your pastor as a son or as a daughter, ready to help him in everything he does for Christ.

THE BENEFIT.

I want to point out in a few words the benefit of this course. In the first place, it does that which young men and young women have not imagined it did. It actually trains them to be regular Christian workers, to be ready to do anything the pastor suggests. If the pastor wants the corner of the church swept up, or half the night spent in copying something important, there must be somebody ready to do it. Whatever he wants, stand by him, and work with him, and so multiply his power. Remember when you join the church that you belong to that particular church, and that its services and its work have the first claim upon you.

Working along these lines the young man will be surprised to discover that he finds time to do three times as much as these promiscuous, multitudinous, evangelical tramps, whose names are upon the church roll and who belong to everybody and to nobody. My experience has been that the young men and women who have worked in the Christian Endeavor Society in our church have found more time for our mission work and more time for the Young Men's Christian Association, which we must always look after. I am not less a friend of the Young Men's Christian Association because deeply interested in the Christian Endeavor Society. The men who are trained in their own church and first of all do their work there, somehow find time to do ever so much beyond. It is a wonderful trainer that way. Try it until we come back to the next annual convention. Above all say: "I will not go anywhere until I have taken care of my own church, and when that is done I will go to my pastor and say, 'Is there any other thing that I can do? Is there any other work in hand?'" Then if there is time, go beyond. Do this and you will soon see that when you go abroad people will respect you.

YOUNG MAN GO HOME.

I will now tell you a story. Once upon a time there was a man who was smitten all at once with a great desire to be philanthropic and he commenced; he laid out his money carefully; he employed it in buying bread; he took that bread all around through the city. Every day and every evening of his life that man took a basket of bread and went somewhere and gave that bread away. One day his wife and three children were found actually starving to death. He had become such a philanthropist that he fed everybody he could reach outside of his family, day and night, with his food, and left his wife and children to die. How his reputation as a philanthropist collapsed. Whenever a minister in one church finds a young man flitting around the work in his parish, he goes to his pastor and says: "Do you know such a young man? What is his name?" "No; I have a dim recollection that he joined our church two or three years ago." "Does he come to your prayer-meeting?" "Never saw him in our prayer-meeting." "Does he not belong to your Society of Christian Endeavor?" "I do not know, but I think I know every member of the society in my church." What does he next do? The next time the young man presents himself that pastor will probably give him some good advice, and close it by saying: "Young man, go home."

How do men apply that passage of Holy Writ: "If any provide not for his own, and especially for those of his own house, he hath denied the faith and is worse than an infidel?" Who are the preachers of infidelity in this country? There are worse men, according to Holy Scripture, than Robert Ingersoll. They are the men who do not take care of their households. What is my household in the sight of God? My family first, my church next, and then my country. A man that does not take care of his own household, and does not work in his own church, to the extent of his ability, is a man that is worse than an infidel, and would, perhaps, be better out of the church.

SETTING MEN TO WORK.

In regard to the outside work. There is so much economy of time in this thing and there is so much more power. The trouble with most men in the world is they have too much fat and too little muscle. We do not want fat churches; we do not want fat societies. We want societies with so much muscle in them that they will work off every single particle of the adipose tissue. That is what the Society of Christian Endeavor is doing. It is setting men to work with all their might inside of their own churches and then outside of their own churches.

Then there is so much in being together. An old lady down in Norfolk, Virginia, a friend of mine, was sitting among several ladies and they were telling about their talents. One had more talent for house-keeping; another for marketing, and so on. This old lady for thirty years never missed being at church, and so when it came to her talent she said: "Oh, my sisters, I reckon the Lord has given me one talent, and that is the talent for *going to meeting*." Being in your places every time your minister preaches is a wonderful talent. Nothing but the last emergency should keep you from that.

I know your honored fellow-citizen, Mr. John Wanamaker, and like thousands of others, have rejoiced in his great Bethany work; but if our friend Wanamaker belonged to any church in this city when he started the great Bethany idea and carried it on, John Wanamaker had no business to be at Bethany when his pastor was preaching; he was bound to be in his own pew at that church; he was bound to find time for both, and I have no doubt he did find time outside of his own church work to do the other. My friends, you will find the same advantage.

POWER IN NUMBERS.

There is so much in masses. Look at this assembly. Do you not think that this vast gathering is going to have a great influence upon the whole country! I know it is making a great impression on the people of Philadelphia. They see you going in and coming out in great crowds. Suppose this whole assembly had reached the city by the Purgatory train,* or the other trains that arrived, and upon arriving here Thursday morning had said: "We will divide and conquer Philadelphia," and one portion had gone to Girard College and another portion to the Water Works, and another portion to the Zoological Gardens, and another portion had walked, straying along, man and woman, on the banks of the Schuylkill, and another portion had gone to Independence Hall — what kind of an effect would this Convention have had upon Philadelphia? Would it have the effect of this immense gathering of thousands of men and women under one roof, massed together in this great work? There is power in discipline. The Duke of Wellington said he could take 50,000 arrant cowards and drill them into heroes and veterans. So it is if we keep together and mass together we shall come with tremendous power.

---

* Allusion is made to an excursion train from New York, the passengers of which will never forget it.

I must close this speech. I have endeavored to bear upon one point as closely as I could. I love you; I love the cause of Christian Endeavor. I want it to prosper more and more. I pledge to it all of my ability for the rest of my life. I thank God that I lived to see the Christian Endeavor Society; that I lived to come to Philadelphia. Fifty-eight years and six months ago I first saw Philadelphia. I thanked God I lived to come to the centennial of American Independence in Philadelphia, and now again I thank God that I am permitted to come to Philadelphia, to see the Eighth Annual Convention of the Young People's Society of Christian Endeavor, and this great hall crowded with these servants of the Lord.

A POEM.

I am going to give you one of my last poems. Do not let any of the reporters get it in the papers that I am a poet, because that may ruin my reputation as a preacher at my time of life. But as you are all my friends I will tell you how it was. Last September, when I fell while conducting Divine service, I was banished from my pulpit for five months, and the doctors said, "You have got to learn to go more slowly," and I have learned to go a great deal more slowly. A few weeks ago I went into my study and saw two boxes of letters to be answered. I saw all this and I thought of Dickinson College, from which I was graduated just fifty years ago, and to which I was going to make the alumni speech. I thought of the Summer School of Philosophy over which I am soon to preside, and I felt the old rush. But a suggestion of self-preservation came to me. I sat down and pushed all work aside and said: "Do not do it, but keep quiet; sit down and write a poem!" I said: "Go to, I will write a poem; that will be soothing employment." So I swept the whole desk clear and wrote my poem. It is only four lines long. They are these:

> The world is wide
> In time and tide;
> And God is guide;—
> Then do not hurry.

That is the poem and that is all.

I went out and washed my face and came back and looked at it and cooled off, and said a short prayer, and went to work and got through the day tranquilly. The next week I went to Dickinson College and there was a gathering of orators; there was Bishop Foss of Philadelphia, preaching as if heaven and earth were coming together, and there was my neighbor, Gov. C. A. Woodford, employing all his marvellous arts of oratory, and there was Dr. Reed, the new president, leading out his forces of enthusiasm, and I had no more speech prepared than I had when I came to Philadelphia yesterday. When I went to bed I was much concerned and said, "What is to become of me?" Whereupon I comforted myself by adding another stanza to my rhyme, which I venture to give you as my contribution to Christian Endeavor.

> That man is blest
> Who *does his best*,
> And *leaves the rest*;—
> Then do not worry.

LOYALTY TO CHRIST.

By Rev. L. T. Chamberlain, D.D., Pastor Classon Ave. Presbyterian Church, Brooklyn, N. Y.

With great delight, my young friends, have I united with you in this wondrous service. With profound gratitude have I listened to the words which have re-enkindled our devotion to both duty and the church. It has seemed as if there scarce was need of further speech; as if, with the Holy Spirit's blessing, we might now wisely dismiss ourselves to reflection on what has been so nobly said.

Yet not without reason, I perceive, has there been included the theme on which I am to speak. It is fitting—especially in this presence—that the personal Christ should be exalted with distinct, supreme exaltation. It is fitting that fealty to Christ should, on our part, be recognized, and anew proclaimed, as the very motive of motives. By that confession, that faith, we stand or fall.

Christ has, indeed, been before us this morning at each moment and in every utterance. Toward Him thought and affection have been constantly pointed. We have had inspiring forecast of the hour when, at mention of His Name, "every knee shall bow, of things in heaven, and things in earth, and things under the earth." Still, even the transfiguration glory is not complete until Moses and Elijah—the Law and the Prophets—have not only come, but also gone, and the disciples "see no man save Jesus only." The love of Christ is the inspiration to duty. The place of Christ is above the invisible church. His is the glory which fills the upper temple, so that there, for brightness, they need neither candle, nor star, nor sun. Christ Himself is all and in all.

CORNER-STONE AND TOP-STONE.

Assuredly, this Christian Endeavor movement stands for loyalty to Christ. Such loyalty is both corner-stone and top-stone in its structural plan. Or, changing the figure, though in this movement there is the likeness of Ezekiel's cherubim, with faces of angel and man and lion and eagle; though there are wheels which stand and move and mount, the spirit in the midst is the spirit of Christ, and the goal toward which faces look and wheels revolve, is the throne of Him, who, dying once, is alive forevermore.

Yet, even thus, have you fully considered the blessedness of the fact that an incarnate Christ is the permitted object of our allegiance? Have you thoughtfully compared that blessedness with whatever felicity belongs to searchers for the abstract truth and goodness, or with the advantage of those who, in earlier times, knew and loved the Father only? Such comparison is both reverent and helpful. It reveals to us, in surpassing degree, the holiness of the ground on which we stand. It moves us, as perhaps nothing else might, to the putting off our shoes from off our feet

Take, for example, the splendor of truth's inspiration, the power of duty's appeal. I love to think that to the Christian, Christ's man, belongs the very fulness of that inspiration and appeal. Indeed, I am apt to conclude that no man knows Christ aright who does not know the absolute royalty of truth, the sheer sovereignty of conscience. Believe it! Into sublime fellowship do we ascend when we rise to the company of those who have been able to say: "Pure knowledge at any cost; right duty at any hazard;" and then, in the comparative gloom, have been true to that valiant confession.

CHRISTIANITY WITHOUT CHRIST.

I sometimes half wish that, for the moment, I might veil Christ from the Christian soul, and thus, perchance, the more disclose the soul to itself. Possibly, it were not an ill thing to challenge even the gentlest as to their abstract allegiance. To ask of them: "What would be your attitude, your purpose, though there were no Christ? What—your other possessions being retained—would be left to you, though the fear of Mary had been realized, and they had taken away the Crucified, none finding, thereafter, where they had laid Him? What though the rock had never been rolled from the sepulchre's door, and no ascension had closed the mighty drama of redemptive grace? What though you were yet waiting for the Messiah's advent, the Day-star not yet above the horizon, the gloom ever deepening! Yes, what, though for righteousness' sake, they stoned you to the death, and, looking up, you saw no opened heavens and no Son of Man at God's right hand?" I assure you that you do not fully know either Christ or "the power of His resurrection," unless to those inquiries you are able to answer, "I should still have my own allegiance to truth and right. So far as in me lies, I would still seek for the light; I would still intend to obey the inner voice." You might not be able to continue the desperate fight, and finish the solitary course, and keep the abstract faith; yet such should be, at least, your endeavor. Though going down at last, it were fitting that you should go with sublime, eternal protest against the overpowering evil.

INDEPENDENT TRUTH.

Or, again, what would you conclude—your other knowledge remaining—though the existence of God Himself were hidden in darkness? With the perception of right and wrong which you now have, what would you do, though your relation to the Father were only a blind groping after Him, if, haply, He might be found? What if there had been no rewards or penalties beyond the grave? What if heaven and hell were known to be idle dreams? What if neither the Father nor the Son had revealed to you your personal immortality? Yes, what if, presumably, your breath was in your nostrils, and the grave ended all? Would you still seek to be faithful to truth's discovery, and try to be loyal to right's perceived demands? If you might not thus conclude, if you cannot thus avow, you do not realize the mark of the prize of your Christian calling! Speaking with all reverence, is truth whatever God may choose to make it? Is right dependent on His mere will? Is conscience to be forced into subservience by even omnipotent power? No. Truth is truth. Right is right. Conscience is conscience. The soul is responsible in, and to, itself. These are, for us, ultimate realities. In the beauty and majesty of them we are ever to live and move.

But there, precisely there, is the deep, unchanging ground on which rests the glory of the revelation of Christ. Therein is the profound significance of the words: "He came to His own." In behalf of those who were thus formed in the divine image; those whose fall had been from such heights; those whose restoration, if worthily accomplished, must be to such allegiance—in behalf of those Christ Jesus came in his lowliness and might. In their behalf He still offers Himself as both the light and the life.

CHRIST IS TRUTH.

For, mark this, Christ is the truth, all blessed realities centering in Him. Does day speak unto day, and night convey knowledge to night? But the converse, the disclosure, is really with regard to what Christ is and has done. The rosy-fingered morn, the dewy eve, the star-pierced darkness are of His ordering. The seasons, the elements, heights of air and depths of ocean are by His appointment. "All things were made by Him, and without Him was not anything made." The entire subject-matter of science is furnished by Christ's creating and sustaining power! Nor is the subject-matter of literature and art in any less degree identified with Christ. The laws of language, the rhythm and rapture of poetry, the march and majesty of prose, the rules of form and dimension, the harmonies of sound and color, the force of external likeness and contrast,—these all are the devisings of His wise love. Of universal knowledge it may be affirmed that Christ is its beginning and end. Though unanointed eyes may be blind to Christ's indwelling, it is there, even as Wordsworth writes:

> "A motion and a spirit that impels
> —— —— all objects of all thought
> And rolls through all things."

CHRIST IS RIGHT.

Mark this, moreover, Christ is the right, all moral verities cohering in Him. Does deep call unto deep in the realm of the soul's convictions, the necessity being laid and the woe threatened? But the call, the urgency is all from Christ. It was He who thus made man but little lower than the angels, crowning him with glory and honor. The dictates of conscience, the sense of obligation, the joy of holiness, the shame of sin, the appeal of duty, the dissuasion of retribution,—all are the expression of Christ's thought and Christ's choice, There is no perception of right and wrong; there is no inward approval of the right and condemnation of the wrong; there is no realization of the morally better and the morally worse which is not the reflection, the embodiment, of the will of Him whose name we bear, and in whose service we are to find our unfailing delight. Yes, the capacity for worship itself, the feeling of filial dependence, the outreaching of prayer, the possibility of self-consecration,—this, also, is part of the plan of which Christ is both author and upholder.

CHRIST IS GOD.

Christ is God, all divine attributes His forever. Eternity, omniscience, omnipotence, omnipresence, infinite wisdom, infinite love, are Christ's inherent powers. "In him dwelleth the fullness of the Godhead bodily." "But of the Son he saith:

> "Thy throne, O God, is for ever and ever;
> And the sceptre of uprightness is the sceptre of thy kingdom."

"And again, when he bringeth the first-born into the world he saith: And let all the angels of God worship him." "In the beginning was the Word, and the Word was with God, and the Word was God." "I and the Father are one." To the absolute divinity of Christ all His other glories pay tribute, as to Joseph's sheaf paid obeisance the sheaves of Joseph's brethren!

LOYALTY TO HIS ATTRIBUTES IS LOYALTY TO CHRIST.

When, therefore, we are gloriously loyal to abstract truth; when we sublimely devote ourselves to abstract right; when we worship Divinity itself, then we are in the truly Christian spirit; we are substantially confessing Christ. To us in that attitude Christ comes as comes the morning to those whose faces are eastward, or as the sight of home to those who are returning from weary exile.

What blessedness, then, in having the incarnate Christ as the object of our loyal love! One who thus gathers in Himself the absoluteness of truth and right, the very divinity of the Godhead, and yet comes near to us, and becomes dear to us in all the ways of personal kinship and personal affection! This is the mystery, the matchlessness of our most holy faith. Other religions have exalted faulty men to the rank of gods; or have fashioned the divine after the likeness of the unworthy human; and sowing thus to the wind of folly, they have reaped to the whirlwind of deeper degradation. Our religion alone keeps for us the genetic tie, exalts the essential bond, yet carries fellowship into worship and makes our stainless Elder Brother "very God of very God."

FAMILIARITY WITH CHRIST.

"It is good to be on familiar terms with our King of Kings." I look tenderly on Him in the Bethlehem manger; dwell with Him in His childhood's home at Nazareth; toil with Him at His carpenter's trade; share His hunger and thirst and fatigue; attend Him in His public ministry of teaching and healing; grieve with Him as He is rejected and despised; sit by His side at the Last Supper; watch with Him in the garden; go with Him to Caiaphas' palace and Pilate's judgment-seat; behold the mocking and scourging; witness the crucifixion, the darkness, the bitter cry; see the spear-thrust and the flowing of the water and the blood, and toward Him my gentle affection is enkindled, is inflamed. I wish it might have been mine to minister to His necessities, bathing His feet, anointing His head, gladdening Him by a free confession of my regard. All the friendship of friends, all the fondness of kindred, all the love of lovers, is less than my esteem for the pure, perfect, human Christ.

DIVINITY JOINED WITH HUMANITY.

Yet even that esteem is but the beginning of the Christian's loyalty! As in Christ divinity is joined with humanity, so the lowly, spotless life, the ignominious, awful death, are revealed as an atonement between earth and heaven. It is all "that God may be just and the justifier of him that hath faith in Christ." For redemption's sake, the only begotten of the Father is the endurer of Gethsemane's pain and Calvary's anguish. The very Son of God is the self-devoted sacrifice for sin—your sin and mine. What wonder, accordingly, that natural affection rises into grateful adoration, and that fealty sweeps beyond all finite bounds! What wonder that the soul, consecrating itself in an unconditional covenant, cries gladly: "For me to live is Christ!" "What things were gain to me those I have counted loss for Christ. Yea, verily, and I count all things to be loss for the excellency of the knowledge of Christ Jesus my Lord!" "That I may know Him and the power of His resurrection, and the fellowship of His sufferings, being conformed unto His death!" What wonder that loyalty to Christ delights to challenge all utmost trial, proclaiming in advance: "I am persuaded that neither death, nor life, nor angels, nor principalities, nor things present, nor things to come, nor powers, nor height, nor depth, nor any other creature, shall be able to separate us from the love of God which is in Christ Jesus our Lord." Yes, we say: "What wonder!"

IS LOYALTY TO CHRIST UNDERSTOOD?

But when I look at the multitudes who now name Christ's name, and hear the ascriptions which rise in song and prayer, I sometimes question whether the meaning of Christian loyalty is now understood; whether or no supreme devotion still lingers in the church. I somewhat distrust the current "nursery endearments," such as rugged Chalmers could scarce abide. There comes the fear that a mystic, emotional fervor is bearing souls on dreamy, deceptive currents. I start, as though I had heard the doom of those at my very side, when the Master declares: "Many will say to me in that day, Lord, Lord; and then will I profess unto them, I never knew you. Depart." It is written: "Whose fan is in his hand, and he will thoroughly cleanse his threshing-floor; and he will gather his wheat into the garner, but the chaff he will burn up with unquenchable fire." I remember with awe that to those who would sit on His right hand and His left, Christ only promised that they should drink of His cup of suffering, and be baptized with His baptism of blood. Similarly, when I turn to the early pages of Christian history—yet history succeeding the apostolic days—I find that there, also, loyalty meant a devotion which feared not death itself. In the unsympathizing Latin of Tacitus, I read of the persecution of Nero: "Some were clothed in skins of wild beasts, and left to be devoured by dogs; others were nailed to crosses; numbers were burnt alive; and many, covered with inflammable matter, were lighted up, when the day declined, to serve as torches during the night." Their Paul beheaded, their Peter crucified, their John banished, yet Christ, none the less, their acknowledged king! The persecutions under Domitian, Trajan, the two Antonines, Severus, Maximin, Decius, Gallus, Valerian, Aurelian, Diocletian—it makes one weep to read, yet the dauntlessness of the Christian disciples is everywhere revealed. They could say with Tertullian: "Though we are slain, we are conquerors. Though we fall we are victors. The fagots are our robe of state. The flames are our triumphal chariot." Thank God, in many an age since, believers have witnessed a like good confession.

WORLDLINESS VS. CHRISTIAN DEVOTION.

Therefore, I will not doubt that the Lord still has many who are ready to lay down their very lives for Him. Confidently, hopefully, will I continue to set forth Christ as worthy of a devotion which not even our modern civilization can mislead, which not even a pervading worldliness can seduce. I am sure that there are not a few in this assembly whose unalterable allegiance is to duty, to the Church, and thus to Christ Himself. Many young men, "not pale in virtue and faintly dyed in integrity;" not given over to compromises, and fertile already in deceits; but intelligently pledged, within and without and forevermore, to the absolute right and the holy Christ. Womanly young women who, since truth is deathless and no stab save that of sin can kill the soul, since Christ needs the service of tender hearts and gentle hands, are, and always will be, Christ's, in an indissoluble bond. In truth, I hail this Christian Endeavor movement, for the very reason that, honoring duty and serving the church, it puts the living Christ first and highest. To me, then, is added presage of the day of which sweet prophecy tells, when there shall be a new heavens and a new earth—Christ on the throne—in this marvellous uprising of young disciples enlisted in the cause of sound Christian living, and, therewith, in the winning of others to the same true life.

CHRISTIAN PURITY IN TOIL.

I say, "enlisted in sound Christian living;" such living in the home, the school, the place of business, the church. Thought and word and deed kept pure and faithful. Toil glorified. Drudgery ennobled. Disappointment bravely endured. Affliction trustfully accepted. Patience allowed her perfect work. Unselfishness constantly cherished. Cups of cold water given to thirsty little ones. A helping hand for all, since for all Christ died.

And I repeat, "enlisted, therewith, in the winning of others to the same true life." Loyalty to Christ means bringing the world to Him. This morning, in this presence, I think of the mount in Galilee and the risen Redeemer's great command. I see the uplifted hand which the cruel nail had torn. I hear the voice which aforetime had been tremulous with anguish. And lo! the hand points afar, and the voice says, "Go into all the world. Make disciples of all the nations." That is still the message of our King! There is, consequently, no true loyalty to Him which does not seek that result. The conversion of the world, the persuading of those at our side, the doing all we may toward saving all,—that is obedience, that, for us, is "keeping faith."

THE STRENGTH OF LOYALTY.

And forget not, my friends, that such loyalty may, and must, ever derive its strength from the very One to whom you are loyal. We may think of truth's embattled legions; the terribleness of Christian armies with banners; the fairness of the hosts whose raiment is white and whose hands bear aloft the emblems of triumph; yet for us there will be no steadfast part in either the service or the triumph, unless we are first baptized into the spirit's baptism; unless, with regard to our very allegiance itself, we can say, "It is no more I that live, but Christ that liveth in me." There was one who sincerely declared his loyalty to Christ in the words, "If all shall be offended in thee, I will never be offended; with thee I am ready to go both to prison and to death." Yet before the cock crew twice, those same lips had denied the Master thrice.

Neither forget, I pray you, that your loyalty is to a Christ, who loving His own trusting ones, will finally take to himself the greatness of the dominion. I know they smote Him once. They lifted him up to the fatal wood. They cried in scorn, "He is the King of Israel; let Him now come down from the cross, and we will believe in Him." They rolled a great stone to the sepulchre's door, and set a watch. But, on the third day, the tomb was rent. He who laid down His life took it again. For forty days He mingled with the disciples, the same Jesus, yet supreme over time and space. He ascended from Olivet's height. It is as if He were there beholding. We see the heavens open to take the Conqueror home. The eternal gates are lifted high. The King of glory, our King, His sword on His thigh, His victor-title on His vesture, enters in. Angels and archangels, cherubim and seraphim, the ranks on ranks of the unfallen, the throngs, the hosts of the redeemed, ten thousand times ten thousand, and thousands of thousands, give Him welcome. As He takes again His sceptre, they cry in joyful worship, "Worthy is the Lamb that hath been slain, to receive the power, and riches, and wisdom, and might, and honor, and glory, and blessing!"

CHRIST'S TRIUMPHS INCREASING.

Yes, the tokens of Christ's triumph among men are increasing every day. We are in the closing dispensation. If we do our duty, if the church believes and works and prays, the day is not far distant when there shall be heard great voices from heaven, saying, "The kingdom of the world has become the kingdom of the Lord and of His Christ; and He shall reign forever and ever." In the delight, the power, of that assurance, go ye forth to your service and your success.

They tell us that when, a year ago, the German Emperor visited the seven-hilled city, and stood at night on the crest of the Palatine Mount,—Tiber and Via Sacra, Capitol and Coliseum, Arch of Titus and Arch of Septimius Severus, Forum and Temple of Peace, alike hidden in darkness,—the whole was suddenly made visible. Floods, coruscations of light, of apparent flame, turning arch and temple, palace and ruin, into one vast, resplendent glory! Then, when the colored gleams began to fade, there shone forth, from above the Capitol's summit, a majestic star, pure and white, emblem of Italy's hope, of Italy's patriotic devotion; its beams reaching far out, over both land and sea, still steadfast, though all other lights had paled and disappeared.

Let duty be your holy watchword; let the church be your "City of God"; let Christ Himself be your Light, your Star, and for you the glory shall break forth, the desire of all nations shall reappear. You shall have your great reward. Your loyal hearts shall hear the word, "They that be wise shall shine as the brightness of the firmament; and they that turn many to righteousness, as the stars forever and ever." Over all Christ shall reign,—"King of kings, and Lord of lords."

THE MISSIONARY UPRISING.

By R. P. Wilder, New York City.

It gives me the very greatest pleasure to bring to your notice this afternoon the most important theme mentioned in the Bible—a subject that is older even than the Old Testament. For when God planned the Redemption, then the work of foreign missions had its beginning, and the charter for this work we find in the very first promise, and the golden thread of foreign missions runs through the Bible from the Book of Genesis to the Book of Revelation. God's covenant with Abraham was a missionary covenant, "In thy seed shall all the nations of the earth be blessed." Though the Jews, to a large extent, were exclusive, yet when David prayed for himself and his people, what was his prayer? We find it in the sixty-seventh Psalm: "God be merciful unto us, and bless us; and cause his face to shine upon us." Why? "That thy way may be known upon earth, thy saving health among all nations. Let the people praise thee, O God; let all the people praise thee. O let the nations be glad and sing for joy."

We turn to the Prophet Isaiah, and from the second chapter to the last, allusion is made to this greatest of all themes. Daniel refers to it, Zechariah refers to it, and even in Malachi we are told that "from the rising of the sun even unto the going down of the same, my name shall be great among the Gentiles." But as we reach the New Testament, the door, which had then been held ajar, is thrown wide open.

Who came to our Saviour's cradle? Gentiles from the far East. Who bore the cross with Him? An African of Cyrene. What was His last command? "Go ye into all the world, and preach the gospel to every creature." The most important theme in the Bible is this: "Christ for the world and the world for Christ." Not only has God given us the charter for this work in His own Word, but He has set His special seal of approval on the work of foreign missions. Thousands of church spires mark the graves of Cannibalism and Witchcraft. Whole nations are turning from darkness into light. Look at Madagascar, the Fiji Islands and Japan. Go to the New Hebrides. On one of these islands is a slab, which marks the resting-place of a man known to few; but I wish no better epitaph for myself than the one inscribed upon that slab. The words are: "When he came, there were no Christians. When he went away, there were no heathen."

So marvellously has God blessed this work, that in the decade between 1873 and 1883, the average foreign missionary had thirty times as many converts as the average minister in the United States.

SUCCESS IN PROPORTION TO EFFORT.

If the success is so great, why am I before you this afternoon? The success has been great in proportion to the efforts put forth. My heart has burned within me as I have read the story of Gideon,—how he went with his handful of men against the one hundred and forty-five thousand Midianites. But if Gideon had gone against the enemy with the same proportion of men that we send to the foreign field, how many men would he have had? He would have had a fraction of one man. He would probably have sent a pitcher or a lamp!

I wish every one of you could see that familiar chart and those black squares, and I do hope that those figures may be burned into the hearts of every one before me. One thousand millions without a knowledge of Christ! God forbid that that I should say anything here this afternoon to disparage the claims of work in our own country. I realize that there are ten million youth in our country who are without proper education in religion or morals. I realize that one hundred thousand drunkards are passing every year from a drunkard's hovel to a drunkard's hell. It is a black picture. But turn to the land of my birth, and we must multiply the population of the United States by nearly five to equal the population of India. We must multiply the population of our country by nearly seven to equal the population of China. Those people have souls as well as we. Christ died for them as well as for us.

When, as a young man, I stand face to face with my life work, and the question comes, "Where are you to invest the capital of your life?" I think of the illustration used by the President of Princeton College: "Suppose that there are ten men here who have plenty of bread, but will not eat it, while off yonder there are a hundred who have no bread, and can get none; shall we go to the hundred, or shall we give the ten tonics and stimulants to create an appetite?" Shall I remain in the United States to give men tonics and stimulants to create an appetite, while millions in foreign lands know nothing of the Bread of Life?

I find in the United States an average of one minister to every eight hundred of the population. Counting the three classes of Christian workers,—the lay preachers, the ordained preachers and the Sabbath school teachers,—there are in the United States workers enough to make the average of one to every forty-eight of our population, and there is in our country an average of one Protestant church communicant to every five of our population; while out of every three persons born into this world, two look up into the same sun into which we look, and die without hearing the name of Christ. Is it fair? Is there not truth in what Stanley Smith said?—"When our Lord gave the bread and fishes to His disciples, and told them to feed the multitude, suppose that they had commenced at the first row and continued feeding until the eighth row, and then had returned to the first row, piling up the bread and fishes in the laps of the people, feeding eight rows over and over again, while the multitudes behind were starving, what would Christ have said to them?" Are we not in danger of doing the same thing?

HEATHEN ENOUGH AT HOME.

I know the cry that is raised: "Heathen enough at home." Dr. Phillips Brooks says that the excuse of "heathen enough at home" is getting more shameful every year. It is like the patricide asking the judge to have pity upon his orphanhood. There was a young man who was tried and convicted of patricide, and he was condemned to die because he killed his father. The judge said: "What plea have you for leniency?" He said: "Please, your Honor, have pity on my orphanhood." We are making the imperfection of our Christianity at home an excuse for neglecting it abroad. "This ought ye to have done, and not to have left the other undone."

I have not yet come across any church or any denomination that has hurt itself by doing too much for foreign missions. God's Word says: "There is that scattereth, and yet increaseth; and there is that withholdeth more than is meet, but it tendeth to poverty."

Seventy-six years ago there was a division in the ranks of the Baptist church, and some became anti-missionary. When they divided there were about thirty-five thousand in each body. According to the census of 1880, the anti-missionary Baptists numbered forty-five thousand, and the pro-missionary Baptists numbered two and a half millions "There is that scattereth and yet increaseth; and there is that withholdeth more than is meet, but it tendeth to poverty." Some one has said that the majority of us are not *anti*-missionary but *O*-missionary.

I hope there is no one before me this afternoon who belongs to the *O*-missionary class. My prayer is the prayer of the stroke of the Cambridge University boat. He prayed that there might be such an outlet of men and money from his country that it would lead to an inlet of blessing from heaven. God grant that there may be such an outlet of men and money from the United States that it will be followed by a great inlet of blessing upon our country. The outlet is coming.

INCREASE OF VOLUNTEERS.

Three years ago this month, two hundred and forty of our college men assembled near Mr. Moody's home in Massachusetts. We gathered there to study the Bible. Twenty-three of us met in the little Museum back of Croasly Hall and dedicated our lives to the work of foreign missions, and before that summer's school had closed there were one hundred men pledged to go into the foreign service unless God clearly blocked the way. It was deemed advisable that a tour should be made through the schools and colleges of our country, and two young men, one of whom is now in India, started out. They visited one hundred and seventy-five institutions, and, before the year closed, twenty-two hundred students signified a willingness and desire, God permitting, to be foreign missionaries. The movement has been increasing, until to-day there are three thousand nine hundred and thirty-eight enrolled on our list as volunteers for foreign service. Most of these are still two or three years removed from the completion of their courses of study; but I am very glad to say that we know definitely of one hundred and ten who have already sailed and are on foreign soil.

It seems to me that I have seen that cloud the size of a man's hand; and now for one hundred Elijahs, each on his Mt. Carmel, crying to God for rain. The showers are coming, and the time is not far distant when our young men and women will go into this work by the thousands. Let us ask for it; let us expect it.

NEED OF MONEY.

We find that not only workers are needed, but money is needed also. One of the secretaries of the Presbyterian Foreign Boards says that the Boards are lame in both feet. They go to the churches and ask for money. The churches say, "Where are the men?" And they go to the men, and the men say, "Where is the money?" Some of the colleges are trying to help in raising money. Two colleges in Canada, Knox and Queen's, have each sent out a man to the foreign field, and have promised to support him there. Knox sent out Mr. Goforth, a very appropriate name for a foreign missionary. The first college in our country to adopt this plan was Princeton. A year ago Mr. Forman and I went to Princeton, and told those men that they ought to work twenty-four hours in each day. They asked how they could do it. I told them about that woman who said she worked twelve hours here, and when she laid down her work at night, she had a representative in India, whom she supported, who worked for the next twelve hours there.

I find that nearly every college thinks it is poorer than every other, and Princeton is no exception to the rule; but within twenty-eight hours the undergraduates of Princeton College promised $1,300, and three days after the money was pledged Mr. Forman sailed for India, where he is working during the twelve hours that the Princeton men sleep here.

Then the students of Princeton Theological Seminary pledged $850, and sent out one of their number to Siam, under the Presbyterian Board of Foreign Missions. The Union Theological Seminary, New York, with only one hundred and thirty-five students, pledged $1,130 to mission work, and sent a man to Syria under the auspices of the Presbyterian Board. A theological seminary with only forty-four students, pledged $625 to support an alumnus in the foreign field. There are at present forty-nine institutions in the United States and Canada contributing toward sending out or supporting workers in the foreign field. During the past eight months $26,000 have been contributed by these institutions for this work.

I find, and the committee which I represent finds, that the student missionary uprising needs not only extending but conserving; so we have appointed a committee of three to stand at the head of this movement. The 3,900 volunteers represent three classes of students: women in our colleges, men in our colleges, and the students of our Theological Seminaries. There are three student organizations that correspond to these three classes: the Young Women's Christian Associations for college women, the Y. M. C. A. for college men, and the Inter-Seminary Missionary Alliance for theological students. The executive committee of the Student Volunteer Movement for Foreign Missions is composed of three members appointed by the Y. M. C. A., Y. W. C. A. and the Inter-Seminary Missionary Alliance respectively. The work of this committee is to conserve and extend the volunteer movement, also " to act as a clearing-house between the church boards and the volunteers."

WOMEN IN LONDON.

In the closing moments I want to again bring before you the claims of these heathen millions. My heart fairly burns within me when I think of that field in India, where my own mother and sister are working. Within a radius of fifteen miles from one of our stations are one hundred and twenty-five towns and villages. They are calling loudly for help. If the women of India are ever to be reached with the gospel, they must be reached by Christian *women*. Men cannot reach them. Among those women in India are 21,000,000 widows. They are clad in the coarsest garments. They live on only one meal a day. They are the slaves and drudges of the household, with no enjoyment in this life, and the future is all dark. There is only one thing that can bring peace to their hearts, and that is Christianity. Christian women must carry this to them. Men cannot enter the zezanas. Among those 21,000,000 widows are 10,000 under ten years of age. Why is it that more women do not go out to those needy fields? I ask you, first of all, to give yourselves, and, secondly, to give your money to this work. I find that it takes only one hundred and thirty-five people, each giving ten cents a week, to pay the salary of a single man in a foreign field. That is the average salary under most of our Boards. It seems to me that nearly every Christian Endeavor Society can find one hundred and thirty-five persons, each willing to give ten cents a week for this work, and to give this over and above what they are already giving.

But the money matter is not the most important matter. As Mr. Forman and I went through the colleges, there was one hymn which we did not like to hear sung. It was this hymn :

"If you cannot cross the ocean," etc.

The organist would strike the first note, and the students would join in on the second word. They would sing it thus :

"You cannot cross the ocean,
    Nor the heathen lands explore;
  You can find the heathen nearer,
    You can help them at your door.
  You cannot give your thousands,
    You can give the widow's mite;
  And the least you give for Jesus,
    Will be precious in His sight."

Let us remember the "if." If we cannot cross the ocean, let us stay at home. But why not cross the ocean? Possibly some one says, "I am afraid I cannot endure the climate." We have any variety of climate from the North Pole to the Equator. If India is too warm you can go to Japan, and if that is not cool enough, go to Mongolia, where 3,000,000 are without a resident missionary, and you can have the 3,000,000 to yourself.

NEED OF VARIED ABILITY.

In one of the colleges we visited, a man said he could not be a missionary because he had no executive ability; that no one should go to the foreign field unless he had great executive ability. At another institution we met a man who said that God had given him special talent in the line of executive ability, and therefore he ought to stay at home. One man could not go because he had no executive ability; the other could not go because he had executive ability. The fact is, the Lord wants men and women of every kind of ability in these foreign fields. There is a call for medical workers. Ten of our students have gone to Japan as teachers. There is a call for preachers; there is a call for journalists; there is a call for men and women of every variety of talent for these fields. The question is not: "Why should I go?" but "*Why should I not go?*" One of our students in Princeton said: "Yonder is a vineyard. Right near the gate I find a great many pickers and few grapes. Further on I find more grapes and fewer pickers. But far off there are millions of clusters, dead-ripe, and not a single man picking." The question is not: "Why should I go where the grapes are thickest and the workmen fewest?" Not, "Am I *called* to go?" but, "Am I *exempt* from going to the neediest portions of the vineyard?"

When I think that millions are without a knowlepge of Christ, the one thought that thrills me is this—that every man, woman and child can hear of Christ in the present generation. If you forget everything you have heard here this afternoon, please carry away this one thought: if there were only one Christian in the world to-day, if he should work a whole year to get another, and these two should toil on another whole year before they obtained two more, and the work keep on in that ratio, in thirty years the whole world would be brought to Christ,

I began with only one and gave him only one soul as the result of a whole year's effort; but when I think that nearly five hundred thousand young people belong to the societies of Christian Endeavor, it seems to me that it is not only possible, but very probable, that this whole world will hear of Christ during the *present* generation.

Two days ago, at Northfield, Mass., where five hundred of our students were assembled, a cablegram from Japan was read. It informed us that five hundred Japanese students were assembled in Kioto for the same purpose for which we had gathered at Northfield. In it were the words, "Make Jesus King; 500 students."

BEAT A CHARGE.

When that cablegram was read, the thought came to me, the time is not far distant when the Lord Jesus will be made King in Japan, India, Africa, and the islands of the sea. God grant that the young people belonging to this Christian Endeavor organization may take the position that the little drummer boy in Napoleon's army took. When the commander said, "Boy, beat a retreat," the little fellow did not stir. He repeated, "Boy, beat a retreat." The boy looked up into the face of the commander and said, "Sire, I know not how. Desaix never taught me that. But I can beat a charge. I can beat a charge that will make the dead fall into line. I beat that charge at Lodi; I beat it at the Pyramids; I beat it at Mt. Tabor. May I beat it here?" And over the dead and wounded, over the cannon and batterymen, and over the breastwork and the ditches he led the way to victory. God grant that we young people may take the stand that the little drummer boy took, and in the face of obstacles say, "We know not how to beat a retreat. But, in the strength of the Lord and the power of His might, we will beat a charge that will make the dead fall into line, and over India and Africa and the islands of the sea we will lead the way to victory and accomplish the evangelization of the world." Let us fall in line for this charge.

Before I close let me repeat those figures. One minister in the United States to every eight hundred of our population; one Christian worker in the United States to every forty-eight of our population; one church communicant in the United States to every five of our population, while two-thirds of our race have not heard of Christ.

THE WORLD FOR CHRIST.

By Rev. Arthur T. Pierson, D. D., Pastor Bethany Presbyterian Church, Philadelphia, Pa.

The bill of fare is inverted. Having had the dessert as the first course, you are coming to plain graham bread as the next. First of all, I wish to say to you that if any of you should be in the city over the Lord's day, you shall have a most cordial welcome to the capacious accommodations of Bethany Church, Twenty-second and Bainbridge Street, and I should like to have you see the gentleman whose munificent generosity has decorated this hall conduct a Sunday school of twenty-five hundred people and himself teach a Bible class of eight hundred. I should like to have you meet in the evening of the Lord's day at the Lord's Table, that great mass of communicants in Bethany Church. Kindly feel yourselves our guests, in case you remain over Sunday.

Now for the speech. I heartily hail the representatives of five hundred thousand people committed to Christian Endeavor, for I think I have, for thirty years of ministerial and pastoral life, known about five millions of people who were apparently committed to Christian laziness.

Those two words, "Christian Endeavor," were divinely chosen as the motto and watchword of your organization. You owe your rapid growth, you owe your enthusiasm, you owe your acceptance with the community, and you owe your position in the Christian church largely to those two words which form your designation. I beg you to notice that the word "endeavor" is of French origin; *en devour*—endeavor—means *in the line of duty*. Christian Endeavor represents the highest form of activity, for it is activity in the line of duty, on the track of right and righteousness, in accordance with gospel principles and actuated by a gospel spirit. God bless the societies of Christian Endeavor.

It is a very necessary thing that our Christian Endeavor should be thoroughly normal and spiritual, that it should not become formal and external and mechanical, a mere noisy bustle; instead of devoutness and devotion, substituting mere mouthing and motion.

HOLY ENTHUSIASM.

The question to-night of supreme importance is this: What are the mainsprings of Christian Endeavor, especially with reference to the work or winning a world to Christ? Give me your silent prayer as, in the presence of this gigantic audience, I seek to set forth two simple secrets of Christian Endeavor. The first of them is a *holy enthusiasm*. We use that word, "enthusiasm," very often without a really adequate sense of its grand significance. It used to be said that enthusiasm was probably compounded of *en* and *Theos*, the two Greek words, and that it really means *God in us*, an *entheism*. There way never a man who did much for the world in any department of activits who was not a man of enthusiasm.

Take Michael Angelo when he attacked that yellow, dingy block of marble in the streets of Florence with hammer and chisel, declaring that within it was imprisoned an angel, and that it was his office, as a sculptor, to set the angel free. Think of Da Vinci when he painted the "Last Supper," consuming ten years of work on the canvas. Think of him going at midday from the cathedral, where he was engaged on his colossal horse, to the convent where his picture was, that he might stand and look at it and add, perhaps, a single line or touch of color. Think of Palissy, the potter, accidentally coming in contact with some elaborately ornamented porcelain, and giving sixteen years to the discovery of the secret of laying on that enamel, reducing himself and his family to the verge of starvation, and breaking up the very furniture of his house that he might have fuel with which to feed the furnace fires that did the glazing of his pottery.

We must be enthusiastic. We admire enthusiasm, even if we see it in misguided men, like Francois Xavier, who, when the crew was attacked with scurvy on board a certain vessel, washed their sores and even their clothes, and went ringing his bell through the streets of Goa, so that he might call together the people to instruct them, and in the course of a life that ended at the age of forty-six, going himself into fifty-two different kingdoms, over nine thousand miles of territory, and preaching the Word of God to upward of one million human beings.

I say that for all Christian Endeavor we need such enthusiasm, a burning, divine passion for God, for souls, for the achievement of high and noble and heroic results. It is a blessed thing that the societies of Christian Endeavor have taken hold, as never before have any other agencies, of the great mass of the young people of our Christian churches, in whom especially there is the capacity and the preparation for a divine and holy enthusiasm, when they are touched by the spirit of God, and when they engage in the various departments of truly Christian work.

HOLY ENTERPRISE.

My second observation, and that upon which I especially desire for a few moments to dilate, is this: that, while back of all Christian Endeavor there must be holy enthusiasm, in carrying out Christian Endeavor there must be holy enterprise.

I know of no word in the English language that so well expresses the exact conception which I desire to put before you as that one word, "Enterprise." It means a combination of dash and push. We see it in the world. The children of this world are wiser in their generation than the children of light, and they carry their enterprise from the rising to the setting sun with a celerity of movement, with a grandeur of absorption and with a readiness of self-sacrifice, which, up to this the present hour of the nineteenth century, has scarcely ever been imitated very largely even in the church of Jesus Christ.

I have heard that the gospel has thus far been carried into no hitherto unexplored territory, where they have not found within the last thirty years the kerosene lamp. That is to say, for the sake of introducing a new invention in the line of illumination, the men of the world manifest more enterprise than the children of God ever manifest in carrying the Light of God for the spiritual illumination of the millions who sit in darkness and in the shadow of death.

I ask you to-night, my young friends in the societies of Christian Endeavor, what is the church of God doing that nineteen centuries have passed and the world is not yet claimed for Christ?

I shall probably never look into your faces again. It would not be among the possibilities of earth that I should ever address, even though it were to-morrow, exactly the same collection of Christian people that I confront to-night, and, with the emphasis of a dying man, I want to put before you, in the moments that remain to me, that great enterprise of a world's evangelization that has absorbed my own mind so completely for the last fifteen years that I think of it by day and dream of it by night, and have given tongue and pen to its ad voccy.

POSSIBILITIES OF THE PRESENT GENERATION.

I am going to say to you what I have said before on many a platform, that I believe it is within the power of the Christian church of the present generation to give the gospel to the entire family of man before the present generation shall have passed away from this world, and I know no place to project such enterprise, more appropriate to the suggestion, than here in the presence of the representatives of a half a million of young people who are committed to Christ and the church for endeavor in behalf of the world.

I have stated that I am entirely satisfied that before the people to this generation shall descend to their graves, the whole world may be evangelized. That is to say, that every man, woman and child on the face of the earth may have heard the gospel before, in the ordinary course of things, the present generation passes from the stage of human history.

First, look at the simple proposition mathematically. There are on the earth to-day about thirty millions of Protestant church members. I will not say a word at this time of those who are within the Papal church, or those who are within the Greek church, but inasmuch as almost, if not quite, without exception, we ourselves belong to the great Protestant churches of Christendom, I speak of those who are your constituency as a body of delegates, namely, the thirty millions of people who profess the Protestant faith, and are gathered within the membership of Protestant churches. On the other side, there are a thousand millions of human beings on the face of the earth that have yet to be reached by the sound of the gospel trumpet, or touched with the sublime contact of Christian Endeavor.

It takes but a very simple sum in arithmetic to show that if you divide one thousand millions by thirty millions you have about thirty-three. That is to say, if every one of the present thirty millions of Protestant church members can be brought into contact with thirty-three of the human race who have never heard of Christ, and would never have heard of Christ but for the agency of that Christian disciple, within thirty-three years, at the rate of only one new soul a year, the thousand millions of the human race may have the gospel from the thirty millions of Protestant disciples.

Will you allow me to ask whether there is any assignable reason that can be presented in this assembly why that enterprise should not be taken up on the basis of such a distribution of labor?

THE PRINCIPLE OF DISTRIBUTION.

When Christ fed five thousand with the five loaves and the two fishes, on what principle was the distribution conducted? He did not undertake to give those five loaves and two fishes to a mob that was disorganized or disorderly. Where those that were especially hungry or especially selfish pressed to the front and crowded others into the rear, those who were more timid or feeble were almost certain to go neglected and unsupplied, but Christ said: First of all, make them to sit down on the grass in companies, in ranks of hundreds and fifties; and then, being thoroughly organized in small companies, the disciples could pass with the bread, which multiplied as it was divided and distributed to all those multitudes.

On precisely the same principle must the Bread of Life be given to the one thousand millions of the human race, if it shall ever be given to them.

We must take the race, not as a disorganized mob, where the most selfish press to the front and crowd the others into the rear, where the few are looked after because of their geographical proximity, where the great mass of those more remote are overlooked on account of distance; but we must organize this great mass. We must distribute it among the Christian Endeavor Societies and the humble Christian workers of the whole Christian church, and then going forth with that mysterious Bread of Life that strangely multiplies as it is divided, and increases as it is imparted, we must give to this entire race of men the gospel of our salvation.

I have frequently in public addresses, as also in that little book that I have written on the "Crisis of Missions," referred to an ancient enterprise that puts the blush of shame on the Christian church of this day. A secular king, a king of worldly principles, and worldly passions, and worldly methods, undertook to rescue in behalf of a Jewish wife, an imperilled Jewish people. They were scattered over one hundred and twenty-seven provinces, that reached two thousand miles from east to west, and fifteen hundred miles from north to south in the great Persian Empire, from the Bosphorus and Golden Horn and Nile on the west, to the Indus and Ganges on the east, over the lower portion of Arabia and the Red Sea on the south, to the Caspian Sea and the Black Sea on the north. He had no printing-press; he had no telegraph or telephone; he had no steam-engines or carriages or vessels; he had nothing but dromedaries and camels wherewith to facilitate the progress of his posts and messengers in carrying the news of salvation to the Jews; and yet, over all those one hundred and twenty-seven provinces, to every man, woman and child in that vast territory, within the space of less than nine months, that decree of Ahasuerus was successfully borne! Yet in the nineteenth century of the Christian era, with a thousand facilities of which Ahasuerus never dreamed, and of which the wildest prophecies of the Arabian Nights could never have had the remotest foretaste, we of this generation stand comparatively still and let a thousand million of human beings go down to hopeless graves and enter upon an Eternity without promise, while we have the Bread of Life, steam-engines and steamships, and printing-presses, and sanctified scholars, and telephones and telegraphs, so that we can girdle the earth with steam in ninety days, and girdle the earth with electricity in ninety seconds!

RESPONSIBILITY OF THE CHRISTIAN CHURCH.

I say again, What is the matter with the Christian church? How are we going to answer to Almighty God? How are we to confront at the Judgment Seat of Christ the fifteen hundred millions of human beings of which we are a part, and a thousand millions of whom are in the darkness of the death shade, and answer to Christ that we have done comparatively nothing, and some of us absolutely nothing, to give them the Gospel within the range of a lifetime?

It is an awful responsibility. It takes away my relish for my food when I think about it, and takes away the restfulness of my sleep when I dwell upon it, and I cannot get peace save as I push this great subject before my brethren in the Christian ministry and in the Christian churches, as I now put it before my dear young friends of the societies of Christian Endeavor.

I have passed the meridian hour of my life; I have gone beyond the age of fifty. I cannot look forward, in the ordinary course of things, to more than fifteen or twenty years of active labor. There are some of you who, if you give yourselves to Christian Endeavor in the sublime spirit of your motto, may yet live, after I am dead, to see this world filled with the knowledge of the Son of God, and to see Christian flags floating on every hill and in every valley the wide world round.

Let us vote before God to-night in the solemnity of Christian consecration that, by the help of God the Father, and God the Son, and God the Holy Ghost, before, in the ordinary course of things, you who are here present to-night shall be called to your final account, you will see to it that every man, woman and child on the earth has had the knowledge that Jesus Christ came into this world to save sinners.

That is what I understand by Christian Endeavor prosecuted with a Christian enthusiasm and methods of Christian enterprise.

I will shorten my address for another brother who is to come after me, and I will forego fifteen minutes of my forty-five that he may have a longer time in which to address you. I am very desirous that this greatest problem that was ever put before the human race should be appreciated by you and taken up by you in the sublime spirit of consecrated enterprise.

THE DARKNESS OF PAST GENERATIONS.

I have referred to the fact that we are here in the nineteenth century of the Christian Era, and that as yet only one-tenth of the world really has been reached with the pure gospel of the Lord Jesus Christ. Do you know what that means? A generation passes from this earth every thirty-three years. Consequently, three times in every century the earth is virtually depopulated. Consequently, in the course of eighteen centuries more than fifty generations of human beings have gone down to the grave. In other words, if the average numbers of a generation may be supposed, as they have been supposed, to be about one-half of the number now dwelling upon the earth, this amounts, in the course of nineteen hundred years, to twenty-five times the present population of the globe . stupendous numbers that it is impossible for us to grasp. Imagination vainly seeks to take in a calculation so colossal. Twenty-five times the present population of the globe since Jesus Christ ascended into heaven have passed away, and the Christian church, as yet, embraces only thirty millions of Protestant church members, and only about one-fifth of the entire race of man, to use liberal estimates, has been reached with a pure gospel.

This is a marvellous era. We talk about such a man as Methuselah living for nine hundred and sixty-nine years before he died. He needed to live nine hundred and sixty-nine years in those days to live at all. While he was putting on his coat and turning around we put on new civilization and sweep around the globe. Look at this age. I have said that I am fifty years of age, which you would probably have known without having been told. I have seen, in my short period of life, more new inventions, more new discoveries, more of the secrets of nature penetrated, and more of her resources utilized, than the human race has seen in the entire thousands of years that have preceded my advent on the earth. That will give you some conception of the wonderful rapidity of modern progress.

IN FIFTY YEARS.

Fifty years ago there was but one line of railroad in this country, and that but five hundred miles long. There was no such thing known as palace cars, sleeping cars, vestibule cars or dining-cars. We knew nothing of electricity as either a motor or illuminator, or a medium for sending messages; we knew nothing of anæsthetics in surgery; we knew nothing of the spectroscope, with its wonderful unveiling of the physical constitution of the stars; we knew nothing of those giant explosives like dynamite and nitro-glycerine or giant powder that are revolutionizing modern science in the globe with their great powers of destruction and their force in the removal of the masses of debris. We knew nothing of the sewing-machine, one of the most important improvements of modern days. The ladies had no sewing-machines fifty years ago, and when you remember that a sewing-machine represents the work of two hundred and fifty women, and can do three thousand stitches in a single minute, you will see what means this one indication of the vast and rapid accumulation and acceleration of the human energies in these latter days. When you think that fifty years ago there was no such thing as photography known, with all the twenty methods of reduplicating pictures by the aid of sunlight that now engross the attention of the artistic world, you will get another insight into the marvellous progress of this day.

What I say this for, beloved, is this: that I may enable you to feel what vast results ought to be accomplished within the time of your life, with all these million springs which your Christian Endeavor must touch and which you can utilize and sanctify for Christ.

A LOOK FORWARD.

The probability is that the next ten years will show discoveries, inventions and the mastery of the elements of more importance, in some respects, than the fifty years that have preceded. Look what Mr. Edison has done in the last fifteen years for the development of the marvellous uses of electricity. Just think of the phonograph as one of the ripest inventions of human times; an instrument which may yet be made so complete that it can take down accurately every word, articulate every utterance that is made in a colossal gathering like this, and put them in such shape that at another convention held one hundred years hence, every one of the addresses made to-night might be repeated in the actual tones of the orators themselves.

With these magnificent appliances before us, everything is moving, not at the rate of the old stage-coach or elephant team, but even beyond the speed of steam, with the rapidity of lightning, which Robert McKenzie says, in his grand book on the Nineteenth Century, represents the first of the last inventions of man, for, as he says, for once man has touched the highest summit of possible invention. There can be no transmission of intelligence that is more immediate than instantaneous; and it may be one indication of the approaching beginning of the end, that in one invention, at least, man has struck that principle of transmission of messages which cannot be exceeded for celerity, or rapidity, or accuracy by any method or agent known or unknown, for such a thing is inconceivable.

GOD HAS CALLED.

You see, my friends, the trend of my argument is this: that God has called upon the men and women of this generation to do a work that no previous generation could possibly have accomplished within the same space of time. My Saviour and your Saviour has been waiting on the throne of the universe for nearly nineteen centuries. He has looked down upon a sluggish, lethargic, inert and apathetic church; and, one hundred years ago, upon a church that even disputed the principle of foreign missions, when Dr. Ryland could tell William Carey to sit down and let God take care of the heathen and that God needed no such agency as his; when the Scotch assembly could rebuke foreign missions as absurd, and when the American Board, which now stands on the vanguard of missionary labor and effort, could be so timid and so discouraged as scarcely to dare to send its four pioneers to the Eastern World, lest the great church of America should not sustain such an expenditure.

We can hardly understand these things as we are in the presence of God and each other to-night, but I pray God to let me live long enough, after having given twenty years of the best of my life to the study and the advocacy of this great proposition, to see this enterprise of Christian missions taken up by the Young People's Society of Christian Endeavor, by the Young Men's Christian Association, by the Young Women's Christian Association, by the Young Women's Temperance Union, by the great Missionary Crusade in the colleges, as well as by the churches of Christ in general, with a determination that before this generation shall pass away the world shall have known that Jesus Christ died for sinners.

THE SPIRIT OF MARTYRDOM.

I remember that when Ignatius stood in the arena about to sacrifice his life for Christ, and was entreated by friends to make the simple sign of obeisance to the false gods and escape the fearful death, he folded his arms over his breast, his white hair and beard mingling as they met over his shoulder, and said: "I am grain of God; I must be ground between the teeth of lions to make bread for God's people." There never was a man or woman who accomplished much in this world for God or for man that had not the martyr spirit, and back of your Christian Endeavor, with its holy enthusiasm and its enterprising method, there must be that supreme spirit of sacrifice for Jesus Christ that shall make it possible for God to make you co-workers with God, the Father, co-Saviours with Christ, the Son, and co-witnesses with the Holy Ghost.

When the Emperor of China told Poussa, who was the Chinese Palissy, to make him a set of porcelain for the royal table, he five times made the experiment of constructing a set of china that would dignify the royal board, and when he had made the fifth and had placed it in the glazing furnace and was watching the process of its enamelling, in sheer despair of ever being able to do any work that was fit for the acceptance of his royal master, through the open door of the furnace he flung himself into the raging flames, and perished; and the Chinese sages say that from out that furnace there came a set of porcelain so magnificently enamelled and gilded and painted that out of sheer jealousy that it should ever be set upon a human table, the gods caught it up into their paradise.

The Chinese sages wrote wiser than they knew. You never make a work that is fit for God to accept until you fling yourself into the furnace, and then from that furnace there come out wares that shine with the splendor of the stars and seem to have been decorated by the hands of angels.

CHRIST FOR THE WORLD.

By Rev. O. P. Gifford, D. D., Pastor Warren Ave. Baptist Church, Boston, Mass.

John Milton, the prince of English poets, in the matchless poem of "Paradise Regained," pictures the Son of man on top of a high mountain. The Prince of this world causes the kingdoms of earth to pass in review before Him. There is Assyria with its ancient boundary, the Parthian power, Greece with her culture, and Rome with her might, and Barbaric thrones lying like uncut gems waiting to be cut and set in their conqueror's diadem. All this he offers to the Prince of light if He will bend the "pregnant hinges of the knee" in one short act of worship.

We stand to-night at the close of eighteen centuries of Christian work and worship, and the kingdoms of the world pass again before us in review, lying as yet in the power of the wicked one. Yesterday, in common with many of you, I stood in the Cyclorama of Jerusalem, and saw the distant road that leads to Damascus, the winding pathway over the shoulders of the mountain to the Bethlehem tower, the far-off blue hills of Moab, the proud city sitting like a queen upon her throne, the two crosses for the robbers, and the world's great Altar of Sacrifice, and over all the darkness of the hours that waited for the offering to be finished. When Christ was on earth, turning to Peter, He said: Satan hath begged for thee, that he may sift thee like wheat, but I have prayed for thee that thy faith go not into a total eclipse.

The Son of man saw the dark body that should roll between Him and the apostle's faith, and shut out the light of His countenance, and leave the apostle in darkness.

THE ECLIPSE OF UNRIGHTEOUSNESS.

To-night the world lies in the eclipse of unrighteousness. The Christian part of it is but a crescent burdened with the black ball of millions who have never heard the truth as it is in Jesus Christ. The need of the world to-day, as when Christ came, is the Christ of God. Instantly we say Christ, there flashes upon us a question, "What do you mean?" From the sunny South there comes a report that the negroes are turning by hundreds to follow a false Christ; from Rockford, Ill., comes the report of a false Christ who has gathered about him hundreds of followers and accumulated millions of money.

All their passions are to thine like the moonlight unto sunlight, like the water unto wine, O Christ of God! Not the Christ of the South, nor the Christ of Rockford, nor the Christ of Unitarian Boston, but the Christ of God is what the world needs.

Who is this Christ of God? Pliny, the younger, in a letter to the Roman Emperor, written in the year 70, said, "The Christians are wont to meet before daybreak and sing the praises of Christ as God." Paul, in the epistle to Timothy, gives us a quotation from one of the early Christian hymns. He calls it the setting forth of "the mystery of Godliness."

"Who was manifest in the flesh, justified in the spirit, seen of angels, preached among the nations, believed on in the world, received up in glory," the center of Christian thought, the inspiration of Christian action, is the incarnation of the Son of God. He whom the world, by searching, could not find out, has by searching found the world out. He has become human that man might become divine. He has lived, Himself, in our humanity that He might lift us into the likeness of God. The manifest, personal Christ, the creator of the ends of the earth, the Father of the ages, the Wonderful, the Counsellor, the Prince of Peace, He, who is the brightness of God's glory, who is the express image of God's person — here is the Christ we must carry to the world.

THE REASON OF OUR SLUGGISHNESS.

Our brother told us that Ahasuerus carried the pardon to the end of his empire in a few short months, but Ahasuerus did it because he felt the danger of the Jew and love for the woman who shared his throne.

We are backward because we do not realize this danger; we are sluggish because the Christ of our conception is not the Christ of the early church, God manifest in the flesh.

Did you ever cross the Atlantic? Do you remember, when the steamer is midway, how the mighty engine throbs like a heart through all the length of the great steamer, how it laughs at the current, sneers at the cyclone, defies the storm, and, with strained muscles, bears its burden of humanity towards waiting shores and greeting friends; but when the great steamer arrives near New York, the engineer slows the speed, and she creeps into New York Bay as slowly as the summer shadow creeps over the shoulder of a New England mountain; she comes up to the New York dock hardly disturbing the friends who are waiting.

Out of its precious heart pours the stream of human life, and out of its full hands the burden of gold that makes the new world richer.

Christ slowed down the mighty energy by which He had created the world, came within the narrow bounds of our humanity, tied up to the little cradle in Bethlehem of Judea, unloaded the burden of His divinity into the lap of the world's great need. This is the Christ we must carry to the world. Not the Christ of modern speculation, not the Christ of negation, but the Christ of burning affirmation, who shall blaze His way through the darkness of unbelief, and leave the world lying in the light of God, as the child lies upon its mother's breast,

"Where the wicked cease from troubling,
And the weary are at rest."

Paul tells us that the Christ of the early church was justified in the spirit. God is just and the Justifier of them that believe on Him, but Jesus needeth no Justifier.

The Roman Catholic Church puts purgatory between the grave and the throne of judgment; the Protestant Church puts the cross and Christ between the world's sin and a righteous God, but Christ needs neither cross nor purgatory. In Him is no sin at all. He lies in the palm of God's judgment as clear as the light that flashes upon Him from the throne. Our lives are like cathedral windows; they break the light of God's righteousness. Christ's love is like a plate glass window, through which the light shines without refraction.

Never yet did a human soul empty itself through the banks of obedience and faith into the life of God but it carries with it something that needed cleansing and purifying; but when Christ emptied His life back again into the life of God, it went as pure as when it leaped from the presence of the infinite Father.

The Christ the world needs is justified in the Spirit.

SEEN OF ANGELS.

He was seen of angels. The same word is used in Paul's Epistle to the Corinthians, where he speaks of the resurrection of Christ. "He appeared to Cephas, then to the twelve; then he appeared to above five hundred brethren at once." He showed Himself to them. In His incarnation and life in the flesh He showed Himself to angels.

Christ says, in the Gospel of St. John, "No man hath seen God at any time; the only begotten Son, which is in the bosom of the Father, He hath declared him." In God's presence the angels bow and the archangels veil their faces. The highest of created beings cover their faces with twain of their wings in God's presence. They serve and worship, but never see the face of God. But now word goes out through heaven that the fulness of time has come. The Word is to become flesh. The uncreated Son is to declare the Father.

There is to be a manifestation of the Son of God. They crowd from heaven to earth; they come and go like white clouds in a summer sky, and when He is born in Bethlehem of Judea they burst into unutterable ecstasy, and sing, "Glory to God in the highest, and on earth peace and good-will toward men."

They crowd around the cradle, warn the wise men, guide the family into Egypt and Nazareth; they watch the struggle in the desert; they glorify Him on the Mount of Transfiguration, minister to Him in the Gethsemane of agony, hover over Him on the cross.

They tarry by the tomb until He takes up His life; they roll away the stone and proclaim Jesus of Nazareth the Lord of life. He declared Himself unto angels.

Then Christ was preached unto the Gentiles, was believed on in the world, received up into glory. He ascended up on high, leading captivity captive and giving gifts to men.

He is the brightness of God's glory and the character of the divine essence; He is the outpouring of the divine splendor.

HIM WHOM THE WORLD NEEDS.

This is the Christ the world needs. The Creator of the ends of the earth, by whom and for whom and in whom all things were made. The heavens declare God's glory, but the Christ unfolds God's love.

There is in the seminary a study called Exegesis, where we lead out the meaning of a text. Christ says no one has seen God at any time; but Christ has given the exegesis of God, and we want God's exegesis to go out, and to bring the world back to God's way of life.

Yonder lies the world in darkness, yonder waits the love of Christ. How shall we carry the Christ to the waiting, needy world? What is the point of contact? "As the Father has sent me, so have I sent you." "Lo, I am with you always," when you go, where you are. Yonder lies the great city in the darkness of the midnight hour, and yonder is the magnificent dynamo, the bright source of life; its wheels are flooded with the splendor of its own begetting. How shall the light of the dynamo become the blessing in the darkened city? From yonder forest, trees must step out and stand like sentinels by night and day in crowded city streets, robbed of their sap, shorn of their leaves, stripped of their bark; further, from yonder heart of the mighty mountain there must come the ore worked up into wires, stretching through the darkness of the city like nerves through the human body, and these poles and these wires must submit themselves unconditionally to carry the splendid power of the dynamo, and the world at midnight shall be as bright as at midday.

THE SECRET.

There is no other secret of carrying Christ to the world. We must step out from the forests of our selfishness; we must get out of the mines of our self-seeking; we must yield ourselves absolutely to God until looking down upon us He can say, "My thoughts are your thoughts, my ways are your ways, and as high as the heavens are above the earth so high have I lifted you into communion with myself, saith the Lord of hosts."

The great city is perishing in flame, the great reservoir is forcing its way through miles of pipe leading to disaster and conflagration. How shall the reservoir be brought to bear upon the burning city? The engine must give itself absolutely to completing the union between the reservoir and the city.

Yonder on the mountains of light are the reservoirs of eternal life. Yonder lies a world wrapped in the flames of selfishness, perishing before God, and between God and the world must stand a busy, throbbing church, every power of its being surrendered to God in Christ that He may bring God in Christ to a world that needs Him and that will perish without Him.

WENDELL PHILLIPS.

We had in our section of the country a man of whose memory we are very proud, a man in whose veins was the bluest blood of Boston, who wore on his brow the coronet of culture, who had within his reach wealth and station and all that men hold most dear, but who gave all his life to the service of the Lord. Wendell Phillips stood like a marble cliff, thrust into the bitter prejudices of New England's conservatism. When he was an old man, and stood on the earthly side of the valley of the shadow of death, a personal friend of his and mine said to him, " Mr. Phillips, did you ever make a consecration of yourself to God?" And he said, "Yes, when I was a boy fourteen years of age, in the old church at the North End, I heard Lyman Beecher preach on the theme, 'You belong to God,' and I went home after that service, and threw myself on the floor in my room, with locked doors, and said, 'God, I belong to you; take what is thine own. I ask but this, that whenever a thing be right it take no courage to do it; whenever a thing be wrong it may have no power of temptation over me.' Whenever I have known a thing to be wrong it has had no power of temptation; whenever I have known a thing to be right it has taken no courage to do it."

That is the mainspring of the life of Wendell Phillips. That must be the mainspring of every soldier in the Christian Endeavor army, "I belong to you, Christ. I ask but this, that whenever a thing be wrong it may have no power over me; whenever a thing be right it may take no courage to do it;" or, in the words of one of our latest poets:

> " If Jesus Christ be man and only man, I say
> That of all mankind I will cleave to Him,
> I will cleave to Him alway.
> And if Jesus Christ be God, and the only God, I swear
> I will follow Him through Heaven and Hell, the earth
> The sea and the air!"

CHRISTIAN YOUNG PEOPLE AND TEMPERANCE.

By Rev. J. W. Hamilton, Pastor Saratoga Street M. E. Church, East Boston, Mass.

I have been honored with the invitation to speak in this city at the opportune moment. I have craved the privilege all my life long to speak in the crisis periods of the nation's history.

The city of Philadelphia has recently rendered the decision, enforced by the significant majority of more than 92,000 votes, which made "liquor men jubilant," as we were told in Massachusetts by the dispatches found in our papers the morning after the election. The emphasis given to similar decisions by the no less decisive majorities in Oregon, Michigan, Tennessee, Texas, West Virginia, New Hampshire and Massachusetts, with the majority of 189,038 votes in this great Keystone State, and lastly, the turning back of the shadows on the dial by Rhode Island, have all but set the hearts of gladness, inflamed with zeal to strains of worship, for the dealers in drinks which intoxicate have poured their spirits forth with shouts of thanksgiving and praise all over the land. A day or two after the last decision—that in Rhode Island—I received the following letter from the distiller in Massachusetts who is sending the products of his still to the pagan purchasers or traders "up the Congo":

"*Dear Brother Hamilton:*—Don't it sometimes seem to you that the ministers are rather on the side of *Baal* than the *true* God; their prayers are not answered like Elijah's, especially so far as prohibition is concerned. How is it? Is there a Devil greater than God?"

The time of rejoicing *is* come to evil-doers. Like the enemy mentioned in the book of Micah they cry out to the preachers of righteousness, "Where is the Lord thy God?" They have found a divinity in numbers. They have multiplied their defense with figures. The multitudes are gone after them.

WHO ARE THE MULTITUDES?

But what are numbers? Who are the multitudes? "Even a popular orator or a popular journalist," said Matthew Arnold, "will hardly say that the multitude may be trusted to have its judgment generally just and its action generally virtuous." Quoting Isaiah, he said: "The actual commonwealth of the 'drunkards' and the 'blind,' as he calls them, in Israel and Judah, of the dissolute grandees and gross and foolish common people, of the great majority must perish; its perishing was the necessary stage towards a happier future." Mr. Arnold was right, as Isaiah was right. The multitudes who have kept holiday shall come to see how they have mistaken their fortunes. "Death is the universal salt of States."

Money, like numbers, dazzles the eyes of the timid and blinds the eyes of the weak. It will purchase the flattery of the crowd, and even the favor of men in high places. It will give to the conscience

"Vacation,
As well as other courts o' th' nation."

It will make of the small men the great, and call the feeble the strong. But the timid and the weak do not rule, neither do they lead. The crowd will scatter and in a little time be gone; the men in high places will be brought low. "The jingling of the guinea helps the hurt that honor feels," as bribery helps crime. And it will make no small man great to hang a golden girdle about his loins; nor of the feeble the strong. No man is strong who for any reason espouses the claim or cause which is wrong.

A NATIONAL DISGRACE.

We have had an instance during the past few days where the shame of the land, and with it the disgrace of the city in which I live, have forced themselves into the homes and faces of people who have been sickened with disgust for their kind. My morning paper, like yours, has had its columns crowded with the brutal details of a vulgar crime. The ink on the type has been mixed with mud and blood. And yet they are managers of a great railroad whom we have seen conspiring with the basest of criminals to violate the law, and both railroad officials and criminals have been joined by the telegraph and newspaper to help on the conspiracy, when the aim of all parties has been no higher motive than "to pick up a dollar." We have seen the streets in our cities crowded before the bulletins, with a hooting, howling mob, all classes represented in it, and all bent on taking some part with the principals in resisting the authorities in Mississippi. Money has been shared without stint to make this the most notorious encounter between men-beasts in all modern times. But what has been the measure of influence exerted in all this expenditure of money? Every man who has given a wink of approval to this shameless exhibition of brutal instinct has sinned against his own sense of honor, and must feel his loss of manhood, whenever in the presence of the wife and children of his home, he may consider his humiliation. He will not be able to look himself in the face when he recalls the part he has taken in this great public misdemeanor, and conceal his feelings which must "cower and brood among the ruins of his peace." No pure-minded woman has been able to read the daily papers for a week, without a blush of shame.

How far then shall the mere numbers and money of the multitudes influence your convictions and mine? How far shall they go toward determining what I am to say and you are to do? I do not under-estimate the noise of popular clamor. I know full well the force of the all but resistless torrent of public opinion. I know that there have been times in the history of all great movements when not only the voice of the people but the persecution of the people have been lifted up against true men. I know that weak men, then, have wavered, and that there has been no strength in them. The persecution of strong men has been so bitter and overwhelming that the cause of truth has seemed to suffer—has seemed to lag or fall behind. I know that in all such times

> "It is hard to work for God,
>   To rise and take His part
> Upon this battlefield of earth,
>   And not sometimes lose heart.
>
> He hides himself so wondrously,
>   As though there were no God;
> He is least seen when all the powers
>   Of ill are most abroad.
>
> Or he deserts us in the hour
>   The fight is all but lost,
> And seems to leave us to ourselves
>   Just when we need him most.
>
> It is not so, but so it looks,
>   And we lose courage then,
> And doubts will come if God hath kept
>   His promises to men."

But it is just then I look for true men to withstand the odds of majorities and to prove themselves God's noblemen. I have come to put so little confidence in the kind of numbers which so unworthily constitute majorities, and in the boasted wealth and position of persons who support the cause which I know to be wrong, that I simply stand and wait for them to vanish away.

GOD IS AT THE HELM.

The problems of a century puzzle the people of a generation; not unfrequently the puzzle runs on into the succeeding generation, and it may be generations. Few men have scope of vision far-reaching enough and sagacity with largeness of soul adequate to compass and comprehend the problem of a hundred years. But there is a presiding genius in every nation whose counsel and control will not permit a people to live and thwart the purpose and plan of human history. In some way and at some time the problem will be solved. There may be times of ignorance which God winks at, but He commandeth all men everywhere to repent because He hath appointed a day in which He will judge the world in righteousness by that man whom He hath ordained.

I have been most impatient with men from whom I could have expected better things. When the voice of numbers in this conflict was uttered against them they turned aside and have fallen away. They have said: "What is the good? The country is against you; the elections have gone; they have left behind them such majorities as generations may not overcome." Faint-hearted men! How they do err, not knowing the Scriptures nor the power of God? I had scarcely finished the reading of the distiller's letter when the words of the Prophet flashed through my mind: "Woe unto them that call evil good, and good evil; that put darkness for light and light for darkness; that put bitter for sweet and sweet for bitter. Woe unto them that are wise in their own eyes and prudent in their own sight! Woe unto them that are mighty to drink wine and men of strength to mingle strong drink: which justify the wicked for reward and take away the righteousness of the righteous from him. Therefore, as the fire devoureth the stubble, and the flame consumeth the chaff, so their root shall be as rottenness and their blossom shall go up as dust; because they have cast away the Law of the Lord of Hosts and despised the Word of the Holy One of Israel."

Brothers, if you would be statesmen, " whatsoever things are true, whatsoever things are honest, whatsoever things are just, whatsoever things are pure, whatsoever things are of good report; if there be any virtue and if there be any praise think on these things."

"That," said Mr. Arnold, " is what both Plato and the prophets mean by loving righteousness and making one's study in the law of the Eternal."

"Now the matters just enumerated," he continues, "do not come much into the heads of most of us, I suppose, when we are thinking of politics. But the philosophers and prophets maintain that these matters and not those of which the heads of politicians are full do really govern politics, and save or destroy states. They save or destroy them by a silent inexorable fatality; while the politicians are making believe, plausibly and noisily, with their American institutions, British constitution and civilizing mission of France. And because these matters are what do really govern politics and save or destroy states Socrates maintained that in his time he and a few philosophers who alone kept insisting on the good of righteousness and the unprofitableness of iniquity were the only real politicians living."

A SIGNIFICANT HOUR.

My dear young friends, there could be no more significant hour for you to be here. If the temperance issue in this state is what men call a forlorn hope then I covet the honor to speak in this hour to the thousands of young people who are before me, through you to the ten thousands, and further through them to other tens and hundreds of thousands on whom is built the hope of this great Republic. If I may be able to articulate what God says and good people believe, my humble speech in this wide open air will be irresistible to a thousand such elections as have just passed in this city and throughout the state and states which have made happy the King's enemies. The simple truth stands, and will stand here as everywhere, the rock of offense against which the ages have dashed their maddened floods of selfishness and sin ; it will stand as a monument to the man and men who have successfully withstood both the floods and ages which have come and gone. Selfishness was doomed before all the selfish men now living were born. And all arguments against the truth are as pitiable as Liebnitz declared them to be when unintelligible.

The American people were committed to an idea which landed on Plymouth Rock that must yet have supremacy and sovereignty over all the broad acres of this fair land. "It was the simple truth," says Mr. Fiske in "The Beginnings of New England," "that was spoken by William Stoughton when he said in his election sermon of 1688 : ' God sifted a whole nation that He might send choice grain into the wilderness.' " This matter comes to have more than a local interest when we reflect that the 26,000 New Englanders of 1640 have in two hundred and fifty years increased to something like 15,000,000. From these men have come at least one-fourth of the present population of the United States." He might have added that the principles and spirit which animate this one-fourth already leaven the whole lump. And when rightly aroused both principles and spirit can now, as ere long they will, control the whole American people.

THE NATION'S HOPE.

Here then, in the presence of the Christian young people, who are the hope of the nation, let us endow the forum from which must go forth the proclamations of government, both divine and human. I stand with reverence to honor the fathers who have gone before us— men whose ages entitle them to a becoming reverence ; but I stand with more profound reverence to honor the young men who are to come after us. Martin Luther studied at Eisenach under a famous master, John Trebonius, rector of the convent of the Barefooted Carmelites. It was the custom of Trebonius to give his lessons with head uncovered, to honor, as he said, the consuls, chancellors, doctors and masters who would one day proceed from his school. "Though you do not see them with their badges," he used to say, " it is right to show them respect." I have learned much from this teacher who taught the child, whose words, when a man, shook the world. What the young men and young women of this decade plan to do will determine what this whole nation must do ten years hence. The resistless grasp of power is already in their hands. Hinder them who may, they are our rulers —their rule only a little delayed. The men and the women who are now fifty years old are already losing their hold on the guidance of the nation's destiny. " The mill will never grind with the water that is past."

In twenty years from to-day the young people who are now under twenty years old will be teachers of all the world's schools, preachers in all the churches of the world, masters of all the world's business; they will be the men and the women who will mould all forms of the world's thought and the world's life, determine the whole trend of the world's history.

Then, as one has wisely said: "Youth should be a savings bank." The sublime moments in which the men and women who are now the young people will be called to act well their part, do their best work, will make such demands on their resources that all possible accumulations will be required to meet their expenditures. No merely rich inheritance can furnish qualifications adequate to the sublime duties which await the next generation. No industry, economy and thrift can exaggerate the needed preparation for the opportunities which stand like an open door before American young people.

Up to the point where the young men and young women whom I am addressing to-day will begin or have begun some things are settled in this great controversy—there are questions which will never be raised again.

SIN AND CRIME OF DRUNKENNESS.

Drunkenness is a shame and a sin. No weakness can justify the indulgence; no position can offer for it an apology; no talent can withstand its humiliation, and no society is safe where it may exist. The higher the position and wider the influence of the person or persons who give themselves up to the sin and crime of drunkenness the greater the shame. For four years this nation has had to bear the humiliation of knowing that one of her highest functionaries at Washington has periodically trailed the habiliments of his office in the gutters of the nation's capital. When through a kind of sentimental deference to the high position he held, the newspapers patiently but inexcusably reported him from time to time to be sick, it was well understood in the circles where he was familiarly known that he was only helplessly drunk. Never was it more a shame and sin, national humiliation, and high crime for men and women to be drunken than at the great ball connected with the centenary of the presidential inauguration at New York. They are the drunkards whose end is destruction, whose God is their belly, and whose glory is in their shame; who mind earthly things.

It is no commendation for a young man who may be seeking employment to say that " he drinks," if it may be only " socially " or never so "moderately." Employers are not seeking that kind of young men to conduct their business. It is a reflection on the quality of the society which exists where the family training produces young men of this character. It is no fitting for the ministry, no qualification for the practice of medicine, and no endorsement for a place in the legal fraternity. The humblest artisan, to be the safest mechanic, must be a sober man.

"Health consists with temperance alone." A sound mind in a sound body consists only with sobriety. Drunkenness invokes disease and death. The drunkard who may escape either or both for a long series of years, can never prove his soundness; he can make no claim to encourage another to do as he is doing, or as he has done.

I was visited at my home, in the early part of this week, by a gentleman who seemed to be as vigorous in mind and body as he could have been thirty or forty years ago, and he is soon to celebrate his eightieth birthday. I asked him how he would account for his good health and long life. He replied instantly, "I was born in the Orkney Islands, which furnished the English army to fight Napoleon, 5,000 soldiers from the 30,000 inhabitants. I was reared, sir, on oatmeal and poverty, and I have always despised *grog*, but never my training." His age and strength may be matched by the age and strength of men who have had other inheritance less favorable to good health and long life. But it is too late in the history of the world's work to discredit good stock and right habits in strengthening and lengthening the life of the race.

Drunkenness can never comport with good morals; the drunkard is a sinner and his sin is sure to find him out. He is the companion of sinners and has his portion appointed him with the unbelievers. Be not deceived; neither fornicators, nor idolators, nor adulterers, nor effeminate, nor abusers of themselves with mankind, nor thieves, nor covetous, nor drunkards, nor revilers, nor extortioners shall inherit the kingdom of God.

If drunkenness is a sin, drunkard-making by the manufacture and sale of strong drink, or by the force of example, is a joint sin. "Woe unto him that giveth his neighbor drink, that puttest thy bottle to him." The social glass is a symbol of the sympathetic sinning which would curse the weak with the force of destructive example. If the apostle's example is to be commended when he says: "It is good neither to eat flesh nor drink wine nor anything whereby thy brother stumbleth or is offended or is made weak," there can be no defense for moderate drinking in this day. "Sympathy," says Mr. Spurgeon, "is especially a Christian's duty." Every professedly Christian man who drinks strong drink moderately is selfishly unsympathetic; he substitutes his own selfish pleasure for his neighbor's well-being and peace. The sideboard with glasses, in the home, stands for such selfishness as is deaf to all entreaty and dumb before the drunken, — nay, such selfishness conspires with the tempter to defeat the tempted. The decanter in the light of the human havoc it now makes, can have only men of poor heart-quality to defend it, and havoc must soon be made of the decanters.

OUR BROTHER'S KEEPER.

What can be said of brothers who have no helpfulness for a helpless brother? Cain has not been alone in his answer to the inquiry of the Lord, Where is Abel, thy brother? when he would excuse himself to his conscience and God, by saying: "I know not; Am I my brother's keeper?" If there may be persons whose environments or personal habits restrain them from an unselfish ministry to the fallen, what justification can they plead before the consciousness of their own moral responsibility?

"They are slaves who fear to speak
For the fallen and the weak."

We are come to times when the preaching of the preacher who may assume for himself the right to drink intoxicants, will avail nothing with the drinkers. The drunkard will say, "Physician, heal thyself." He knows no distance between moderation and immoderation. He never will deny that total abstinence is an absolute safeguard, and the only perfect security for men whose habits and lives have been endangered by heredity and circumstance. But no preacher who will drink, do whatever else he may, can influence the drunkard to believe he is sincere, in any desire he may express, to do the most good in the best way. If he may be sincere, his very tears shed through solicitude for the recovery of the drunkard, will be mere water-drops to mock the drunkard's despair.

The preacher whose lips close on the wine cup is a teacher of weak men who look to him in vain for example, which is always the best part of teaching and preaching. The reform of criminals can never be secured by teachers or preachers who, themselves, do not abstain from all appearance of evil.

The names of prominent preachers were secured in Boston, as I presume they were in Philadelphia, to aid in the interests of the saloon, when most good men combined to oppose the saloon. One of the most prominent preachers who was thus associated with the saloon keepers in Massachusetts was noticed in the daily papers a few days later as one of the best whist players in Boston. Another has long been discredited with good men, because he is reputed to excel (?) in the vein of vulgar or indecent story-telling. Still another, a moderate drinker, had a brother gathered from the streets of Boston and cared for by friends when he was found in a state of helpless intoxication. I do not recall the name of a single person in all the list of clergymen which was printed to help the saloons, that has been prominently associated with the names of the men and women to whom we are indebted most for the promotion of the temperance reform.

I do know that the most prominent name printed was that of the clergyman who refused simply to preside in one of the most notable temperance meetings ever held in Boston, and where a brother clergyman of his own denomination, who was one of the most widely known and reputable of Englishmen, was announced to be the only speaker. Indeed, it was a public reception extended to him, in one of our largest halls, by the temperance people.

One of the first clergymen to identify himself with the saloonists secured to himself the tribute of having a certain mixed drink called after his name by the common bibblers who ordered their drinks in shameless fashion at the open bars.

On the day of the election a lithograph book which contained the opinions of these celebrated clergymen, was sold in the streets of Boston to advertise a certain brand of German beer.

When clergymen are more ambitious to secure the favor of the world's people, than the approval of the self-sacrificing and devotedly pious people, or when they are more commonly identified with the world's people in their sympathies and activities, than they are found to be engaged with the spirit of self-denial in the lowliest offices of mercy, to lift and save the fallen,—and the most fallen—they endanger more the interests of the people they are made to serve, and certainly nullify their own influence more than they ever can hinder the spirit and work of reform.

There were able and doubtless conscientious preachers who opposed the adoption of the constitutional amendments which were submitted to the people, but we found them in Massachusetts to be clergymen who are so far removed from the "common people" as to know little of the great wrongs and temptations which threaten and often overcome them. Without exception the preachers who were down among the struggling poor, and who went about in mission stations to care personally for the widows and orphans of the drunken, knew no compromise with the sin. The great denominations which outnumber all the others, and whose preachers are in the forefront of every reform, stood together like the great divisions of the army, and as they stand to-day, ready for the war of a hundred years, or until the islands shall flee away and the mountains shall not be found.

The personality and following of certain prominent men may give them a present success, for, as Dr. Bowne says, in quoting Malebranche, "if a person expresses himself with facility, is a person of quality and reputation, has a following and is intimate with minds of the first order, he will be right in all he may advance, and there will be nothing, even to his collars and cuffs, which will not prove something." But this is not the working of "the law of the eternal."

THE COMING BATTLE.

The battle which Christian Young People will wage against the enemy of all righteousness, who may be full of all subtlety, has the pledge of the Lord of Hosts. The eternal years defy the armies of the saloon. The principle of prohibiting crime is not defeated—only delayed. The license expedient cannot command a single text book on jurisprudence, nor a reliable precedent in the laws of God or man. Some of our western cities have carried the expedient to quite consistent lengths in the license they have given to lust. The libertine who frequents the brothel, exhibits his license with as much complacency as Christian parents frame their marriage certificates. But when the family compact and relations find no more favor in the eyes of the municipal law than the *liaison* of the dissolute, for a fixed fee, suspicion is cast on the virtue of all women in that city, and the men who prefer marriage certificates should pay for them the same price which other men pay for licentious ones, for they are neither better nor worse.

The methods adopted by aggressive temperance people in averting the evils of intemperance may be modified, as the local or temporary success of saloonists may make it necessary to modify them—the appointments and assignments of the temperance armies may be changed, but the siege about this great citadel of sin will never be lifted, until the unconditional surrender of the saloon forever shall be put in writing, and the red armies of this fierce alien shall be put to an honorable livelihood.

Already the American people are driving the business of the saloon out of the keeping of native Americans. I was told a few years ago that only one American woman could be found who was identified with the business of the saloon in Philadelphia; it may be different now. The properties of brewers and distillers are passing into the hands of foreign purchasers. Let no American interfere. When it may be announced that the great syndicates which manufacture the ruin of our sons and daughters are all in the hands of foreign capitalists, the sentiment of patriotism will come to the help of our great reform, and we will bid the foreigners with their blood-money begone.

OUR STRONGEST ALLIES.

I build my hopes for the triumph of our armies, sisters, brotheis— I say sisters first, for our sisters are the strongest allies we have—on the forces bound about the hearthstones of our Christian people. Woman is the savor and saver of our homes; she will yet be the saver of the Republic. She has more moral courage than man. I have no fear of her political influence; it would be ingratitude unworthy of a citizen of Boston to discredit the influence which overturned the wrong Boston and upturned the right Boston in the elections of a year ago. It is woman who consecrates the hearthstones of our people, and I repeat that it is hearthstones which are the safeguards of the nation.

Adjutant-General Schouler of Massachusetts, while travelling in the Highlands of Scotland, found a man kneeling in the ruins of a cottage. He was curious to know what interest had led him there, and approaching him, he ventured to say that he had seen him kneeling in that humble place. "Yes," said the man stoutly, "I was kneeling at the hearthstone, where there were raised up four major-generals of the English army, and I am one of them."

The defenders of the saloon may pursue us to the doors of our own homes; they may succeed, even in burning down our houses; but up and out from their ashes will come whole armies of victors, every man and woman of whom shall come to honors not unworthy of English major-generals. The echoes of the ages, then, shall resound in the ears of saloonists, keepers and drinkers, forever and forever, "Depart from me, all ye workers of iniquity; I never knew you."

CONVENTION SERMON.

(ABSTRACT.)

Preached by Rev. Geo. H. Wells, D.D., Pastor of the American Presbyterian Church, Montreal, Canada.

(TEXT: EPH. vi, 11–17.)

The Christian is a soldier, and Jesus Christ is the captain of salvation in a war to which death alone brings release from the soldierly duty. This figure is a favorite one with Paul, who speaks of the "fight of faith" and encourages his followers to "fight the battle of Christ." When Paul wrote to the Ephesians he was a prisoner at Rome. In some passages he calls himself the prisoner of Christ.

Paul had often seen the Roman soldiers fall in line and march before their haughty Emperors, and heard the word of life and death passed upon them by their masters. He was a man of quickest and tenderest sympathy and spiritual discernment, and it was not surprising that he should catch the spirit of soldiery and figure the Christian as a soldier of Christ.

The first soldierly duty is to understand the conflict at hand and know his enemy, and so St. Paul tells his followers that their enemies are not human only, and describes them.

There are the vicious, the indifferent, the weak and silly adherents who never stand in line nor march in step with the hosts of Christianity. Muster all these opponents, call out the Christian soldier and say, "Brother, with these you must wage war." But your count is still incomplete. Above, beneath, before, behind, sweeps another dark and threatening host. (See Ephesians vi, 12) The pen of inspiration points us as Christian soldiers to a heavenly armor forged by a Divine hand. ("Put on the *whole* armor of God.") It is to put on the law of God, and to bring the whole will into subjection unto Him. "Having on the breast-plate of righteousness." When we put on Christ's righteousness and plead that, and not our own, then we have a breast-plate that Satan cannot pierce. "And your feet shod with the preparation of the gospel of peace." To have peace with God and to be ready for any service to which he may call — to stand upon the Rock of Ages and know that Satan cannot dislodge us. "Above all, taking the shield of faith." The Christian's shield is large and strong. With it he is "able to quench all the fiery darts of the wicked." Joseph wore that shield, and overcame evil. The Hebrew children had on that shield when the king pointed in fury to the blazing furnace, if they should *dare* to disobey. Peter and John put on that shield when straitly charged not to preach or teach in the name of Jesus. (See Acts iv, 19.) Learn, too, the lesson of Christian unity and co-operation. Learn to *lock shields* with all your Christian neighbors. Our shield bears *our* coat-of-arms — *the cross of Christ!* Its motto is: "The Lord is my Helper; of whom shall I be afraid?" (See Romans viii, 35, 38, 39.) "And take the helmet of salvation." We ought not to be sad, we ought to lift up our heads and rejoice. (See Isa. xxxv, 10.) This is all *defensive* armor, not a weapon of attack. The most blessed word ever spoken by mortal lips, is, perhaps, "peace." May God speed and bring the day of peace! but it is foolish and wicked to cry "Peace, peace," when there is no peace. Even Christ, the Prince of Peace, did not bring peace. (See Matt. x, 34.) The apostle Paul gives his Christian warrior two hands — the left, strong and steady to hold the shield, the right firm and good to grasp the sword, and turn it against the foe. "And take * * * the sword of the Spirit, which is the word of God." It is remarkable that there is only *one* weapon. (See Heb. iv, 11; II Tim. iii, 16.) May it be given us all to put on the *whole* armor of God. Notice *one* thing, there is no armor for the back. Run away from the devil and he will be sure to pursue and overtake you. Let us stand and fight together till victory is proclaimed. Let us stand until the Master calls us to come up higher: then we can say, with the apostle: "I have fought a good fight, I have finished my course, I have kept the faith; Henceforth there is laid up for me a crown of righteousness, which the Lord, the righteous Judge, shall give me at that day."

PASTOR'S HOUR AT THE PHILADELPHIA CONVENTION.

Conducted by Rev. B. B. Loomis, Ph.D., Pastor Trinity M. E. Church, West Troy, N. Y.

When President Clark, a few week since, requested me to take charge of this Pastor's Hour, he was not generally recognized as a doctor of divinity, but was quite worthy of the honor, for there is no other living man who has done so much to doctor the divinity of the age as our esteemed president, and every pastor, whether he endorses this Christian Endeavor movement or not, ought to be profoundly thankful to Dr. Clark for the great doses of tonic of heroic Christian effort that he has been pouring down the Christian churches, and for the effect that he has had in the healthful exercise of earnest Christian work, himself setting the example, and bidding us to follow in his footsteps.

I doubt whether I should have been willing to stand in this presence and open the discussion of the hour, but for the fact that when I invited President Clark, a few weeks since, to attend and speak on Christian Endeavor at two of the great Sunday school assemblies of the land, in whose management I am interested, though he had already more engagements for the summer then fixed than his wise and excellent wife thinks he ought to have undertaken, yet for the sake of the cause he said, "I will come." So we are to supplement this great gathering on Saturday and Sunday next by similar assemblies by the sea, at the Ocean Grove camp-meeting ground, and President Clark and the New York State officers are to be with us there. We invite you all to come. We have abundance of room, and if it rains we have a shelter as broad as this.

In view of these facts, when President Clark wrote to me, saying, "You must take charge of the Pastor's Hour at Philadelphia," I said, "In my heart I can refuse such a man nothing within the realm of possibilities."

I am very glad, however, to remember that I am not alone or chiefly to be responsible for this hour. There are a multitude of brethren in the ministry who can and will bear testimony, from their own personal experience and observation, to the power and adaptation of the Society of Christian Endeavor to help the pastor in his great work. As for myself, I have but two thoughts resulting from my own experience to offer in answer to the inquiry, "How does the society aid the pastor?"

First, I remark that it aids the pastor, as many of us can so well testify, by lifting from his heart one of his heaviest burdens. I envy that pastor neither his head nor his heart, neither his intellect nor his conscience, who can look out over the scores and hundreds of young people of his charge, without deep solicitude for their present and future welfare.

With such possibilities for success, and with such possibilities of peril as are wrapped up, the young men and maidens of this eventful age of the world, no light responsibility rests on the heart of him who is set to guard and guide them. And when as has been too often the case, he sees these dear young people giving their powers to frivolous things, devoting their energies to pursuits and pleasures that are low and unworthy, the sight is so sad that many a pastor has carried a heavy burden in his heart by day and by night. But when young people are set at work in honest, earnest Christian Endeavor for Christ and the Church, when the object of the daily life is to minister to others rather than to be the selfish object of ministry of others; when our young people go out through the length and breadth of the land, impressed with the sublime and solemn idea that they are actual laborers together with God, then no longer does the pastor feel weighed down with intense anxiety for a little flock to be guarded and kept from devouring wolves; but that anxiety is supplanted by gratitude to God for a force at His own right hand of earnest, consecrated, devout Christian workers, ready to second His efforts, and by the Divine blessing push them to success.

And there are many pastors here to-day who have had such an experience as this, and here are some pastors, of whom I know, who have reason to thank God forever for what Christian Endeavor has brought to their own homes in the blessing of their own sons and daughters.

From all such, as far as the time shall permit, we shall be glad to hear.

Just one thought more. In the second place, I have found what God has wrought and is working through this new and divinely-ordained institution. It strengthens the pastor's faith in the speedy triumph of Christ and His church in the earth. The pastor has a great deal to discourage his heart and weaken his faith; but when he finds that the spirit of Christian heroism still lives among the young people of the age, that there are some of them who are not asking for an easy style of religion, that there are great multitudes who are, in fact, saying, "Give us something worthy of our powers, something in keeping with the great sacrifice of the Lord Jesus for us, and we will enter into it and push it with all our God-given energies."

When a pastor looks upon, or even reads about, this magnificent assemblage of the flower of our Christian chivalry, and reads the comments of thousands whom you represent, all pledged to earnest, self-denying, cross-bearing work for the Lord Jesus and His cause, he hears behind these hundreds of thousands the tramp of the on-coming millions in the near future, he has no longer any ear for the pessimistic cry of the infidel that religion is dying out, that Christianity is defeated; but his soul thrills, and his pulses leap for the old refrain, with a higher, holier meaning than ever before, and then himself he sings, " Glory, glory, hallelujah, our God is marching on!" and has fuller, purer faith in the speedy fulfilment of the divine prediction that the kingdoms of this world shall all become one united kingdom in our Lord Jesus, and He shall reign forever and ever.

Brother pastors, what have you to say this morning? What words of testimony as to your appreciation of this great religious movement of the age, and this power to help us in our divinely-appointed work?

Rev. J. L. Scudder, Jersey City, N. J.

I am not here to make a speech, but simply to give testimony, and when you give testimony in your societies, you should always be brief. I wish to say this: that we have in Jersey City, in a church with which I am connected, a society of about one hundred and seventy-five members, and they are not only a Society of Christian Endeavor, but also a society of Christian accomplishment. They can do anything the pastor asks them to do. I regard this society as the hot-house and conservatory next to the church. The atmosphere there is of such a character that it causes everything within it to bloom and come into fruitfulness. This society's influence has been good upon the church upwards and upon the young downwards. Let me tell briefly its influence upon the Friday night prayer-meeting.

This society has driven the pastor out of his seat in that prayer-meeting. I rejoice in it, for I believe no pastor should take charge of his own prayer-meeting. One of the best prayer-meetings I have ever attended was held in our church about two weeks ago, led by a young lady, a member of the Society of Christian Endeavor, who, a year ago, could scarcely open her mouth in the house of God. This was a regular church prayer-meeting, not a prayer-meeting of the Society of Christian Endeavor.

We have coming on a young society. They are not called the Junior Endeavor, but if my wife has anything to do about it, — and she has a great deal to say about these things, — we shall make them a Junior Society. There are some sixty or seventy little ones there. They are learning the spirit of the senior society, so they can lead a prayer-meeting. It interests you to see boys and girls leading a prayer-meeting and speaking almost like clergymen.

I believe that, in this age, we are coming into contact with a new power of organization. What is the new power? It is electricity, which is to supplant steam. I have seen great powers in our churches. The missionary is a great power. It is only one power. The Sabbath is a great power. Printer's ink is a great power. Our railroad system is a great power. There is a new power, and that is this power which comes through the Society of Christian Endeavor and the banding together of our young men and young women in a systematic work for Christ. I thank God for this day.

Rev. William Liske, Philadelphia, Pa.

I have feasted upon the good things that we have already heard here within three days, and I am very glad to bear my testimony, as a pastor, to the excellence of this institution. I recall the answer of a little girl when she was asked what it was to be happy, and she said, "Well, it is to feel that you want to give away all your playthings to the other little girls." It seem to me the pastors who have successful societies of Christian Endeavor feel just like sharing their good things with the others and especially with the young people. They feel that the young people are going into possession of a very great deal of that which is incident to service for Jesus, "Not to be ministered unto, but to minister," and that, to my mind, is one of the very happy features of the Society of Christian Endeavor in its relation to the pastor and the church. The pastor is happy because he sees his young people happy; their hearts are drawn out; their talents are made use of, and they find service on every hand for the work of their blessed God.

Rev. W. H. Tracy, Albany, N. Y.

The Christian Endeavor Society in my church in Albany has been a help to me because of the reasons embraced in each word that forms the name "Christian Endeavor." Our society is an earnest and endeavoring society. They are pushing forward enthusiastically in the work that seems to be mapped out before them. They are natural in their work. They are determined in their work, — not all, but a great many of them, and some who began very feebly, have tried to take steps in Christian labor for Christ, and have determined to push forward.

They are displaying an eagerness to go out into different fields of work connected with the church that is delightful. When I have called upon some of them to come into our general meeting, again and again they have responded by prayer, by short testimony and in a variety of other ways.

They have been aggressive in trying to reach others. We want this aggressiveness among our young people, that they may go out and reach a great many others, especially in the southern part of the city of Albany, where my church is located.

Again, I notice that they have been vigorous. They have been growing and developing. It has been encouraging to me.

We have heard this morning from Dr. Hoyt that the members of the Apostolic Church did not stay away from church because Peter might have been officious and prominent. I think the tendency in our societies is for young people to be a little backward because some one else is too forward. I think that our young people are growing in power, and that they are not going to stay away because some one else may be too prominent in the work.

They are growing natural, determined, vigorous, aggressive and religious in every line of endeavor, so the Christian Endeavor Society is a matter of encouragement and a cause of blessing to our church.

Rev. W. W. Stevens, Oshkosh, Wis.

A little more than a year ago I had in my church a young people's Friday evening prayer-meeting that gave me more trouble than anything else. The question was how to keep the meeting going for an hour. We organized a Young People's Society of Christian Endeavor a year ago last April. To-day I take my place among the boys, and listen to the exhortations and earnest words of the young people. We have a very large meeting. A week or two ago, when the church voted me a vacation, the young people said: "The warm weather is coming and the preacher going, and how shall we keep our meeting up and keep up our society?" Since coming to this convention I received a letter from the president of the society, saying: "We had one of the largest and best consecration-meetings we ever had; four young people arose for prayers." This has been our experience almost weekly for five or six weeks, and our spirit has been contagious. We have now six societies in our city and a growing, flourishing local union. God is in this movement in Wisconsin, and by His help through this society we expect to take Wisconsin for Christ.

Rev. M. H. Bixby, Providence, R. I.

For several years in my church in Providence, R. I., we have had a Society of Christian Endeavor, which has proved a nursery to the church. It has been very successful in bringing souls to Christ, and as God has given to us converts, they have been immediately gathered in and prayed for and developed, so that we have often been surprised at the vigor and earnestness with which these young converts spoke and prayed and worked for Christ.

I do not know of any instrumentality that is so effectual in developing the spirit of prayer and in giving to young converts the power of expression, so that they can come into the regular meetings of the church and speak and pray with freedom and with propriety. Even little children do this sometimes coming from the Society of Christian Endeavor. Not long since we had occasion to plant a new mission, where we needed a superintendent. We went at once to the president of the Christian Endeavor, for he had learned to work for Christ. He gave up the presidency in order to give himself wholly to the mission, and another young man was called to the presidency of the society, and if we had another mission, in all probability we would go for him to be the superintendent of the new mission.

About one year ago God gave me the privilege of baptizing eighteen in one day, and the eighteen were taken at once into the Society of Christian Endeavor, and now they are vigorous workers for Christ. It is a real help to the pastor.

Rev. W. J. Peck, Corona, L. I., N. Y.

I want to testify for my Young People's Society of Christian Endeavor, that, first, they are like the file-leaders in an army; they are file-leaders in their work. In the second place, they are like scouts. They go out and bring in information, and, better than that, they bring in captives to the good idea of Christian Endeavor. And in the third place they keep me awake. They make me study. If I am asleep they rouse me. They make me vigilant. There is spirit in the army that makes the leader awake, and my young people do that for me.

Rev. J. P. Green, Baltimore, Md.

I want to say a word in regard to the value of the society in case of a necessary absence of the pastor. In company with another student I went from Princeton to Baltimore, and the Lord blessed our work so that there were about sixty persons who professed faith in Christ. Of course it was necessary, after a few days, to return to Princeton, and the trouble was, what were we to do in regard to caring for those who professed faith in Christ?

We organized this society, and those who had never taken the name of Jesus upon their lips joined it, and nearly all of those who had recently come into the church became members. What is the result? The most aggressive, active, earnest, consecrated members of the church, so far as you can tell by outward actions and results, are those who lately professed faith in Christ, and who are under the training of the society.

Rev. B. B. Loomis, West Troy, N. Y.

I wish we might all have had an opportunity to speak. I am sure, President Clark, that these young people who are such strong supporters of the church will be glad to know how many pastors there are in this assemblage this morning who appreciate their work and are glad of their help. I wish, whether you are on the platform or in the audience, you would stand up for a moment, so that they may see the number of pastors here.*

A large number of pastors arose in response to this invitation.

REPORTS OF CONFERENCE ON PRACTICAL METHODS.

PRAYER-MEETING METHODS.

Led by V. Richard Foss, Esq., Portland, Maine.

Many preconceived plans and arrangements regarding the conduct of a prayer-meeting may be entirely disarranged by the Holy Guide and Teacher, so that it is all important that His direction should always be sought. The successful leader must depend wholly upon the Holy Spirit, not only for guidance but for power and inspiration. The leader should prepare for the meeting by careful and prayerful consideration of the subject, looking up all Scripture references bearing thereon. Continue much in prayer, both in secret and with others, prior to the meeting, for the outpouring of God's Spirit upon the service and the conversion of souls. Burden yourself for the lost, and take especial pains to invite personally, and get promises from them to attend the service. Ask the workers to sit in the front seats to encourage and help you, and arrange with a few of them to immediately lead off in prayer and testimony when requested. Expect immediate results from the service, and bend all your energies and faith to this end.

Very much of the success or the service depends upon the thoroughness of the preparatory work. The leader should not be the only one concerned, but all should be made to feel their responsibility. A few ought to meet for a brief season of prayer before the hour of service, beseeching for a special outpouring of the ·Holy Spirit upon the meeting.

Commence and close promptly on the hour. I would emphasize this, as many meetings have been spoiled by negligence of the leader in this respect. Have a good organist and chorister that can be depended on. The first five or ten minutes should be used for a praise service. Don't be afraid of too much music. Bring constantly into use new hymns of a lively meter that shall stir the blood and give impetus to the spirit of the occasion. Remember it is not a funeral, and all hymns of a dirge nature should be discarded. Appropriate hymns should be sung spontaneously and sandwiched in during the testimonies, not more than one verse, however, being sung at one time. The leader may read a brief Scripture lesson, or Scriptural quotations may be given from all parts of the house in quick succession. Then should follow twelve or more brief prayers, and those who participate should be requested to ask of God just the one absorbing or chief desire of the heart. Long prayers as well as long exhortations will kill any meeting. They are the "vain repetitions" similar to those uttered by the Pharisees and which Christ so severely condemned. May the Lord deliver us from those who desire to be heard for their "much speaking." In some large meetings twenty-five or even fifty sentence prayers can be offered with great impressiveness. As a rule we do not pray enough in our Young People's Christian Endeavor meetings. Fellow workers, let us encourage more and more the spirit of prayer. The leader should not occupy more than five minutes, except in small meetings, in giving an exposition of the lesson. His remarks should be of a suggestive character, to stimulate rather than to cover the thoughts of the subject. Now, after a hymn is sung, testimonies should be called for, and let the leader suggest that as every Christian is to be heard from each one should occupy only a very brief time. The leader should hold the reins and not lose control of the meeting for an instant. He should be constantly alert and prepared to repeat a passage of Scripture, such as: "Ye are my witnesses, saith the Lord"; "I am the vine, ye are the branches"; or, "Deny self, take up the cross and follow me"; or, if the leader is a singer, he should be ready to start up a suggestive hymn, such as, "Now just a word for Jesus," "Come ye that love the Lord," "Stand up for Jesus," "Work for the night is coming," etc. If the leader is not a singer the chorister should sit near at hand so that he can be used upon the spur of the moment. Five minutes before the close of the meeting the leader should arise and ask for just a word or two from all who have not been heard from. Then let every Christian unite in silent prayer, taking firm hold upon God's promises, that never fail, while the leader throws the net for new volunteers. Don't ask for interested ones to rise for prayers. There is no Scripture authority for such a proceeding. Ask for definite acceptance of immediate salvation. After the meeting closes seek for inquirers. Use not your own words so much as God's Word. Wield the Sword of the Spirit. The old self of sin and rebellion must be slain before the regenerating Spirit can enter and take possession of the soul. A prominent pastor once said, "A prayer-meeting is of but little value unless some one is converted." I hardly agree with him, but do think we should expect and strive for conversions in all our meetings.

Mr. Foss was followed by J. L. Beacham, of Ohio, and Rev. J. W. Chapman, of Albany. Referring to the duty of leaders and the hesitancy of some of them in approaching their work, one speaker exclaimed, "I think any leader ought to be willing to break down for Christ." This exhortation to courageous leadership provoked much applause.

A very spirited discussion ensued, several being upon their feet at once. One question evoked a division of sentiment; that regarding rotation of leaders. The majority decided that the success of the meeting did not depend upon experienced leaders, hence all the active members should be called upon to lead in turn.

The time passed very quickly and all regretted we could not have had more time for the consideration of this important topic.

WORK OF THE LOOK-OUT COMMITTEE.

Led by Mrs. M. L. Selden, Gainsville, Fla.

The meeting to discuss the work of the Lookout Committee was held in the audience room of the Arch St. Methodist Church, at 3 o'clock, Wednesday afternoon.

The large church could not seat the crowds who were interested in the work of this Committee, perhaps the most important of all Christian Endeavor Committees. Many remained standing throughout the session. Nearly every one present had a note-book.

Mr. Howard Terry, of Haddonfield, N. J., conducted the singing.

The session opened with singing, followed by prayer by Rev. Mr. Haines of New York. The leader made a few remarks and closed by saying, when asked to lead this conference, "I could not refuse, as *endeavor* is an important word in our organization. I remembered a gentlemen, who read a paper on "Helpful Committees," at the last convention, and I wrote and asked him to assist me to-day. He kindly consented, and I now have the pleasure of introducing to you the Rev. H. N. Kinney of Connecticut, a "Helpful Committee," who will open our discussion.

Mr. Kinney's suggestions were applauded by all, and his happy manner of putting our duties before us won friends at once. A time-keeper was appointed, and requested to stop all speakers at the end of two minutes.

The leader thought the most profitable way to spend the time, would be to hold an informal discussion, any one asking questions or making suggestions. Immediately several rose; and throughout the entire session the greatest interest and enthusiasm prevailed.

A very pleasant thought suggested was that it was our duty to look out for others, as somebody had once looked out for us. The question, "What shall we do with unfaithful members?" was naturally among the first.

Suggestions in reply included : " use tact, to win them back ; " " set a better example ; " "make meetings more interesting ; " " be patient in your Christian endeavors ; " " have faith and courage ; " "do not reprove, but show your real interest in the delinquent."

How shall the Lookout Committee best act when they think it wise to reject an applicant?

The answer was: "Simply see that the name of such a person never comes before the Committee."

Many societies complained of *inactive* active members. They were advised to reorganize if no other means were effective, and be more careful that those joining as active members knew their duties.

Some questions were answered by a vote of all present, thinking the majority of such an assemblage *must* be right.

A very animated discussion was brought forth by the question: "Should the names of members be brought before the Society, when dropped for absence from three consecration meetings?" Delegates seemed about equally divided both as to methods really existing, and the most advisable methods. Some claimed the Society ought to know it. Answered, "that they had best learn it quietly, as there was much more chance then of reclaiming the indifferent member." The question was about to be decided in the negative, when a gentleman produced the Constitution and proved that he was right, and that names should be brought before the Society. However, the prevailing opinion remained that no action was necessary by the Society, as the member dropped *himself* by absenting himself.

The other work of the Lookout Committee was being briefly discussed, when the hour of closing arrived. The desire was expressed by many that all future Convention programmes would contain conference meetings.

HOW CAN WE HELP OUR ASSOCIATE MEMBERS?

Led by Rev. D. R. Lowell, Pastor of the M. E. Church, Rutland, Vt.

The large church was full, and all seemed eager to speak or to catch every word.

Not a moment was lost, many being on their feet at the same time, to make suggestions, ask questions, or to give information.

After singing "All hail the power of Jesus' name," in which all joined heartily, the leader briefly said: "This Christian Endeavor movement attempts two things: first, to establish and develop Christian character, and, second, to reach out after the unsaved. We are concerned in this conference only with the latter, "How can we help our associate members?"

The Christian Endeaver individual or society lacking this spirit of a burning desire for the unsaved, is not possessed of the real Christian Endeavor spirit.

Now, mark, we are to confer as to *methods*. The fundamental principles of the plan of salvation are *settled*; God has settled them; they abide forever and may not be changed by us. But methods are human, and we are here to confer as to the best methods of helping our associate members.

Now, while I am on my feet let me suggest:

First, use live and persistent efforts to secure their attendance at the weekly meetings.

Second, when there, let them be surrounded by a warm, spiritual, stimulating atmosphere.

No unsaved person can, as a rule, long stand out against such a spiritual meeting. Now, how secure such a meeting?

First, be warm and spiritual yourself.

Second, by frequent, hearty and spiritual singing.

Third, by prompt speaking, praying, etc. Let no time be wasted in the meeting.

Another and the chief means of reaching and helping them, will be by tender, loving, wise, personal appeals.

Remember that they will be very quick in discerning between *real* and *spurious* interest; the former will *win*, the latter will *disgust* and *repel*.

In the conference many questions were asked and answered, and much valuable experience was elicited.

The prevailing sentiment seemed to be that kindly and personal effort was the most important and successful agency. Many illustrations of this were given, several delegates telling how a large proportion of the associate members in their societies were brought into the active membership in this way. In some cases an active member would take an associate member and personally pray for and labor with that member, and in nearly every case, in a very short time, the associate became an active member. Sometimes, two active members would unite for an associate member; sometimes, one of the committees would divide up the associate-member list and give a portion to each active member. In all these cases, the same result followed, and the associate members were reached and saved. One society could get more associate members than they could care for, but most societies found difficulty in getting enough associate members, because they were so easily and constantly being transferred to the active list.

Several delegates gave their experience in securing associate members. The most successful method was to divide up the list of eligible persons and give them to active members, to be looked after. In most cases such efforts were successful.

Several cases were reported where persons who were members of the Church, had been admitted as associate members. This was conceded to be wrong. How prevail upon them to become active members was discussed. In some cases it was easy to persuade them to the change, in others very difficult. Personal appeal seemed the most effective agency here.

The sentiment prevailed very strongly that when the society was faithful and really spiritual there was no trouble in reaching the associate members.

The whole conference revealed a most earnest desire to reach out after and help the associate members. It was an hour memorable to those who were present.

JUNIOR SOCIETIES.

Led by Miss Mary F. Dana, Manchester, N. H.

The element of vitality in the Christian Endeavor movement is evidenced by the changed conditions in junior societies since the convention a year ago, when "nothing like tabulated statistics or especially successful methods could be offered." This year's conference was marked by a readiness to discuss practical suggestions and to interchange experiences.

There was a rapid filling of note-books as the attempt was made to show the supreme excellence of Christian Endeavor principles for junior societies. Loyal to the organization that has helped us, believing that nothing has equalled it in power to create a stalwart, enthusiastic Christianity among the young, we would enroll the boys and girls in the same army. There can, however, be no advantage in, and no authority for, adopting the name of an organization without the essential features of its government. The question, therefore, is: Can the distinctive elements of this movement be successfully worked with children? The prompt reply comes from various quarters, Yes, and the same grand results will follow.

First, there can be no Christian Endeavor society without a pledge. Is this too hard a test for children? The advocates of the little ones rise to their feet in indignation asserting that the fidelity of little children to their promises is such as to put their older brothers and sisters to shame. Taking this for granted, then, it hardly seems that after some preparatory gatherings in which the one party may learn the demands of the society and the other the capabilities of the children, constant attendance upon and participation in their own little meetings is too much to ask. The promises of Christian living in the Model Constitution are helpful additions for active members, and associate members can pledge interest and attendance as in the older societies. The ease and naturalness with which children meet these obligations is the very reason why they should enter the ranks now, and escape the pressure of reserve and formality which has so deadened the enthusiasm of young Christians in the past.

The monthly consecration meeting, so precious a feature of our societies, can be made an equally sweet and tender service with the children, and as one listens to their simple, touching responses during the roll-call one feels that it is pure, natural, honest consecration.

Pledged work for others in the various committees is another essential. Can children meet this demand? It is this very feature which is hailed with delight. Children have no longer only to listen while adults seek to instruct and amuse. Here it is "not to be ministered unto, but to minister." The desire of young folks to be busy is taken advantage of and consecrated. The only limit to the number of available committees is the ability of the leader to instruct and keep them at work. Voices of experience testify to the success of Lookout, Prayer-meeting, Social, Missionary, Temperance and Flower committees in junior societies. Without doubt the Christian Endeavor Society with its broad sympathies and elastic principles is just the place for the children, with methods properly adapted to their nature. Instead of talking about the doctrine of original sin, take particular sins—lying, quarrelling, selfishness. Let discussion of the plan of redemption become familiar talks on Christ's love for children, and on how they can serve Him. Remember that a child loves variety, and take advantage of the many-sidedness of religion and present its every aspect: home and foreign missions, temperance, purity and peace. Teach the children how to pray by praying with them, sentence by sentence, or by naming special subjects for petitions to individual members. Teach them how to gather information on various subjects in marked envelopes or scrap-books. Direct in everything, but let the children work. Provide social attractions for the fun-loving child: games and sports at suitable times, and books, papers and cards whenever possible. Do not attempt to do everything at once. The majority are forced to experiment awhile. Only get the children together and try them. Keep them interested and add new features as the way opens. Enlist the children, everyone, under the Christian Endeavor banners, and hold them "for Christ and the Church."

WORK OF THE SUNDAY-SCHOOL COMMITTEE.

Led by Mr. C. H. Parsons of Salt Lake City, Utah.

Mr. Parsons is Secretary of the Utah Christian Endeavor Union, and also of the Utah Sunday School Association, and is therefore interested in both lines of work.

The meeting was well attended, and a practical discussion on plans, aims and methods of work followed.

Not a moment was lost, several trying to obtain the floor at once.

Methods of work were compared, and successes or failures noted.

It was a success in every particular, and the young people in attendance voted that longer time be given to it another year.

The Endeavor movement is a great aid to the Superintendent of the Sunday School as well as to the pastor, and could the pastors have heard the way they planned to assist both Superintendent and Pastor, they would gladly welcome a society in every church.

The following suggestions may prove helpful to committees:—

First.—Co-operate with the Superintendent, always bearing in mind that he is the commander-in-chief of the Sunday-school forces.

Second.—Don't wait to be asked to do something, but go to the Superintendent, and tell him that you are ready for work if he will find you something to do.

Third.—Prepare a list of all the young people in all the families of your congregation and find out how many of them are not members of the school. Divide up the names of all such among your committee and see that every one has a personal invitation to the school. Also find out if they have any intimate friends who are members of the school, and if so, secure their co-operation and urge them to bring their personal influence to bear on the person in question. The result of this will be that in nearly every case you will gain a member.

Fourth.—Remember that when you have secured their attendance, your work has only just begun. Make it your business to see that they receive a cordial welcome, and that they are introduced to other members of the school. Secure the help of the Social Committee at this point.

Fifth.—Invite them to your Christian Endeavor prayer-meetings, and be there to welcome them when they come. Introduce them to the Lookout Committee.

Sixth.—Search out the strangers who do not attend any church or Sunday-school, and try to get them in. If you succeed, be sure and give your pastor their name and residence, that he may call upon them.

A Sunday-school committee in a California town increased the attendance of their school from about fifty to one hundred and seventy-five in three months. Many others increased the attendance from ten to twenty-five per cent. Every school can be enlarged if the committee will *pray* and *plan* and *work*.

THINGS TO DO.

Consult with the Superintendent. Get the names of those who do not attend Sunday-school.
Send them a neatly printed card of invitation.
Give them a personal invitation.
Interest others in them.
Give them a cordial welcome when they come.
Follow them up until they accept Christ and join the Church.
Pray. Plan. Work.

LOCAL AND STATE UNIONS.

Led by Rev. H. H. Hall, Pastor Congregational Church, Meriden, Conn.

The conference on local and state unions divided the three-quarters of an hour about equally in practical suggestions on the following themes: "How to Work up a State Meeting," "How to Work up a Local Union Meeting," "How to Work a Local Union after its Organization," "Social Gatherings of Local and State Officers," "Presidents' Exchanges."

Rev. J. L. Sewall of Plymouth, Mass., discussed the first of the five topics:

HOW TO WORK UP A STATE MEETING.

First.—Begin twelve months ahead to pray and plan. Note any failure or mistake in this year's meeting, any place for possible improvement while freshly in mind.

Second.—Capture and imprison in memorandum book every bright idea which flashes upon your mind: a timely topic, the name of a good speaker, a new method.

Third.—As to place of meeting: see that the greatest possible Endeavor enthusiasm is previously aroused in the community and adjoining towns, as by a local union or similar meeting; local interest is a great help.

Fourth.—Secure as chairman of the committee of arrangements a *genuine business* man, and let all local responsibility centre in him.

Fifth.—*As to programme:*

(*a*) Arrange it three months before the meeting; this will give none too much time to secure a speaker for every part: six weeks before the convention the complete programme ought to be ready and printed.

(*b*) Have some reliable "all-round" men ready to fill vacancies which are sure to come during the sessions.

(*c*) Use lay talent as much as possible, in a few ten-minute and more five-minute addresses; let those who take these parts understand that time limits will be strictly enforced; if they are inexperienced in public speaking, earnestly advise them to submit their papers to their pastors for criticism.

(*d*) Have every part of the state represented in the list of speakers, not slighting the smaller societies. Try to discover new talent by inquiry of pastors and local union secretaries.

(*e*) *As to character of topics:* divide about equally between those of instruction upon specific points of Christian Endeavor work and those of broader inspiration to better Christian service. Rely on the question-box for all matters of detail in the work of the societies.

(*f*) Secure, if possible, one of our trusted leaders from the National Society, and give him a fair chance, that is, if he gives an evening address, shorten the preliminaries, and have only one address (not exceeding thirty minutes) before his, so that he may have a fresh and not an exhausted audience.

(*g*) Plan places for business where it will not find uninterested audiences; for example, put in a half-hour at the close of the afternoon, when the local audience, but not the delegates, will be anxious to get to their homes.

(*h*) Have frequent devotion interspersed throughout each session, rather than concentrated at its beginning. For good singing, get the

Society of Christian Endeavor books, a cornetist (indispensable) and a chorus choir (very helpful).

(*i*) Remember that the two best parts of the programme are the model Christian Endeavor prayer-meeting (an early morning one, if possible, led by the best leader in the state) and the consecration meeting. If you cannot have Mr. Van Patten lead this last, do the next best thing you can.

Mr. George T. Lemmon of Troy, New York, gave many practical suggestions on working up a local union meeting.

Rev. W. S. Kelsey, president of the Willimantic Union of Connecticut, gave the following article as to the working up a local union after its organization:—

First.—The union must have a good head in its *president*. He must be a live man. The president must not be a figurehead, nor an honorable head, but a *working, planning* head. There must be work done—the president must plan it and see that it is executed.

Who shall be president? Not a minister unless no other suitable man can be found. A business man—a professional man if he is business-like—a young man.

Second.—The local union must have an *object* in all its work. An *object general*, as to be an evangelistic power in the community and a help in the cause of Christian Endeavor. An *object special* for each meeting, as to help the society with which it meets in some weak point.

Third.—As to meetings. Not best generally to hold them often; bi-monthly or quarterly, as often as needs demand. Meetings have been held once a month for a time with profit.

Fourth.—Begin early to plan for each meeting. Plan to bring out local talent. Do not have many speakers from abroad; one such is enough generally. Have printed programmes. The more attractive the better, if inexpensive.

In a word, a local union cannot be kept up well without good *management and work.*

Mr. W. H. Childs of Manchester, Conn., spoke on the value of social gatherings of local and state officers. These meetings should be held at sufficiently long intervals. Themes should be discussed of special interest to the state work. Suggestions would naturally come from the various local unions as to any special success in either new or old forms of Christian Endeavor work. The invitation should include pastors who have shown interest in local or state work. Such meetings would be of great value not only to the State Executive committee but also to all the societies represented.

Mr. A. H. Warner of Bridgeport, Conn., commended heartily the custom of exchanging programmes of the various local union meetings. The advantage was seen in many ways. The outward make-up of the programme, the themes discussed, the best place for devotion in the meeting, the apportionment of time, and the character and quantity of the music. By this "presidents' exchange" each local union, through its presiding officer, could profit by the information given in this easy and natural way.

The various subjects suggested at the conference were discussed by questions and answers. Some of the most eager delegates who were seeking light were from Canada. This conference, as was doubtless true of all the others, showed very clearly that some states are far in advance of others in methods of local and state work.

WORK OF THE MISSIONARY COMMITTEE.

Led by Stephen L. Mershon.

From the Missionary Conference was gleaned the following :—
First.—Every Society should have a Missionary Committee.
Second.—The Reports from every Society where this Committee existed showed that it had greatly increased the missionary zeal of the young people.
Third.—Societies representing churches having the largest number of Missionary Societies reported that the Young People's Society of Christian Endeavor Missionary Committee had been of great assistance to those Societies in supplementing their work among the young. In no case reported had the contrary been found.

SUNDRY SUGGESTIONS.

(*a*) An uninteresting Missionary meeting implies a Missionary Committee not interested.

(*b*) Lack of Missionary enthusiasm proves the lack of Missionary information.

(*c*) Loyalty to Christ's command, loyalty to the Church in its great conflict, and loyalty to our model constitution demands the complete equipment of every Society for the conquest of the whole world to Christ.

FROM FAITHFUL MISSIONARY COMMITTEES.

CEDAR FALLS, IOWA.—Are taking care of a little church out in the country that cannot afford to pay a pastor's salary.

DES MOINES, IOWA —Make it a point to write encouraging letters to Missionaries plodding away in discouraging fields. Have the responsibility of making up the programme of the regular church missionary meetings.

WESTBORO, MASS.—Each small child given 5 cents, to invest and re-invest for a year, and give the profit to the missionary fund.

PROVIDENCE, R.I —Are doing personal work in the Seamen's Bethel prayer meetings.

MINNEAPOLIS, MINN., WESTMINSTER CHURCH. — The members hold themselves in readiness to respond to any summons from three city missions when needing extra or substitute teachers. The Mission Superintendents notify the Chairman of missionary committee, and he issues the notice to report "next Sunday" at Blank mission. This church spends $8000 per annum on these mission schools.

EAST HARTFORD, CONN.—Have started eight circles of King's daughters.

LIMA, IND.—Sustain a public reading room.

EVANSVILLE, IND., GRACE PRESBYTERIAN.—Appoint a Missionary Reporter for each Missionary field in which the Presbyterian Church is engaged. They are to keep the Society posted on all points of their respective fields at every meeting, except consecration meeting, and *very briefly*.

CHICAGO UNION PARK CONGREGATIONAL.—To provoke to good works, the lady members contribute to the Woman's Board, and the gentlemen give to the American Board.

ROXBURY, MASS., WALNUT AVE. CHURCH.—First month is jelly month. Each one attending our missionary meeting is expected to bring a glass of jelly. This is taken by us to the sick during the month. Second month is orange month. Third month is toy month,

This gives us an opportunity to visit the poor, the sick and the children.

EAST BOSTON, SARATOGA ST. CHURCH.—Have given some money at various times to the Children's Mission band fund to encourage them in their efforts.

PHILADELPHIA, WEST SPRUCE ST. CHURCH.—The young ladies, the Home Mission, and the Foreign Mission bands each constitute a Committee to report at regular intervals to the Young People's Society for Christian Endeavor in their missionary meetings.

THOSE NOT OBEDIENT TO THE GREAT COMMAND.

———, OHIO.—We have no missionary committee, and we do *very little* in the missionary line.

———, MASS.—We have *no* missionary committee, and are *not engaged* in missionary work.

———, MASS.—We have *no* missionary committee, but a *few years ago* we raised seventy dollars for missions.

———, N. Y.—*No* missionary committee, *no* plans for making interesting missionary meetings, are doing *nothing* for missions. (NOTE.—A prison with thousands of inmates at their very doors.)

COMMITTEE WORK.

Educate.
Interest.
Incite to individual effort.
Guide into practical channels of Missionary need.

'TIS SO!

Information $+$ consecration $-$ selfishness $\times$ by activity and $\div$ by every individual Christian Endeavor $=$ successful missionary effort.

PHILADELPHIA MINT-INGS.

By Rev. James L. Hill, of Medford, Mass.

Ho! for St. Louis! Two young ladies inquired the way to the Armory. "Follow the crowd! everybody's going!" was the reply from a Philadelphian. —— The delegates were as closely placed in that great auditorium as the rows of pins in a paper. —— Under a heavily-inked picture in a Philadelphia paper were printed the words Rev. F. E. *Black*. Correct! —— How smoothly everything went! Thanks to President Clark.—— Everybody remarked that the delegates are increasingly satisfied with a discussion of the deeper subjects. —— And where were the cranks? Well, we suppose that there are few places so uncongenial for people of that ilk. —— If anybody wants to know how to prepare for a convention, write to the committee of nine, in care of Mr. Shumway.—— Telegram: "President Harrison sends greeting to this convention. Public business prevents his attendance."—— After one has visited Europe he desires to go again. So is it in the matter of our conventions. 'Rah for St. Louis! —— "The society not undenominational but interdenominational." A member of the society is not a *mugwump*. Political elections prove that little can be accomplished outside of some party.—— Speakers exceeding their time were stopped by electricity.—— Dr. Deems drops into verse: —

> "The world is wide
> In time and tide,
> And God is guide, —
> So do not hurry.

> "That man is blest
> Who does his best
> And leaves the rest, —
> Then do not worry."

The final prayer of consecration, by Dea. Choate Burnham, seemed like Abrahamic intercession. As if inspired, he lifted up the audience. Would that God would put His Spirit into other laymen! —— Odd, wasn't it, that continual applause of a sermon? But the delegates could not seem to help it; he preached so! —— The dinner given at the Belmont to the trustees and to Dr. Hamilton and Mr. Wilder, was an exceedingly pleasant affair. —— *Kindred Spirits*. Those who catch the idea that animates this great movement, it was suggested, could write as titles after their names " K. S."—— And one clerk at John Wanamaker's asked another, who is a member of the society, " Are all these delegates rich?" " No. They have not gone up into riches, but have gone down into sacrifice."—— *Reaching the Masses.* They were at the Armory. As the delegates thronged out, singing as they went, the unchurched young men caught up the contagious sacred song. That is it. The rich and poor meet together; the Lord is the maker of them all.—— The sermons in this series of summer sessions have been a succession of successes. The audience was electrified! The preacher a pure fountain of eloquence.—— The morning prayer-meetings were wonderful. Speakers stood waiting. Prayers were even coincident. Two hymns would sometimes be launched simultaneously in different parts of the house. —— " I hail five hundred thousand young people committed to Christian Endeavor, for during a ministry of thirty years, I have known five million people committed to Christian laziness."—— In the reports of the convention in other organizations, an omission of the sermon is suggested. It has always been with us of unsurpassed interest. We are not someway impressed by any decadence of the pulpit.—— The conducting of the final consecration-meeting left nothing to be desired. It was perfect.—— Nothing moved the hearts of the trustees more than the eloquent and earnest pleas for next year's convention. Ably done, young men!—— One of the seventeen delegates from a church near Boston, fearing she might not rise early enough to enjoy everything, obtained an alarm-clock. This was not the one told of by Dr. Hoyt that a lady bought one evening, and on her way home stepped into prayer-meeting. By anticipating its morning's work, it cut in two what promised to be a very long prayer.—— Said a lady of acute perception, " How it broadens us to see things done as well as we could do them, yet in such a different way."—— Prof. Wm. G. Fischer, for ten years teacher of music in Girard College, author of " I Love to Tell the Story," " Whiter Than Snow," and "I Am Trusting, Lord, in Thee," had an unlimited amount of animation and magnetism. Two hundred fresh-faced young people of Philadelphia composed the choir.——" I do not object to being notified that my time is up, but I do not like the sneering sound of that buzzing bell. Its tone implies, ' Oh, you are not saying anything to the purpose; stop!' "—— " In view of eternity, I stand to-day in this august presence and declare that I am not less loyal to my denomination after thirty consecutive years of service in its pulpit because I enter my earnest protest against the transfiguration of existing Christian Endeavor Societies into denominational organizations under new names." — *Rev. Dr. Leech of the M. E. Church.*—— Prof. Fischer, the leader for months of the Moody and Sankey choir, said, " Make nothing of me; I am here to cheer for the crowd."—— We confess to some pride in the young men that are applying their business methods to the conduct of our conventions. —— A young lady, in presenting the claims of the Northwest for the next convention, said she remembered the first time she heard a lady pray in public. She found she was from Massachusetts and was a member of a Christian Endeavor Society.——

The bearing of the delegates from the Twin Cities was touched with sublimity when, having lost the next convention, they began to rejoice with St. Louis.——The Armory was hard to leave. Its atmosphere was one of song and prayer. Earnest Christian life hallows all our memories of it.—— "No missionaries go where they do not find the kerosene lamp. Earlier enterprise is exhibited in introducing the light taken out of the dark earth than the Light from heaven. Commercial earnestness exceeds Christian zeal."——Much regret and sorrow were expressed at the enforced absence of Secretary Ward and President Van Patten.—— The custom of starting a hymn as the audience was passing out of the great auditorium seemed new in Philadelphia, and excited wide remark. Sometimes the tune was carried along for several blocks.—— The eloquent and forcible presentation of the claims of the twin cities of Minnesota had behind it twelve hundred miles of travel and an expense of four thousand dollars.—— After the greatest of our conventions, our hearts beat quick with excitement as we anticipate St. Louis.— *The Golden Rule.*

AN OUTSIDER'S VIEW.

(*From The Philadelphia Inquirer.*)

A Glance at the Motives and Movements of the Whole Convention.

The Christian Endeavor Convention has appeared, to the outside observers of their work, to have practically proven Burns' poetic line, "A man's a man for a' that." There never was a great convention of people where such a degree of sociability and a disregard of formality prevailed. There never was a great convention in which everybody knew so little about the personality of everybody else, and yet everybody was willing to trust everybody else to be his or her equal in claims to courtesies. They were nearly all strangers to each other, and yet all were the best of friends at first meeting, their very membership in the society being a pledge of their social worth, good-will and ingenuousness.

At their conferences, dozens of speakers rose and had their say, and none could tell who they were that spoke, not even the chairman or chairwoman of those meetings. They all had note-books, and they took down, not *who* spoke, or did this or that, but invariably they jotted down what they said or did. It was the substance of what was done that they wanted. How many thousands of times was this sentiment reiterated in their meetings, in the phrase, "Quality, not quantity."

Throughout all the debates and programmes, none have heard of any wrangling or hot, wordy contests. Never has there been the slightest obstinacy to the authority of the gavel. Their proceedings have been conducted with such marvelous fidelity to parliamentary rules as to suggest a Utopian order of things. Their rules of order seem not to be enforced by any iron-handed authority, but by the thorough harmony of spirit and intention that pervades their work. The laws of parliamentary proceedings to them have not appeared to lie in the letter, but in the essence and spirit of the rules, in the necessity of order and parliamentary politeness. No biting sarcasm, no ironical indulgence, no scornful flings, or irritating, sour remarks have been heard, and, if there should be, a sweet hush of silence, in keeping with their Christian professions, would immediately put the speaker to blush.

The unanimity of practice and profession with them is further promoted, too, by the place to which the fair sex is elevated in their ranks—to a place of absolute equality. The male members have been the concrete of gallantry in their recognition of women's voices in the convention. The stronger voices of men have never dared to drown out or suppress by sheer masculine strength the rightful speech of a feminine member. Mutual recognition of the smallest rights of thought and speech by all of them prevented any loss of time in convention disputes, although they have all been remarkably quick to seize the chance to say a word, and their thoughts and differences have been expressed with unconflicting enthusiasm. The outsider cannot be present at their deliberations without feeling the existence of a sixth sense in the hall—the sense of parliamentary unity, as though the thousands of voices were but parts of the same conventional being. They have personified the complete subjection of little selfishnesses to the general wish, always manifest and in supreme control of their gatherings.

"How hypocritical is formality!" exclaimed one speaker, during the week, in talking about the best way to bring strangers to their meetings. They put aside formalities and shake hands and talk with strangers as frankly as though they were lifelong friends. They immediately trusted each other to be honest upon meeting. Of the thousands of prayer-books left on the benches not a single one has been carried away. A lost umbrella was returned to its owner on even a rainy day, and the finder had none to go home with. Everything in their affairs has seemed to be, in a great measure, the reverse of what it is in the outside world. They don't feel their dignity so much as to be above recognizing everybody. No one "looks down on" any other. No one sneers at anybody. None deserve a sneer.

In short, as said in the beginning, this Christian Endeavor Convention seems to have personified the "Golden Rule" and Burns' song:

"A man's a man for a' that,"

and to have out-Burned Burns, as they would say, too,

"A woman's a woman for a' that."

OPINIONS OF THE PRESS.

EDITORIALS FROM THE RELIGIOUS PRESS.

One of the most gratifying features of the late convention was the uniformly discriminating and courteous notice which the movement received from the Philadelphia press. Every one of the leading journals devoted a large portion of its space to comprehensive reports of the meetings, and nearly all of them gave an editorial each day upon the society and its work. These editorials, as we happen to know, were the honest expressions of practical newspaper men who are in the habit of estimating the worth of a thing from the standpoint of public interest and utility. They had heard of the movement before this tidal wave of enthusiasm struck Philadelphia; but they knew little of its scope and meaning. The tone of all their utterances is that of great surprise at the sight of so much vital religion and practical Christianity. Some of them had evidently been indulging in Mr. Savage's delusion that the final surrender of orthodoxy is at hand; but the great convention, with its constituency of half a million aggressive young Christians, opened their eyes to the fact that the banner of the cross is not likely to be furled during this generation.

That vast assemblage of nearly seven thousand of the brightest young men and women of the country, the eminently practical drift of everything which was said and done, the administrative and business ability of the young men who managed the details of the convention, the fact that the delegates were manifestly more interested in the order of the programme than in the sights of Philadelphia, the spirit of earnest loyalty to Christ and the church which pervaded the meetings,—all these things impressed an outsider as being decidedly unique and significant; and they were interpreted by the secular press as "a cheering sign of the times," indicating that a new day of Christian life and activity is dawning upon the churches. When we think that to-day the leading journals of the largest city but one in the country are disposed to devote whole pages to reports of a Christian Endeavor convention, and to vie with each other in appreciative editorial comment; when we think that the President and Postmaster-General of the United States saw fit to recognize the importance of the movement, the one by a congratulatory telegram, the other by his personal attendance upon the convention, we cannot help thinking that it was only four years ago that even some of the religious journals refused to give in their columns a respectable report of the annual convention.

It is in no spirit of vain-glory that we speak of these facts, but with devout gratitude to God, in whose hands we believe the Christian Endeavor cause has been from the beginning.—*Editorial in The Golden Rule.*

The Convention of the Christian Endeavor Society has come and gone. It was a beautiful and impressive sight to see five thousand delegates from all parts of the land, in the beauty, vigor and enthusiasm of young manhood and womanhood, assemble in midsummer for prayer, praise and conference. Everything passed off to general satisfaction. . . The topics considered were of a spiritual and practical nature. Good judgment and harmony characterized the discussions and deliberations. Wise and experienced heads guided affairs, and the representatives seemed imbued with a lovely spirit. The prayers were earnest, the singing inspiring, and the remarks generally apt and helpful. Howsoever viewed, truth and candor must pronounce the convention a decided success. . . Its distinguishing endeavor is conformity to Jesus Christ, a growing love for His person, character, life and truth, and supreme consecration to His service. . . . This popular manifestation of how many young Christian workers there are all over the land, has been a kind of revelation to thousands who have been fearing for the foundations of Christianity in an age when infidelity, rationalism and agnosticism are making such loud boasts, and shows that there are myriads who have not bowed the knee to Baal, and that the gospel of our Lord has still an invincible and aggressive might to master man's nature and meet the wants of humanity. In the Christian Endeavor Society we have a demonstration of the efficiency and harmony of the co-operative principle within denominational lines. Here are thousands banded together as an organization, yet composed of separate societies within and in connection with the individual churches of the various denominations of Christ's church. . . . Among other things its late convention proves the great advantage of large and enthusiastic gatherings in a noble cause, with stirring speakers and practical subjects for consideration, the value of the social element in an organization, and the impetus which a movement skilfully engineered and properly advertised receives in a large city. . . . It has untold possibilities of development and usefulness, and needs the prayers and sympathy and co-operation of the aged and experienced as well as of the youthful and the enthusiastic.—*Editorial in the Presbyterian.*

The recent annual convention of Christian Endeavor Societies at Philadelphia is, so far as we recall, the largest delegate religious assemblage that Christendom has yet witnessed; and as such is a noteworthy event. As appears in the report published elsewhere, its meetings were marked by deep spiritual tone, and by a well-grounded enthusiasm in the work of Christ and His Church. Manifestly it required a strong motive to draw so many young people to the necessary discomforts of travel and temporary stay in a city as hot as Philadelphia at this season; and we are glad to believe that the chief attractive force was a genuine interest in Christian living and Christian work. We also note with gratification the general conservative drift and spirit of this body.—*Editorial in the Congregationalist.*

It is not denominational in any sense. If it were denominational, it would be a failure. Denominationalism has seen its day and must henceforth decrease. Any Christian movement inaugurated for the upbuilding of the cause of Christ and the promotion of pure Christianity should not be hampered and ruined by sectionalism and party zeal. The Christian Endeavor movement was inaugurated for the young people everywhere who love the Saviour and who want to serve him acceptably. Most all Protestant churches have such societies, and they are proving to be great auxiliaries to these churches in training young men and women for the various activities of these churches. They are serving a good purpose from another standpoint, in that they are bringing the young people of the various churches nearer together, so that the future churches will standing closer fellowship.—*Editorial in Christian Evangelist.*

The Christian Endeavor movement has much the same meaning as Mr. Moody's Northfield encampment for college students. The Church has questioned what she should do for her young people; the young people have decided to do for themselves. The Church has tried to amuse them; they show that they want not amusement, but work. The Church has attempted to do for them; they now find their satisfaction in an attempt to do "for Christ and the Church." They have not been drawn together by a desire for pleasant companionship; instead, they ask that they may be used for God's glory. "Not to be ministered unto, but to minister," is their motto. Self-consecration has roused their zeal.

These thousands go forth with no flashing of lance; they are not gay with banners; they do not glory in shedding the blood of infidels. The enemies of the Church have gathered for attack; the young men and women have flocked to its help. "The banner of the Great King goes forward;" they will follow the conquest. That is the spirit which they show. Keeping that enthusiasm, they must conquer all lands for Christ.—*Editorial Christian Inquirer, New York.*

Our last General Synod numbered nearly two hundred delegates, and that of the Presbyterian General Assembly between five and six hundred delegates, and both were regarded as large bodies. The last Democratic and Republican conventions numbered between seven and eight hundred delegates, and both were acknowledged large. The Young Men's Christian Association Convention in this city, last May, had 1,000 representatives and required the Academy of Music to hold its evening meetings. But the Society of Christian Endeavor counted 6,500 delegates and required the Armory of the First Regiment, with a capacity of seating 7,000 hearers, and which proved inadequate to accommodate the delegates and the crowds that attended this convention.—*Editorial in the Lutheran Observer.*

The Young People's Society of Christian Endeavor now represents the church in its more progressive and aggressive work. It is a method, not so much for putting young people at work, as for putting all people at work. This method is worthy and wise. Whatever was the original purpose and method of the society, each society may now have, as a part of itself, a "Junior" society. The creation of this annex has been proved to be necessary, and it is as wise as has been the whole course of this movement. Pastors and societies should see to it that "junior" societies are at once formed. In each organization such a branch seemed necessary for doing the work which the society is designed to do. For the society, in all its varied labor, we have the heartiest esteem, and to each of its hundreds of thousands of members we bid godspeed. May they each be true to the motto of the society, " For Christ and the Church."—*Editorial in The Advance.*

Here there is an organization made up chiefly of the young, bound by sacred pledges in various definite ways to endeavor to lead a Christian life and to work for the building up of the Christian church. When we take in view the nature and extent of this organization, we can see what a powerful agency it is and how widespread is its influence. It is a force to be used distinctly and designedly to advance the interests of "evangelical" Christianity. . . . Instead of criticizing this movement cannot Unitarians learn something from it? We see here what a mighty power can be wielded by an effective and widespread organization. It would be wholly foreign from the spirit and ideas for which we stand to attempt an exact copy of this association. But may we not, by the more general organization of the young of our churches in associated action, add to the growth and strength of these churches.—*Editorial in the Christian Register, Boston.*

It seems to us altogether admirable and immensely useful that there should be certain great undenominational movements like the Society of Christian Endeavor, in which the spirit that is larger than any sect may find expression and a theatre of action. . . . . Large acquaintance and sympathy with the work and workers of other churches conduces at once to breadth of view and catholicity of spirit, and it is in great undenominational or interdenominational gatherings that such acquaintance is cultivated.—*Editorial in the Christian Leader, Boston.*

As state after state arrived and was assigned to its section, the delegates immediately made themselves at home. There was nothing formal about the affair, but every one acted like a member of a big family which had gathered for a grand reunion. Such throughout was the character of the convention, and a more fraternal gathering has never been witnessed in this city.—*From The Lutheran Observer.*

Said an eminent clergyman of Philadelphia, "As I sat upon that platform and looked down upon that sea of young faces, I could hardly refrain from a passion of tears." We think a good many serious people had a similar experience as they thought of the tremendous possibilities enshrined within that mighty host of young Christians. The flower and strength of our American churches were represented there. Over five thousand young men and women pledged to the grandest ideal that can fill and possess the human soul—a life of active service for Christ. Beauty and strength, hope and courage, devotion and aspiration, all that makes youth glorious, held for God and His future under the power of an earnest Christian purpose.

This is what gives to the Christian Endeavor movement its phenomenal impulse. This is why it awakens such universal interest, and wins for itself such general sympathy. Wherever its conventions are held, the people are strangely moved by what they see and hear. So many bright, energetic young men and refined young women bent on religion is an unprecedented sight. The saloon-keepers come to their doors, rough men stop and stare, and in a good many hearts hardened by sin and business cares there is kindled by the sight of these earnest young crusaders a feeling akin to that of tears; a half regret over a life misspent, and a half wish that the unspent part of life may be better. A good many people who are generally indifferent to religious matters felt their hearts come to their throats as they witnessed that grand scene of Wednesday evening.—*Editorial in The Golden Rule.*

EDITORIALS FROM THE SECULAR PRESS.

A Cheering Sign of the Times.

The Christian Endeavor Convention, now in session in this city, is one of the most remarkable indications of the real character of modern religious feeling to be found anywhere. Coming so closely on the heels of the debasing New Orleans affair, and thus placed in strong antithesis to that, it furnishes a quick, practical answer to those pessimists who find in the wide-spread interest shown in the prize fight an indication that society is not growing better as it grows older.

There could not be a better answer than the marvelous growth of this young movement—it has not even organization enough to be, strictly speaking, a society—among the more elevated classes of the community. Moral and intellectual elevation is meant, of course, for the Christian endeavor work knows no distinctions of rank, wealth, color or condition. It asks but two questions: "Is he a Christian? Will he work? Then let him come with us."

The Christian Endeavor idea combats all that is debasing or even selfish in human nature. Like the monks of old, he who joins in the work must not only renounce all sinful pleasures but must accept work repugnant to all his natural instincts. He is not asked to be a fanatic, but he is given to understand very plainly that if he wishes to join the ranks of the Christian workers he must do Christian work and his full share of it.

No allurement is placed before him. He is promised no entertainment, nor even a reward of merit in this world. The appeal is wholly to his sense of duty; the only reward offered is that promised to the "finally faithful." Moreover, the originators of the movement did not advertise it. They organized the first society for their own local work and did not tell the world about it until the pressure of inquiry forced them to do so. Then a book, "St. Paul's Problem," was written to explain the motive of the new movement and the readily adaptable methods of working, and when that was published the young people in churches of all denominations, all over the country, took up the idea—and the growth of eight years is exemplified in the 10,000 delegates, from every part of the United States and Canada, assembled in this city to-day.

Now, when it is remembered that this great and rapid growth has been among the very class where it could be least expected, the younger members of society, fond of amusement, little given to serious thinking, not at all inclined by nature to lively religious work, it must be accepted as a very hopeful indication that society is growing better, that under all its froth and foolishness, its open sin and secret vice, there is a strong and very general sentiment of devotion and a desire for the higher life. If it were not so, the present convention would be impossible.—*Editorial, Philadelphia Inquirer.*

The eighth annual convention of the Christian Endeavor Society was yesterday organized in this city, in the spacious hall of the First Regiment Armory, at Broad and Callowhill streets. This body of zealous workers represents a very large proportion of the religious community of the United States, the delegates being of many denominations and all earnestly interested in the promulgation of religious truths and the spiritual helping of mankind. The work of the convention will be important, as it will be done by men and women of eminent ability and distinction, and will be of such a comprehensive character as to cover a wide range of thought and action. The delegates come from every part of the country, and have been chosen for their conspicuous fitness to execute the work in which the society is engaged. Philadelphia's hospitality is never stinted when worthy guests are within her gates, and she could hold none worthier than these of the Christian Endeavor Society, whose vocation is that of seeking and proclaiming spiritual truth. The list of subjects to be considered by the society is a long one, and shows how general is the area of thought upon which the delegates propose to enter.—*Editorial, Public Ledger, Philadelphia.*

CHRISTIAN ENDEAVOR SOCIETY.

The Christian Endeavor Society of the United States, now holding its annual convention in this city, is a new expression and partial realization of the impulse towards union, or at least united effort, on the part of the active members of evangelical Protestant churches. Its aim is to make active Christians as distinguished from professing Christians, and its centre and rallying point is the weekly prayer meeting.

Experience teaches that to make a man or woman thoroughly interested in any enterprise it is necessary to make them take an active and energetic part in promoting it. It is in the practical application of this principle that members and attendants on Christian churches are made zealous Christian workers. The Christian Endeavor Society does not wait to get them into the church before placing obligations upon them, but begins with the prayer-meeting, and there imposes a pledge upon its members which is the essential feature of all the societies. It binds those taking it to attend every weekly prayer-meeting, and to take some part, aside from singing, in every meeting unless prevented by absolute necessity. There are other pledges as to daily prayer, Bible reading and leading a Christian life, which are compatible with a comparatively passive Christianity. It is the obligation to "speak in meetings," with the confidence which it gradually inspires, and the zeal which it confirms, that makes the Endeavor Societies an efficient training school for the early development of promising material for deacons and elders, teachers and class leaders, and a most valuable support to the ministry in maintaining a live Christian spirit among the laity, and especially among the young.

The movement had its small beginning only eight years ago in Portland, Me., but it has grown in this short interval until all the societies include in their membership some half a million members. Their strength, however, lies less in the quantity than in the quality of their membership, for they include in their ranks the cream of the Protestant Church militant—its youth, energy and enthusiasm. They have no use for drones. It is the workers they take in, and the influence of example and the contagion of enthusiasm make workers of nearly all who come within their influence.

Since Robert Raikes organized the first Sunday-school and its subsequent rapid development as an arm of the church, there has been no single church agency set on foot comparable to this Christian Endeavor movement. Its great convention in Armory Hall is a most interesting and impressive sight. Those who are given to bewailing the degeneracy of the times and the decline in the influence and activity of the Christian Church should visit this convention, where they could hardly fail to learn something very much to their advantage.—*Editorial, The Press, Philadelphia.*

THE CHRISTIAN ENDEAVOR CONVENTION.

Those who think that Christianity as a vital force has had its day will not have that impression strengthened by the sight of the Christian Endeavor convention. There is something inspiring in the presence of these 5,000 representative young Christians gathered from all quarters of the land and in their songs and earnest utterances. They are in the hey-day of their youth; they are sincere in their purpose and enthusiastic in performance. The most indifferent observer must be impressed with the thought that they constitute a leaven with power to permeate and influence for good every section of the country.

The bane of Protestant Christianity has been its tendency to divide and subdivide into innumerable sects, many of which spent fighting each other the force and energy that should have been devoted to the propagation of the religion of Christ. The Young Men's Christian Association was the first organization that attempted to promote the principle of co-operation in religious work. The Christian Endeavor movement is an advanced step in the same direction, the most important characteristic of which is that it enlists the young people of both sexes, thus more than doubling its working power, experience showing that women are largely in the majority in the membership of the churches. The movement deserves the highest commendation, as well for its recognition and cultivation of the co-operative principle, as for its recognition of the fact that a working Christianity is the only Christianity that amounts to anything.

There is another tendency in modern Protestantism which is quite as bad as intense sectarianism, and which it should be the particular mission of the Christian Endeavor Association to counteract, and that is the tendency of the churches to exclusiveness. If these young people can break down the wall between the churches and the masses and penetrate the hidden strata of our large cities, mentioned by Dr. Beckley in his address on Tuesday, the community will have occasion to rise up and call them blessed. This is a kind of work that won't figure much in conventions and will have to be done, if done at all, by those who don't sound a trumpet before them. And yet it is the most imperative religious duty of the hour. If the Christian Endeavor Associations demonstrate that they are sufficiently inspired by the spirit of Christian self-sacrifice to do it they will show that they have sized up their work correctly and that the name of their association signifies something more than empty sound. Christianity to-day is in greater danger from the selfishness of its professed followers than from the attacks of all the infidels and free-thinkers in the universe, and the mission of its real followers should be to demonstrate that they practice as well as preach the faith that they profess.—*Editorial, The Times, Philadelphia.*

The Christian Endeavor Convention, now in session in this city, is a midsummer wonder to the thousands of people who have not noted the swift growth and development of this new motive power in church work. Its object appears to be to develop working Christians as distinguished from professing Christians, speaking Christians as distinguished from the silent sort. The enthusiasm and interest of the present convention and the numbers in attendance are something phenomenal, and give an idea of the energy latent in united Christian effort.

The closing day of the Christian Endeavor Convention was perhaps the most interesting of all. Postmaster-General Wanamaker showed his interest in this great moral agency by coming over from Washington to take part in the convention. He was given an enthusiastic reception in recognition of his practical Christian work. Philadelphia has been greatly honored by this great gathering of religious workers, and will be glad to welcome them back at any future time.—*Editorial, The Press, Philadelphia.*

Through its various committees the society takes care of its own devotional meetings and promotes those of the church, it provides flowers for the pulpit and for the sick, visits those who are astray or in need, introduces strangers, looks up recruits for the Sunday school, supplies social and literary entertainments for its members, and co-operates actively in all the work of the church. It supplements the Sunday school and furnishes what has been aptly called a "church porch"—a kind of vestibule to the church itself. Naturally, its growth was viewed at first with distrust by some conservative people, as if it presaged influence which might claim too great independence of church control, but it has justified its existence and proved its value by its direct loyalty to church and pastor.—*Editorial in the Boston Journal.*

In fact, the work of the society, by its very nature, is purely local. It is a branch of the church as is the Sunday school. Its future, if it continues to be guided divinely, as it seems to have been thus far, will, perhaps, secure the evangelization of the world. Certainly nothing has ever so quickened and brought into activity the forces of the church as the methods of Christian Endeavor. If the society succeeds in ridding churches of their drones, in making church-members active, zealous and earnest "laborers together with God," as President Clark put it in his motto for the year, if it can set into motion the dormant forces, it will certainly have a glorious future. No man could have told, ten years ago, the present status of this society. So no man can tell what the next decade will bring forth. It remains for the individual members of the society to be true to their promises, and a great moral reform will surely come, which may do much to better the world.—*Editorial in New Haven Register.*

The Societies of Christian Endeavor have had a famous meeting in this city, marked by great attendance, zeal and enthusiasm. Such an organization of young folks, enlisted for actual work, cannot fail to make itself felt in promoting Christian faith and inspiring faithful observance of that faith. Its influence, powerful and widespread, is wholly for good.—*Editorial, Public Ledger, Philadelphia.*

The swaying from side to side of over 5,000 bodies; the grand outburst of melody from 5,000 and odd throats; a surging line of beautiful women, presenting a broad phalanx filing through the wide portals of the First Regiment Armory, and a rhythmic volume of music, such as has never before been heard in this or any other city; that was the inspiring and picturesque closing last night of the second day's session of the greatest convention ever held in this city. For a full half hour that dazzling throng filed slowly from the great hall out to the street. It was a kaleidoscopic song picture, a grand chorus of 5,000 voices, making the walls of the armory ring with songs of praise, while the tramp, tramp, tramp of the moving throng kept time to the music. As the vast throng marched on, hymn after hymn was taken up, that floated through the hall out into the corridors and down into the street, where they were involuntarily taken up by the crowds of wondering spectators attracted to the spot, and soon Broad street was like one vast camp meeting, through which the beautiful music of Christian Endeavor made an unceasing flow of melody.

Enthusiasm is no word for the spirit with which the Christian Endeavor Convention is being conducted.—*Philadelphia Inquirer.*

I have seen many conventions in many lands, among them the Convention of Christian Endeavor at Saratoga, two years ago; but nothing has impressed me as much as this convention. To see thousands of such persons as are here, packed in such an edifice; to witness the glow of the thousands of eyes under the spell of the eloquence of the speakers; to be in the center of the wide circle of young, intelligent, chastened enthusiasm, and to hear that singing which swells like the mighty rush of many waters, I feel that it would be worth a voyage across the Atlantic to be present at such an assembly of the Lord's army.—*Dr. Dunn in New York Mail and Express.*

CORRESPONDENCE.

Rev. Dr. S. V. Leach, of the First Methodist Episcopal Church, Albany, speaking for the trustees of the United Society, declared with great emphasis and amid much applause: "Each Christian Endeavor Society is as intensely loyal to its own local church and communion as if it constituted, in solitude, the entire organization we represent. There cannot possibly exist under our banner any society that is not as thoroughly subject to local church supervision as any purely denominational association can possibly be. It is peculiarly gratifying to its early and constant advocates to see this principle thus increasingly recognized and insisted upon; and this fact ought to reassure any who have feared that this new organization would in some way rival or harm the local churches."—*Correspondence of Christian at Work.*

Certainly no more enthusiastic religious assembly has ever gathered in Philadelphia than the Eighth National Christian Endeavor Convention which met here last week. It cannot but be that the 6,500 delegates, who spent the three days in the heat of such intense spiritual enthusiasm, must carry to their home work new ardor, new thoughts about duty, new hints for practical work.—*Rev. J. R. Miller, D. D., in The Evangelist.*

The perfect harmony of the convention was a matter of great surprise when it is remembered that there were delegates from all parts of the United States, representing all kinds of political and denominational views. Such a feeling of brotherly love and such an entire absence of rivalry or of personal allusion reminded one strongly of the Apostolic times, when they were all together with one accord and had all things in common. With such a vast amount of young life as was here assembled, it would not have been surprising if now and then there had been some manifestation of exuberance that savored more of youthfulness than of dignity, but to the great gratification of all, every one of the young people deported themselves with a dignity and prudence that would be worthy of any assemblage in the land.—*Rev. W. H. York in Northern Christian Advocate.*

Philadelphia has been a willing captive, this week, to an army such as never before took it or any other city by storm. It was an army with banners and badges, a host bent on peaceful victories, full of enthusiasm, not to be daunted by summer's sultriness or three sessions a day. No wonder that the conservative Philadelphians could not readily comprehend the power and spirit of a society that could draw 6,500 young people to their city from all parts of this broad land in July to attend a strictly religious meeting. Verily it was not so in the days of their fathers. Wonder was succeeded by admiration and congratulation as the daily newspapers acquainted the people with the character and magnitude of the Christian Endeavor movement, and everywhere the delegates met with warm welcome.—*Rev. H. B. Grose in The Examiner.*

To say that enthusiasm has marked the sessions is to convey but a faint impression of the ardor and inspiration that have been two characteristics of this remarkable gathering. The Armory Hall has been packed from front to rear, platform and gallery, with the thousands who have accepted the motto, "For Christ and the Church."—*S., in Christian Union.*

The audiences are worthy of a remark. Those of Wednesday and Thursday evening were immense. Everything was filled, auditorium, gallery, choir-seats and platform. Hundreds besides all this stood, and as the doors were vigorously closed while speaking was going on, many went away unable to enter. The precentor, Mr. W. G. Fischer, aided by his choir of two hundred, used the vast body effectively in the singing, the new book, "Hymns of Christian Endeavor," being used. Indeed, the singing was a prominent feature of the convention. In brief connection with this may be mentioned the unique way (which for two or three years has characterized the conventions) in which the vast audiences retired from the meetings. As it took so long a time to go out, they utilized the time by singing as they retired from the room, and frequently, idlers on the street caught the sweet songs of Zion and joined in them.—*Rev. S. W. Adriance, in New York Observer.*

The largest religious convention that has ever been held on this continent has just concluded. For the last three days, the First Regiment Armory Hall has been the scene of gatherings that have been an astonishment to thousands of the good people in this City of Brotherly Love. Thursday evening's closing session will not soon be forgotten by those who gained admission to the First Regiment Armory Hall. Barring the heat, the meeting was delightful. The devotional exercises were conducted with heart, and the music was beautiful. Dr. Pierson delivered a magnificent address on "The World for Christ," and Dr. Gifford, of Boston, spoke on "Christ for the World." A short speech was given by Postmaster-General Wanamaker, and telegraph communication passed between the convention and the President of the United

States. Three-quarters of an hour were given to a closing consecration service, and what one of the speakers termed "the greatest religious meeting, numerically speaking, in the history of Christianity," was ended at half-past ten o'clock.—*A. H. S., in The Interior.*

In reviewing the convention as a whole, and inquiring the grounds for the universal verdict of success, it should be remembered that bigness is not always greatness, yet there is potency in the consciousness that one is associated with 6,000 fellow-disciples, bound by ties which such an immense gathering makes visible and tangible. The best exhibition of this was in the singing, of such superlative power and majesty, the use of the old favorite hymns of the church largely predominating. The large representation from denominations other than that in which the movement started, is a gratifying token of broad and healthy growth. The predominance of practical topics, the tone of consecrated aggressiveness in service, and, above all, the exaltation of loyalty to Christ and the local church as the true essence and end of Christian Endeavor, were noteworthy features of the gathering.— *Rev. J. L. Sewall, in The Congregationalist.*

Enthusiasm was at its height throughout it all, but everywhere it was mingled, though not modified, by strong common sense and business method. Though all would have been glad to linger on the mount, all seemed to be preparing themselves, by their copious notes and rapt attention, to carry the blessing home with them to their churches, and, through the strength gained by fellowship with Christ and His saints, to cast out the demons of self and Satan from their own hearts and those of their sin-burdened neighbors.—*Rev. F. W. Greene, in Christian Union.*

The religious feature of the movement is the predominant one. It makes not the literary or social gathering, but the prayer-meeting, the attractive center. It makes the public confession of Christ the first duty of every disciple, until the duty becomes his joy. It solves the vexed problem of amusements and restores the true perspective to many a disordered spiritual vision. The very genius of the society renders interference with ecclesiastical affairs impossible. It is not denominational; it is not undenominational; it is interdenominational. There is as much danger of a Sunday-school overthrowing the denominational status of its church as there is of the society weakening its doctrinal integrity. It would be impossible to report the spirit of the convention. There are no parliamentary tangles, no suggestions of friction. There is a naturalness and freshness that fascinate, a consecration to Christ that is real.—*Rev. J. T. Beckley, D. D., in Sunday School Times.*

THE STATISTICS.

[The number of societies has increased to such an extent that it is impossible for us to print the list as formerly. To do so this year would require a book as large as this report for the list alone. We give below the number of societies by States.]

The statistics of the Christian Endeavor Societies to July 1, 1889 have been made up as accurately as possible, and a grand total of 7,672 societies is found on the record, of which 7,586 are reported as in the United States and Canada. These societies average something over sixty members each, and it is safe to say that there are 485,000 members in those reported. There are, however, doubtless hundreds — perhaps thousands — of societies of which we have no record, and these would bring the sum total of members to a much larger figure. In 2,141 of these societies which reported the number who have joined the church, we find that 15,672 have taken this step, which indicates that not less than 45,000 in all, at a moderate estimate, have been received from the societies into the churches of the land.

The following is the representation by States: Alabama, 6; Arizona, 3; Arkansas, 5; California, 241; Colorado, 80; Connecticut, 352; Dakota, 84; Delaware, 24; District Columbia, 19; Florida, 32; Georgia, 12; Idaho, 1; Illinois, 541; Indiana, 169; Indian Territory, 7; Iowa, 336; Kansas, 228; Kentucky, 30; Louisiana, 6; Maine, 184; Maryland, 35; Massachusetts, 742; Michigan, 262; Minnesota, 213; Mississippi, 3; Missouri, 207; Montana, 4; Nebraska, 161; New Hampshire, 135; New Jersey, 279; New Mexico, 4; New York, 1,387; North Carolina, 11; Ohio, 465; Oregon, 41; Pennsylvania, 484; Rhode Island, 68; South Carolina, 18; Tennessee, 23; Texas, 21; Utah, 20; Vermont, 150; Virginia, 4; Washington, 37; West Virginia, 9; Wisconsin, 226; Wyoming, 4; British Provinces, 213. Total, 7,586.

www.ingramcontent.com/pod-product-compliance
Lightning Source LLC
Chambersburg PA
CBHW031350040426
42444CB00005B/251